Peacekeeping
Fiascoes of the 1990s

Peacekeeping Fiascoes of the 1990s

Causes, Solutions, and U.S. Interests

Frederick H. Fleitz, Jr.

Westport, Connecticut
London

Library of Congress Cataloging-in-Publication Data

Fleitz, Frederick H., 1962–
    Peacekeeping fiascoes of the 1990s : causes, solutions, and U.S. interests / Frederick H. Fleitz, Jr.
        p. cm.
    Includes bibliographical references and index.
    ISBN 0–275–97367–0 (alk. paper)
    1. Peacekeeping forces. 2. United Nations—Armed Forces. 3. United States—Foreign relations—1993–2001. I. Title.
    JZ6374.F58 2002
    341.5'84—dc21   2001054588

British Library Cataloguing in Publication Data is available.

Library of Congress Catalog Card Number: 2001054588
ISBN: 0–275–97367–0

First published in 2002

Praeger Publishers, 88 Post Road West, Westport, CT 06881
An imprint of Greenwood Publishing Group, Inc.
www.praeger.com

Printed in the United States of America

The paper used in this book complies with the
Permanent Paper Standard issued by the National
Information Standards Organization (Z39.48–1984).

10 9 8 7 6 5 4 3 2 1

For the eighteen U.S. Army Rangers and Aircrew killed in Mogadishu, Somalia, October 3, 1993, and their families.

Chief Warrant Officer Donovan Briley
Staff Sergeant Daniel Busch
Corporal James Cavaco
Staff Sergeant William Cleveland
Staff Sergeant Thomas Field
Sergeant First Class Earl Filmore
Chief Warrant Officer Raymond Frank
Master Sergeant Gary Gordon
Sergeant Cornell Houston
Sergeant James Joyce
Private First Class Richard Kowalewski
Private First Class James Martin
Master Sergeant Timothy Martin
Sergeant First Class Dominick Pilla
Sergeant Lorenzo Ruiz
Sergeant First Class Randy Shughart
Corporal James Smith
Chief Warrant Officer Clifton Wolcott

They served their country with honor against terrible odds.
We must never let this happen again.

Contents

Illustrations

TABLES

Preface and Acknowledgments

I wrote this book to fill a void in the analysis of UN peacekeeping since 1992. While there have been a plethora of books and articles looking at peacekeeping over the last nine years, most have been optimistic paeans that fail to take an honest look at the historical record of power realities of the post–Cold War world. With the November 2000 election of George W. Bush as president of the United States, I believe America will initiate a comprehensive reassessment of American policy on UN peacekeeping. I am hopeful that this book will aid such an effort.

As a CIA analyst who covered the UN and peacekeeping for the Reagan and (first) Bush* administrations, I had the privilege of working closely with U.S. policymakers as the Cold War ended and the UN gained a new lease on life. I wrote key analyses for senior U.S. policymakers before and during the Persian Gulf War, some of which touched on the legality of the war effort under the UN Charter. In February 1993, I participated in the drafting process of the Clinton administration's policy on UN peacekeeping, Presidential Decision Directive 25 (PDD-25). This assignment required me to cast a wide net to gather the best evaluations of the potential for UN peacekeeping from academics and think tanks across the United States. This experience gave me unique insights into the origins of peacekeeping, its problems in the 1990s, and how it might be salvaged.

I try to be blunt and dispel numerous rumors and discrepancies that have come to surround UN peacekeeping. For example, readers looking for a

---

*This book distinguishes between the "first" President Bush, George H. W. Bush, president of the United States from 1989 to 1993, and his son, the "second" President Bush, who was elected President in November 2000 and took office in January 2001.

peacekeeping doctrine for U.S. troops will be disappointed. I believe the historical evidence clearly demonstrates that peacekeeping is not a task for the United States. This is not to say that I do not have the greatest respect for American soldiers who have been deployed by the thousands to peacekeeping missions from Cambodia to the Western Sahara to Kosovo. I know that the U.S. Army has devoted significant resources to developing a peacekeeping doctrine and to training U.S. soldiers for peacekeeping. In my view, American soldiers are the best in the world and their ability to take on peacekeeping missions is a credit to their professionalism and "can do" attitude. But asking American soldiers to be peacekeepers is to ask the world to forget that they represent the most powerful military force on earth. This makes no sense. Moreover, attempts to shoehorn American troops into peacekeeping roles have diminished U.S. military readiness and put U.S. forces at unnecessary risk.

I also address misuses of the term "peacekeeping" and Chapter VII of the UN Charter in peacekeeping mandates. While these discrepancies have gone unanswered by most American experts, the UN and the British have recognized them. I expect that the United States will follow suit over the next few years.

It is clear that UN peacekeeping was seriously undermined by failed missions between 1993 and 2000. I believe that peacekeeping can still play a role in helping manage or resolve international conflicts if world leaders recognize its capabilities and limitations. It is my hope that this book will help policymakers understand peacekeeping's limitations and deploy any future operations with more realistic mandates.

I owe a lot to my wife, Julie, for being so patient and supportive of me for the years I worked on this book. I also want to thank many experts in the field who advised me and guided my research, including Under Secretary of State John Bolton, Ambassador Jeane Kirkpatrick, Ambassador Charles Lichenstein, Ambassador Hugh Montgomery, former Deputy Assistant Secretary of Defense for Peacekeeping James Shear, former Assistant Secretary of State Leonard Hawley, Perry Pickert, John Herzberg, Margaret Hemenway, William Deere, Donald Daniel, Mark Lagon, Michael Westphaul, Pam Thiessen, Frank Record, Lester Munson, Brian Boquist, Colonel George Oliver, Michael Rohrbach, Tetsuo Miyabara, Daniel New, Colonel Kenneth Allard, Pedro San Juan, and Stanley Meisler. I also am grateful to a number of U.S. military officers, UN officials, OSCE officers, and other experts who spoke to or corresponded with me about their peacekeeping experiences.

I would also like to thank the many people who helped me prepare and edit this book: my wife Julie, Scott Mason, Stephen Elliott, Hugh Burns, Craig McKee, and Perry Pickert. I could not have finished this project without their help.

Acronyms

CIS	Commonwealth of Independent States
CPP	Cambodian People's Party
DPKO	UN Department of Peacekeeping Operations
ECOMOG	Economic Community of West African States Cease-Fire Monitoring Group
ECOWAS	Economic Community of West African States
EU	European Union
FALD	UN Field Administration and Logistics Division
FOD	UN Field Operations Division
FUNCINPEC	Front Uni National pour un Cambodge Indépendent, Neutre, Pacifique, et Coopératif
GAO	United States General Accounting Office
ICJ	International Court of Justice
INTERFET	International Force East Timor
IPTF	International Police Task Force (Bosnia)
KPNLF	Khmer People's National Liberation Front
MICAH	International Civilian Support Mission in Haiti
MICIVIH	International Civilian Mission in Haiti
MINUGUA	UN Verification Mission in Guatemala
MINURCA	UN Mission in the Central African Republic
MINURSO	UN Mission for the Referendum in Western Sahara

MIPONUH	UN Civilian Police Mission in Haiti
MONUA	UN Observer Mission in Angola
MONUC	UN Mission in the Democratic Republic of the Congo
MPLA	Movimento Popular de Libertação de Angola
NATO	North Atlantic Treaty organization
NGO	Nongovernmental organization
NPFL	National Patriotic Front of Liberia
OAU	Organization of African Unity
ONUC	UN Operation in the Congo
ONUCA	UN Observer Group in Central America
ONUMOZ	UN Operation in Mozambique
ONUSAL	UN Observer Mission in El Salvador
OSCE	Organization for Security and Cooperation in Europe
PDK	Party of Democratic Kampuchea (Khmer Rouge)
POLISARIO	Popular Front for the Liberation of Saguia el-Hamara and Rio de Oro
RPF	Rwandan Patriotic Front
RUF	Revolutionary United Front (Sierra Leone)
SRSG	Special Representative of the UN Secretary General
SWAPO	South West African People's Organization
ULIMO	United Liberation Movement for Democracy (Liberia)
UNAMIC	UN Advance Mission in Cambodia
UNAMIR	UN Assistance Mission for Rwanda
UNAMSIL	UN Assistance Mission in Sierra Leone
UNAMUR	UN Observer Mission Uganda-Rwanda
UNASOG	UN Aouzou Strip Observer Group
UNAVEM I	First UN Angola Verification Mission
UNAVEM II	Second UN Angola Verification Mission
UNAVEM III	Third UN Angola Verification Mission
UNCIVPOL	UN Civilian Police
UNCRO	UN Confidence Restoration Operation in Croatia
UNDOF	UN Disengagement Observer Force (Golan Heights)
UNDP	UN Development Program
UNEF I	First UN Emergency Force (Sinai/Gaza Strip)
UNEF II	Second UN Emergency Force (Sinai/Gaza Strip)

UNFICYP	UN Peacekeeping Force in Cyprus
UNGA	United Nations General Assembly
UNGCI	UN Guard Contingent in Iraq
UNGOMAP	UN Good Offices Mission in Afghanistan and Pakistan
UNHCR	UN High Commissioner on Refugees
UNIFIL	UN Interim Force in Lebanon
UNIIMOG	UN Iran-Iraq Military Observer Group
UNIKOM	UN Iraq-Kuwait Observer Mission
UNIPOM	UN India-Pakistan Observer Mission
UNITA	Unitão Nacional para a Indêpendencia Total de Angola
UNITAF	Unified Task Force (Somalia)
UNMEE	UN Mission in Ethiopia and Eritrea
UNMIBH	UN Mission in Bosnia and Herzegovina
UNMIH	UN Mission in Haiti
UNMIK	UN Interim Administration Mission in Kosovo
UNMLT	UN Military Liaison Team (Cambodia)
UNMOGIP	UN Military Observer Group in India and Pakistan
UNMOP	UN Mission of Military Observers in Prevlaka
UNMOT	UN Mission of Observers in Tajikistan
UNOGIL	UN Observation Group in Lebanon
UNOMIG	UN Observer Mission in Georgia
UNOMIL	UN Observer Mission in Liberia
UNOMSIL	UN Observer Mission in Sierra Leone
UNOMUR	UN Observer Mission Uganda-Rwanda
UNOSOM I	First UN Operation in Somalia
UNOSOM II	Second UN Operation in Somalia
UNPA	UN Protected Area
UNPREDEP	UN Preventive Deployment Force (Macedonia)
UNPROFOR	UN Protection Force (Yugoslavia)
UNPSG	UN Civilian Police Support Group (Croatia)
UNSC	United Nations Security Council
UNSF	UN Security Force in West New Guinea (West Irian)
UNSMIH	UN Support Mission in Haiti
UNTAC	UN Transitional Authority in Cambodia
UNTAES	UN Transitional Administration for Eastern Slavonia, Baranja, and Western Sirium

UNTAET	UN Transitional Administration in East Timor
UNTAG	UN Transition Assistance Group (Namibia)
UNTMIH	UN Transitional Mission in Haiti
UNTSO	UN Truce Supervision Organization (Palestine)
UNYOM	UN Yemen Observer Mission

Peacekeeping
Fiascoes of the 1990s

Chapter 1

Peacekeeping in Crisis

I think it was a mistake in the early 1990s to assume that civil wars and collapsed states could be dealt with by the peacekeeping model. Peacekeeping was designed to deal with conflicts and power vacuums between states and was not suitable for the far more complex task of dealing with civil wars. So far, however, the UN's member governments have been unwilling to build new instruments more suited to this task.
—Sir Brian Urquhart, former UN Under Secretary
General for Political Affairs, March 8, 1999[1]

UN peacekeeping's record in the 1990s lends credence to Karl Marx's dark prophecy that history repeats itself first as tragedy, then as farce. A 1993 decision by Western statesmen to expand UN peacekeeping mandates to address civil wars and humanitarian conflicts led to disastrous results. Peacekeeping in Somalia collapsed after the UN became a combatant in the Somali anarchy and 18 U.S. soldiers and over 500 Somalis were killed in an ambush. UN peacekeepers were able to deploy to Haiti in 1994 only after the United States invaded and occupied the island. When the U.S.-led force withdrew, Haiti deteriorated, forcing the UN to pull out. In 1994, UN peacekeepers in Rwanda looked on helplessly while Hutu tribesmen killed an estimated 800,000 Tutsis and Tutsi supporters. UN peacekeepers in Croatia and Bosnia proved woefully incapable of promoting stability or stopping ethnic violence. The UN withdrew its 30,000-man Bosnia force in 1995 after the Bosnian Serbs kidnapped 370 UN peacekeepers to use as "human shields" and overran two UN "safe areas," massacring the inhabitants of one of these supposed UN-protected refuges. By 1995, the world seemed to have learned its lesson that peacekeeping could not work in areas rent by civil and ethnic conflict and returned to the traditional peacekeeping model successfully used during the Cold War.

These lessons were soon forgotten. In 1999, the UN agreed to send 25,000 lightly armed UN peacekeepers to address civil and ethnic conflicts in East Timor, Kosovo, Sierra Leone, and Congo. The East Timor and Kosovo missions are essentially occupation forces. (The Kosovo UN mission actually is partnered with a coercive non-UN peace enforcement mission.) The current UN missions in the Congo and Sierra Leone resemble the poorly designed UN missions sent in the mid-1990s to Somalia and Liberia.

Sierra Leone has been a major embarrassment for the UN. Spurred by U.S. pressure, the UN struck a deal in 1999 to free from prison (actually house arrest in Nigeria) a Sierra Leone rebel leader with a reputation for using children as soldiers and cutting off the limbs of civilians. Once released, the rebel leader quickly turned against the UN, killing seven peacekeepers and taking 500 UN troops hostage. Despite these setbacks, the UN plans to retain its beleaguered peacekeeping force in Sierra Leone through 2002 and is striving to find troops to send to the Congo. The illogic of these decisions gives new meaning to the word "farce."

ROOTS OF THE PROBLEM

It is hard to conceive an international relations concept that is as convoluted as peacekeeping. From 1956 until the early 1990s, the term "peacekeeping" referred to small UN operations, deployed with the consent of state-parties to disputes, that used force only in self-defense. By 2000, it had become a vague label for a wide variety of international operations, some of which waged war to enforce peace accords imposed on warring parties by the UN or the West. Late 1990s "peacekeeping" forces could order airstrikes against recalcitrant parties, dismiss elected leaders, and destroy infrastructure. In the vernacular of many in the foreign policy establishment today, peacekeeping can refer to any multilateral military operation. It slips off the tongues of newscasters so often that the public is unaware that most 1990s multilateral operations dubbed as peacekeeping had little in common with the Cold War variety of lightly armed, blue helmeted troops serving in fairly tranquil situations.

Does the broad use of this term make sense? Are troops with the lightly armed UN Truce Supervision Organization in Palestine (UNTSO) and the heavily armed NATO-led Stabilization Force in Bosnia (SFOR) all peacekeepers? Is it fair to say that the successful First UN Emergency Force (UNEF I), deployed after the Suez Crisis of 1956 with the consent and cooperation of Egypt and Israel, operated on the same principles as KFOR, the NATO-led so-called peacekeeping force in Kosovo? Can peacekeeping troops conduct military operations against disputants and still remain peacekeepers? Can a UN operation be at war in a nation while trying to rebuild it at the same time? Is it justifiable to deploy peacekeepers to civil war situations hoping that their presence will encourage warring parties to make peace?

Many observers answer such questions affirmatively. Some contend that changes in peacekeeping theory reflect new security and power realities of the post–Cold War era, such as the end of the superpower conflict and an increase in civil wars and ethnic conflicts. This argument maintains that changes in peacekeeping doctrine were necessary to allow the international community to respond to "failed" states and humanitarian disasters in states without functional central governments. Implicit here is a related contention that state-parties should no longer be permitted to use national sovereignty as a shield to block international action to address dire ethnic strife or humanitarian disasters.

Regrettably, none of these rationales for expanding UN peacekeeping led to successful operations. Most expanded peacekeeping missions failed, wasting billions of dollars and making dire situations worse. The biggest casualty, however, may have been the reputation of the UN, which was pilloried by some for its ineffectiveness and by others for abandoning its neutrality and serving as an arm of Western foreign policy. After embarrassing setbacks in Somalia, Haiti, and Yugoslavia, the West began to pursue less ambitious UN missions with smaller numbers of troops. It also turned to NATO for peace enforcement operations to address crises in Bosnia and Kosovo.

This book will establish what peacekeeping is and whether it can play a role in the post–Cold War world. It will differentiate between popular misuses of the peacekeeping concept in the 1990s and more realistic definitions. A central focus will be peacekeeping's place in American foreign policy. I will argue that certain bedrock principles enabled peacekeeping operations to succeed during the Cold War and remain just as valid today. My analysis rests on the following assumptions:

1. *There is only one legitimate form of peacekeeping: traditional peacekeeping.* Traditional peacekeeping is a mechanism to manage conflict and facilitate and supervise truces. Traditional peacekeeping forces are unarmed or lightly armed multilateral troops deployed with the consent of state-party disputants. They are impartial and use force only in self-defense. Traditional peacekeeping forces sometimes are permissible to help end civil wars if verifiable cease-fires and the full consent of disputants can be obtained. Traditional peacekeeping operations continue today and remain capable of addressing future post–Cold War international disputes.

2. *Various "improved" models of traditional peacekeeping, a.k.a.* multidimensional, second generation, aggravated, and muscular *peacekeeping, are nonviable experiments without any clear doctrinal or theoretical foun-*

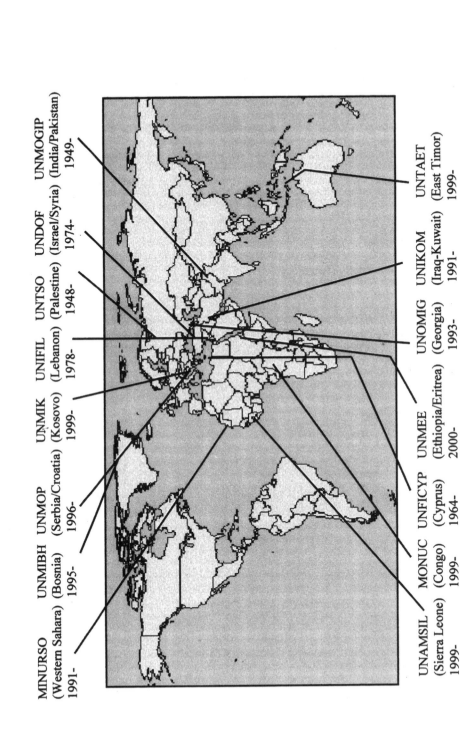

MINURSO (Western Sahara) 1991-

UNMIBH (Bosnia) 1995-

UNMOP (Serbia/Croatia) 1996-

UNMIK (Kosovo) 1999-

UNIFIL (Lebanon) 1978-

UNTSO (Palestine) 1948-

UNDOF (Israel/Syria) 1974-

UNMOGIP (India/Pakistan) 1949-

UNTAET (East Timor) 1999-

UNIKOM (Iraq-Kuwait) 1991-

UNOMIG (Georgia) 1993-

UNMEE (Ethiopia/Eritrea) 2000-

UNFICYP (Cyprus) 1964-

MONUC (Congo) 1999-

UNAMSIL (Sierra Leone) 1999-

Map 1.1: Active UN peacekeeping operations, April 2002. (Julie Fleitz)

dation. Since most of these new terms are deliberately ambiguous, this book refers to them generally as *expanded peacekeeping,* a neutral term for peacekeeping-like operations deployed in the 1990s coined by former UN Secretary General Boutros Boutros-Ghali.[2] In many cases, expanded peacekeeping models gave peacekeeping troops missions requiring the use of military force against local parties, deployed peacekeepers without obtaining the consent of warring parties, or used the veneer of peacekeeping to perform other functions, often rebuilding "failed" states. Many expanded peacekeeping missions were further undermined by contradictory Western political agendas. Mostly due to resource constraints, expanded peacekeeping focused on resolving rather than managing conflicts, often with missions deployed for short periods of time.

3. *There is a clear distinction between peacekeeping and peace enforcement.* Multilateral military operations such as SFOR in Bosnia and KFOR in Kosovo are *not* peacekeeping efforts. They are peace enforcement missions. Unlike traditional and expanded peacekeeping forces, peace enforcement operations are heavily armed efforts prepared to wage war against parties who violate peace accords. They also are not impartial. Table 1.1 illustrates the differences between peace enforcement and peacekeeping.

4. *The dilution of the peacekeeping concept has rendered it convoluted, endangering the safety of traditional peacekeepers and undermining the utility of peacekeeping as a tool to resolve future disputes.* Peacekeeping missions deployed in the 1990s frequently took sides in civil wars or used military force against warring parties. The collapse of such missions squandered the moral authority and reputation for impartiality UN peacekeeping had built up over the previous 50 years. As a result, peacekeeping has become inherently more dangerous, since warring parties are now less likely to regard UN forces as disinterested mediators. This has in turn spurred a shortage of peacekeeping troops and funding.

5. *The Clinton administration's policy of using peacekeeping as window dressing for military operations undermined American security in the 1990s.* From 1993 to 2000, the U.S. military expended significant resources on peacekeeping while taking large budget cuts. U.S. military retention levels plummeted due to a proliferation of peacekeeping-like missions around the globe. Military readiness also was harmed by continuous peacekeeping and peace enforcement deployments. In November 1999, the U.S. Army rated two of its 10 divisions as unfit due to peacekeeping deployments.[3] To compensate for a growing manpower shortage, the Pentagon began a controversial policy of staffing peacekeeping and peace enforcement missions with Reserves and National Guard troops. In 1999, the headquarters of the Texas National Guard 49th Armor Division and its commander, Brigadier General Robert L. Halverson, took command of the American

Table 1.1
Comparison of Peacekeeping and Peace Enforcement Characteristics

	Traditional Peacekeeping	Expanded Peacekeeping	Peace Enforcement
Consent of Parties	Required.	Desired from at least one combatant.	Not needed.
Use of Force	Only in self-defense.	Use of force discouraged. Troops may engage in limited military operations, such as to defend aid convoys. Proposals were tabled in 2000, however, to authorize these operations to use force to fight "evil" (i.e., genocide and rape) and when disputants are not "moral equals."	Prepared to use overwhelming military force to compel parties to abide by peace accords.
Troops	Unarmed or lightly armed.	Unarmed or lightly armed.	Heavily armed combat forces.
Impartiality	Required. Are viewed as nonthreatening by combatants.	Technically required but tends to side against one party.	Generally, peace enforcement efforts ally with one party and identify the other as the aggressor.
Relationship with Parties to Dispute	Traditional peacekeeping forces may not interfere in the domestic politics of the host countries.	Also forbidden to interfere in domestic politics of hosts.	Can be short-duration operations, like Operation Desert Storm, which drove Iraq from Kuwait, or long-term missions that are essentially occupation forces, like SFOR in Bosnia and KFOR in Kosovo.

SFOR sector in Bosnia.* In doing so, the 49th became the first Guard unit ever to provide the command and control element for an active duty maneuver unit, the 3rd Armored Cavalry Regiment.[4]

Clinton peacekeeping policy also proved to be demoralizing and dangerous for the U.S. military. At the abstract level, it runs contrary to the military theorists who have most influenced twentieth-century U.S. military doctrine, such as Carl von Clausewitz and Sun Tzu. Most significant to this debate may be Clausewitz's truism that wars are serious business for serious goals. By contrast, expanded peacekeeping rests on the unserious theory that parties to vicious civil wars and ethnic conflicts in failed states will voluntarily yield to lightly armed UN forces and comply with Western conceptions of international law.

Peacekeeping experiments during the 1990s endangered U.S. soldiers at a more basic level. American troops are trained to be warfighters and to wield high-tech weaponry with devastating destructive power. In Bosnia, U.S. combat troops are conducting crowd control and other police functions. Such tasks cause the technical proficiencies of U.S. soldiers to erode and require that they be retrained after UN assignments and retaught twenty-first-century warfare. Lewis MacKenzie, former Canadian commander of UN troops in Bosnia, made a similar observation in a January 2001 article:

Frequently, when I lecture at U.S. military institutions, I am asked, "Does too much peacekeeping erode the Warrior Ethic?" For years, I said no—that well-trained and well-led soldiers will make the transition from peacekeeping to combat in a heartbeat if that is what the situation demands. But now, based on the experience of my own country, I no longer give that answer. Canadians have discovered that peacekeeping does harm the Warrior Ethic—not so much in the minds of the soldiers, but in the minds of the public.[5]

Finally, the Clinton peacekeeping policy undermined respect for the United States as a great power. The prospect that U.S. military force could be used against a recalcitrant state should be enough to force most malefactor states or groups from taking actions that would risk incurring Washington's wrath. U.S. participation in failed peacekeeping missions with vague mandates damaged America's reputation as a powerful and decisive nation and reduced the prospect that Washington could stare down states that threaten U.S. national interests. On the other hand, peacekeeping cannot perform its vital confidence-building function if peacekeeping troops are armed to the teeth. Washington learned the hard way in Somalia in

---

*The author wants to note here that the controversial aspects of this policy are troop shortages and extremely lengthy assignments for U.S. Army reservists, and not the competence of the Texas National Guard 49th Armor Division headquarters. This unit has performed admirably in Bosnia and trained extensively with the 1st Cavalry Division at Fort Hood, Texas. General Halverson also has prior experience in Bosnia, including serving as the deputy commander of U.S. forces in Bosnia.

1993 that American troops serving as UN peacekeepers must be heavily armed or they risk being targeted by terrorists and insurgents. UN officials know all too well that many of these groups believe the easiest way for them to get media attention is to attack or kill an American soldier. Lewis MacKenzie has argued that the risk to U.S. peacekeepers is so severe that U.S. troops should be kept out of peacekeeping operations for their own safety. He once stated, "You don't get your picture on the cover of *Newsweek* killing Canadians. You've got to kill Americans."[6]

6. *Distortions of peacekeeping terminology and precedents between 1993 and 2001 were an anomaly resulting from a leadership vacuum on the world stage in the mid to late 1990s.* Put simply, weak leaders in a number of Western countries chose to use the peacekeeping concept as a substitute for reasoned policy and decisive action. These leaders engineered operations that masqueraded as peacekeeping with abstract goals that had little to do with their national interests and could not be sold easily to their national legislatures. *Los Angeles Times* columnist and longtime UN expert Stanley Meisler aptly described this phenomenon in his 1995 book, *The United Nations: The First Fifty Years*: "In the long run, both Bosnia and Somalia will surely be regarded as flawed or even failed UN missions. If so, they were dragged down by the lack of resolve in the United States and not by the failings of the [UN] secretary general."[7]

Due to its disastrous consequences, I hold that this is a temporary phenomenon that will not continue in this decade, since the expanded peacekeeping concept will either be completely discredited or, more likely, a new set of leaders with more enlightened views on foreign policy will come to the fore.

DON'T CALL THEM SECOND GENERATION

One of the most misleading monikers for expanded peacekeeping efforts is "second generation peacekeeping," a term that supposedly represents improvements on the Cold War peacekeeping model by redefining the use of force by peacekeepers and the consent and mandate concepts. Experience has shown that rather than being an improvement or a new departure, such operations represent a hopeless dead end. Professor Alan James, a distinguished expert on peacekeeping, is a critic of the second generation peacekeeping concept and has written that, although this term has been widely accepted in academia, new operations deployed during the 1990s differ too radically from traditional peacekeeping operations to be considered their "second generation."[8] He believes that UN missions in Somalia and Yugoslavia might be more accurately described as "a second generation of enforcement."

There appears to be a rough continuum of force separating pacific peacekeeping and forceful peace enforcement efforts. Operation after operation

Figure 1.1
Peacekeeping Continuum of Force

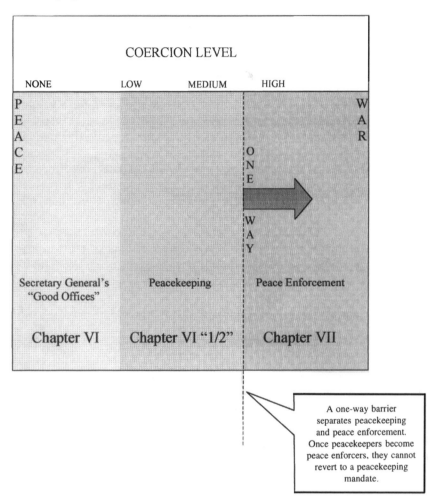

during the 1990s proved that forceful action against disputants is incompatible with peacekeeping. Figure 1.1 illustrates this continuum.[9] Moreover, there appears to be a "one-way door" separating non-forceful peacekeeping and coercive peace enforcement. While it is possible to convert a peacekeeping force into a peace enforcement mission by giving peacekeepers a coercive mandate, it is impossible to move in the other direction, since the international troops in question irrevocably lose local consent and good will and become combatants.

Advocates of "second generation" concepts also contend that such missions improve upon the Cold War variety because they include a host of new non-peacekeeping functions, such as distributing aid, monitoring elections, etc. This argument is flawed, since an examination of prior peacekeeping operations shows that traditional peacekeeping missions have long performed many of these duties. For example, UNFICYP, deployed in Cyprus since 1964, established a humanitarian and economics branch to provide emergency humanitarian assistance. UNIFIL, deployed in Lebanon since 1978, has long been engaged in civilian administration, humanitarian activities, and rebuilding infrastructure. UNIFIL also operates a hospital for the local population in southern Lebanon. UNSF, deployed in west New Guinea from 1962 to 1963, built a police force, performed civilian administration, and helped organize civilian elections.[10]

Finally, liberal internationalists[11] claimed 1990s peacekeeping efforts like UNTAC and UNOSOM II were a new or second generation of peacekeeping because of their enormous size and the complexity of their non-peacekeeping nation-building functions. However, since these extra functions proved incompatible with peacekeeping and contributed to their failures, they hardly count as an improvement or a next generation of peacekeeping. Misleading descriptions of post–Cold War peacekeeping-like missions will be explored in greater detail in Chapter 7.

FROM EUPHORIA TO TRAIN WRECK

No one could have seen in 1992 the dire predicament in which peacekeeping would find itself in 2000. Expectations for the post–Cold War UN snowballed in 1992 after the successful 1991 U.S.-led military operation against Iraq (Operation Desert Storm), a warming of American-Russian relations, and a series of successful UN peacekeeping operations in Namibia, El Salvador, and Iran/Iraq. UN proponents seized on the fact that Operation Desert Storm was authorized by the UN Security Council as indicative of the new role the UN would play in promoting international security in the post–Cold War era. Liberal internationalists also contended that the UN's role in approving the Persian Gulf War meant an end to the unilateral use of military force, at least by the United States. These claims were erroneous and ignored the reality that the first Bush administration used the UN endorsement of Operation Desert Storm largely as a figleaf to protect the sensitivities of America's Middle East allies.

In 1992 and 1993, UN peacekeeping captured the imagination of Western policymakers and analysts wrestling with the question of how to forge a more secure and peaceful world after the Cold War. Peacekeeping had a particular allure to Western foreign policy experts—most of whom were liberal internationalists—since it represented a way to implement their dreams of Wilsonian internationalism while drastically cutting defense spending. Other experts talked about how the new world order meant the lowering of national boundaries, "enhanced" self-determination, and the beginning of a slow movement toward world government.[12]

Traditional peacekeeping had two principal Cold War objectives: first, keeping "peripheral" disputes from becoming part of the Cold War arena, and second, serving as a non-collective security mechanism to manage international conflicts and establish and maintain truces. Traditional peacekeeping operations assumed this second objective by default when it became clear that their original objective—resolving international crises—could rarely be accomplished with peacekeeping forces. Instead, most traditional peacekeeping efforts remained for decades monitoring cease-fires or were withdrawn due to a new outbreak in hostilities. Traditional peacekeeping was used under very narrow circumstances, usually limited to international conflicts and requiring the consent of warring parties. Permanent members of the UN Security Council—especially the United States and the Soviet Union—generally were not permitted to participate in traditional peacekeeping efforts during the Cold War.

A new international relations paradigm was born in 1992 with the unveiling of expanded peacekeeping missions. Unlike traditional peacekeeping, expanded peacekeeping operations were attempts at collective security. Therefore, they did not require the consent of the warring parties and often took sides, using force to *impose* UN Security Council–directed solutions to conflicts. Moreover, permanent members of the council—especially the United States and the Soviet Union—were *encouraged* to participate in these new missions. Expanded peacekeeping operations had ambitious objectives, which included conflict resolution and Wilsonian goals such as nation building and creating democratic societies. As a result of the loose prerequisites for expanded peacekeeping, the UN approved sending more than 182,000 troops to 34 peacekeeping missions from 1992 to 2000 compared with only 61,000 troops to 22 missions in the previous 44 years (see Tables 1.2 and 1.3).

The expanded peacekeeping model seemed to work at first. By mid-1993, new operations in Cambodia, El Salvador, Somalia, Yugoslavia, and Liberia were widely credited with saving lives by ending fighting and, in some cases, forcing warring parties to the negotiating table. There was a widespread perception that some of these missions were the only possible solutions to dire humanitarian disasters. UN efforts in Cambodia and Somalia initially received plaudits for nation-building projects such as rebuilding infrastructure and setting up democratic institutions.

The UN peacekeeping mission in Cambodia (UNTAC), conducted from 1992 to 1993, was considered the prototype expanded peacekeeping mission. UNTAC avoided armed confrontations, took few casualties, and, most importantly, helped put an end to years of civil war. UNTAC succeeded in carrying out a national election for which millions of citizens stood in long lines—many risking their lives—to cast their ballots. The

Table 1.2
UN Peacekeeping Missions Deployed, 1948–1991[13]

	Start/End Dates	Authorized Size	Total Cost ($ millions)
UNMOGIP (India-Pakistan)	1948–	102	163
UNTSO (Palestine)	1948–	572	592
UNEF I (Sinai/Gaza Strip)	1956–1967	6,073	214
UNOGIL (Lebanon)	1958	591	4
ONUC (Congo)	1960–1964	19,828	400
UNSF (W. New Guinea)	1962–1963	1,576	26*
UNYOM (Yemen)	1963–1964	189	2*
UNFICYP (Cyprus)	1964–	1,257	980
UNIPOM (India/Pakistan)	1965–1966	96	2
UNEF II (Sinai/Suez)	1973–1979	6,973	446
UNDOF (Golan Heights)	1974–	1,454	732
UNIFIL (Lebanon)	1978–	7,000	3,240
UNIIMOG (Iran/Iraq)	1988–1991	399	190
UNGOMAP (Afghanistan/ Pakistan)	1988–1990	50	14
UNTAG (Namibia)	1989–1990	7,500	400
UNAVEM I (Angola)	1989–1991	70	16
ONUCA (Central America)	1989–1991	1,098	89
ONUSAL (El Salvador)	1991–1995	1,108	107
MINURSO (W. Sahara)	1991–	3,000	430
UNIKOM (Iraq-Kuwait)	1991–	1,100	496†
UNAVEM II (Angola)	1991–1995	655	175
UNAMIC (Cambodia)	1991–1992	1,504	‡
Total: 22 missions		**62,195 troops**	**$8.7 billion**

Notes: Data as of November 2001. Cost figures are not adjusted for inflation. *Full costs were borne by parties to disputes. †Since 1993, Kuwait has paid two-thirds of the costs of this mission. ‡Costs of this mission were incorporated into UNTAC.

election was far from perfect, and UNTAC failed in many important aspects of its mandate, most notably disarming former warring parties. Nevertheless, victory was declared and the operation withdrew in late 1993. Cambodia remained peaceful for about six months after UNTAC withdrew, spurring liberal internationalists to assert that it was proof that the expanded peacekeeping model worked.

Table 1.3
UN Peacekeeping Missions Deployed, 1992–2000[14]

	Start/End Dates	Authorized Size	Total Cost ($ millions)
UNTAC (Cambodia)	1992–1993	22,000	1,600
UNPROFOR (Yugoslavia)	1992–1995	45,000	4,600
UNOSOM I (Somalia)	1992–1993	4,270*	43
ONUMOZ (Mozambique)	1992–1995	7,100	520
UNOMIG (Georgia)	1993–	136	250
MICIVIH (Haiti)†	1993–2000	100	?
UNOMIL (Liberia)	1993–1997	400	85
UNMIH (Haiti)	1993–1996	6,800	316
UNOMUR (Rwanda)	1993–1994	81	15
UNAMIR (Rwanda)	1993–1996	5,500	437
UNOSOM II (Somalia)	1993–1995	28,000	1,600
UNMLT (Cambodia)	1993–1994	20	5
UNASOG (Libya/Chad)	1994	9	0.7
UNMOT (Tajikistan)	1994–2000	120	30
UNAVEM III (Angola)	1995–1997	4,220	890
UNPREDEP (Macedonia)	1995–1999	1,106	570
UNCRO (Croatia)	1995–1996	7,000	300
UNMIBH (Bosnia)	1995–	2,900	810
UNTAES (Croatia)	1996–1998	5,177	350
UNMOP (Croatia)	1996–	28	26
UNSMIH (Haiti)	1996–1997	1,500	56
MINUGUA (Guatemala)	1997	155	5
UNTMIH (Haiti)	1997	250	20
MONUA (Angola)	1997–1999	3,575	293
MIPONUH (Haiti)	1997–2000	300	40
UNPSG (Croatia)	1998	233	70
MINURCA (Central African Republic)	1998–2000	1,360	73
UNOMSIL (Sierra Leone)	1998–1999	250	40
UNMIK (Kosovo)	1999–	6,000	1,200
UNAMSIL (Sierra Leone)	1999–	17,500	1,300
UNTAET (East Timor)	1999–	10,790	1,300
MONUC (Congo)	1999–	5,537	450
MICAH (Haiti)	2000–2001	100	10
UNMEE (Eritrea-Ethiopia)	2000–	4,200	180
Total: 34 missions		**191,717 troops**	**$17.5 billion**

Notes: Data as of November 2001. Cost figures are not adjusted for inflation. *Only 500 troops deployed. †Joint UN/OAS Mission.

Even the UN's troubled operation in Yugoslavia (UNPROFOR), which was never able to arrange a stable cease-fire between warring parties, was billed by Western leaders as late as 1994 as a success, since they claimed it ended most of the fighting in the region and played an important role in guaranteeing the delivery of humanitarian aid. While it was clear that UNPROFOR would not bring about a peaceful settlement, Western leaders maintained that its withdrawal would lead to enormous bloodshed and possibly genocide.

THE DREAM COMES CRASHING DOWN

During the late afternoon of October 3, 1993, Somali militiamen shot down two U.S. Army helicopters supporting the UNOSOM II peacekeeping mission, touching off a bloodbath in which 18 U.S. soldiers and over 500 Somalis were killed, and more than 1,000 injured. Bullets were fired at U.S. troops in Mogadishu from every direction by men, women, and children. Somalis dragged the naked body of a U.S. Army Ranger through the streets of Mogadishu.

The carnage shocked America. Shock turned to outrage when it was learned that casualties were so high because Washington refused to equip U.S. soldiers in Somalia with heavy weapons or armored vehicles because the Clinton administration viewed Somalia as a benign "peacekeeping" environment. As a result, many U.S. soldiers initially injured in the October 3 violence were shot again while being evacuated in humvees due to a lack of armored personnel carriers.[15]

Somali militiamen brought down more than two U.S. helicopters on that day; they forced the abandonment of assertive multilateralism as an overt U.S. foreign policy and contributed to the resignation of a U.S. secretary of defense. Today, despite the expenditure of over $2 billion on two UN peacekeeping efforts, Somalia remains as lawless as it was when UN forces entered the country 10 years earlier.[16]

UN peacekeeping and assertive multilateralism might have recovered from the October 1993 disaster in Somalia if there had been no further peacekeeping fiascoes and if UN and Western officials had learned from the mistakes of the Somalia operation. Unfortunately, this was not the case.

Two weeks after the Somalia debacle, UN peacekeeping efforts suffered a stunning—but bloodless—setback in Haiti when armed thugs on the docks of Port-au-Prince turned back peacekeepers on board the *USS Harlan County*. Confronted with gangs of armed men and a bevy of television cameras, the *Harlan County* withdrew and the peacekeeping mission was canceled. In March 1994, the United States invaded Haiti under the UN flag to establish democracy and conditions for a peacekeeping force. But neither U.S. nor UN efforts saved Haiti from dictatorship and kleptocracy. Jean-Bertrand Aristide—who was returned to power in November 2000—

has prevented free elections and set up a corrupt regime of his cronies. Five subsequent UN peacekeeping efforts since 1993 failed to bring democracy to Haiti or significantly improve the humanitarian situation in the country. Cost of UN expanded peacekeeping efforts in Haiti, 1993 to 2001: about $440 million.[17] Costs incurred by the United States to invade Haiti and U.S. efforts to reform the Haitian police: approximately $3 billion.

Shortly after UNTAC withdrew from Cambodia in early 1994, its achievements began to unravel. The genocidal Khmer Rouge faction resumed its guerrilla war in the countryside. Hun Sen, former head of the communist government, ran the winner of the UNTAC-brokered national election, Prince Ranariddh, out of the country and killed his top aides. A mid-1998 national election was manipulated by Hun Sen, who used political killings, torture, and blackmail to undercut his opponents. Cost of UN peacekeeping efforts in Cambodia, 1992 to 1994: $1.6 billion.[18]

Meanwhile, while UN peacekeepers in Rwanda looked on helplessly, between April and June 1994, Hutu tribesmen killed an estimated 800,000 Tutsis and Tutsi supporters in one of the worst cases of genocide since World War II. The UN force in the country was woefully understrength and had neither the mandate nor the means to stop the violence.

In Bosnia, UN peacekeeping suffered its most spectacular setbacks. By 1995, it became clear that UN efforts to guarantee the delivery of humanitarian assistance were being manipulated by all sides to serve their war aims. In March 1995, after UN peacekeepers called in NATO airstrikes, the Bosnian Serbs responded with their "human shield" tactic—chaining UN peacekeepers to strategic facilities to stave off more airstrikes. In June 1995, the Serbs overran UN "safe areas" despite the presence of UN troops, slaughtering thousands. Cost of UN peacekeeping efforts in Bosnia, 1992 to 1995: $4.6 billion.[19]

A SOLEMN JUBILEE

As a result of these and other peacekeeping setbacks, the UN's fiftieth anniversary in 1995 was more a wake than a celebration. The United Nations sheepishly backtracked from the activist peacekeeping policy it had championed just two years earlier. In February 1995, the president of the UN Security Council issued a statement reaffirming that peacekeeping is based on "the principles of consent of parties, impartiality, and non-use of force except in self-defense."[20] Secretary General Boutros-Ghali had made a similar statement the previous month.

The UN was lambasted in 1995 from coast to coast in the United States as incompetent and irrelevant. In 1991, a Gallup/Roper poll reported that 67 percent of Americans thought the UN was doing a good job. By June 1995 only 42 percent were favorably impressed, while 46 percent thought it was doing a bad job.[21] The UN's longtime allies in the American press joined in the attacks. Influential liberal journal *The New Republic* ran a feature cover story calling for abolishing the UN with a bullet-ridden UN logo on its cover.[22] Other former American friends of the UN, such as the United Nations Association of the United States of America (UNA-USA), were strangely quiet.

Notwithstanding Western efforts in 1995 to falsely pin the blame for major peacekeeping failures entirely on Boutros-Ghali and the UN, the truth slowly emerged that these failures were mostly the result of negligent policies of the major powers. This is not to say that the UN was blameless; its management of post–Cold War peacekeeping operations ranged from poor to abysmal. But the limitations of the UN system and mismanagement of Cold War peacekeeping was no secret. From 1993 to 2000, Western powers dumped the world's most intractable conflicts on the United Nations without providing it with the necessary funding, logistical support, or political backing needed to resolve them. The cascade of peacekeeping fiascoes which began in 1993 were not only inevitable, they were predictable. Moreover, it is worth noting that Boutros-Ghali was a staunch opponent of most proposals to give UN peacekeeping missions in Somalia and Yugoslavia offensive military missions because he believed that such steps would be counterproductive and endanger the lives of UN peacekeepers.

THE PEACEKEEPING BALANCE SHEET

UN peacekeeping's downfall in the mid-1990s saddened its long-suffering supporters and gladdened its enemies. Like Woodrow Wilson and the signers of the Covenant of the League of Nations in 1919, UN proponents lamented the loss of what they thought was a once-in-a-century opportunity to build an idyllic world order based on international law and collective security. UN opponents were cheered by the demise of a philosophy that they felt would never work and could have endangered the world's democracies by causing them to lower their defenses. Many critics of the 1990s UN revival saw the beginnings of a nascent world government and a majoritarian global parliament.

Regardless of ideological viewpoint on the UN and peacekeeping, one point is clear: there is ample evidence that traditional UN peacekeeping has played a useful role over the last 50 years by filling a niche as the only viable mediator in a number of international conflicts. These conflicts included Kashmir, Cyprus, Palestine, and Iran-Iraq. In almost all cases, traditional peacekeeping served U.S. interests by facilitating truces involving U.S. allies and preventing the outbreak of major conflicts that may have required U.S. military intervention. Given that conflicts between states are certain to continue in the post–Cold War era, maintaining UN peacekeeping as a viable foreign policy tool clearly is in the interests of the United States.

This book explores the questions of whether UN peacekeeping can play a role in promoting post–Cold War world order, whether it can recover from its post–Cold War crisis of credibility and confidence, and what U.S. equities are in the continued development of UN peacekeeping operations. I will try to answer the following questions:

- How does peacekeeping work?
- What was its Cold War record?
- What factors allowed peacekeeping during the Cold War to succeed?
- Has UN peacekeeping been damaged beyond repair?
- How can traditional peacekeeping advance post–Cold War U.S. interests?

NOTES

1. University of California at Berkeley Institute of International Relations Internet conference, 1999, http://globetrotter.berkeley.edu.UN.Urquhart/urqchat99.peace.html.

2. Boutros Boutros-Ghali, "An Agenda for Peace: One Year Later," *Orbis* 37, no. 3 (Summer 1993), p. 328.

3. Bradley Graham, "Two Army Divisions Unfit for War," *Washington Post*, November 10, 1999, p. 1.

4. Diane Tsimekles, "Guard in Charge: Can Part-Time Warriors Command Active Duty Units in Bosnia?" *Army Times*, October 11, 1999, p. 14.

5. Lewis MacKenzie, "A Crucial Job, but Not One for a Superpower," *Washington Post*, January 14, 2001, p. B3.

6. Lewis Mackenzie, quoted in Perry L. Pickert, ed., *Intelligence for Multilateral Decision and Action* (Washington, DC: Joint Military Intelligence College, 1997), p. 523.

7. See Stanley Meisler, *The United Nations: The First Fifty Years* (New York: Atlantic Monthly Press, 1995), p. 289.

8. Alan James, "Is There a Second Generation of Peacekeeping?" *International Peacekeeping* (University of Frankfurt) 1, no. 4 (September–November 1994), pp. 110–113.

9. Figure 1.1 is based on consultations the author conducted with peacekeeping experts and research of post–Cold War missions. Many attempts at this continuum have been made by other authors and analysts studying this subject. The Department of State in July 2000 favored two complex formulations developed by the Rand Corporation for the Pentagon. These continuums, RANDMR583-1.1 and RAND582-3.1, although produced only months apart, have significant differences. One has seven dimensions, the other eight. They typify the confusion among some Western statesmen and foreign policy experts about multinational conflict resolution after the Cold War. See Bruce R. Pirnie and William E. Simons, *Soldiers for Peace: Critical Operational Issues* (Santa Monica, CA: Rand Corporation, 1996)

and Bruce R. Pirnie and William E. Simons, *Soldiers for Peace: An Operational Typology* (Santa Monica, CA: Rand Corporation, 1996).

10. *The Blue Helmets: A Review of United Nations Peacekeeping*, 2nd ed. (New York: UN Department of Public Information, 1991), pp. 134, 175–185, 263–277.

11. For simplicity, this book refers to those who advocated in the 1990s using new forms of UN peacekeeping to address civil wars and ethnic conflicts or to charge peacekeeping with "nation building" as liberal internationalists. This is not meant to be pejorative, and I hope my many friends who are enthusiastic supporters of expanded peacekeeping will forgive me if they find this label objectionable.

12. The most prominent book encompassing this thinking is *Self-Determination in the New World Order* by Morton H. Halperin and David J. Scheffer (Washington, DC: Carnegie Endowment for International Peace, 1992). Halperin and Scheffer were architects of President Clinton's peacekeeping policy and held senior foreign policy jobs in the Clinton administration. Mr. Halperin was named in mid-1993 to a newly created Pentagon post, "Under Secretary of Defense for Peacekeeping and Humanitarian Affairs," but had to withdraw his name in December 1993 due to intense opposition from Senate Republicans and Senator Sam Nunn (D-GA). Another liberal internationalist publication on this theme that significantly influenced Clinton administration UN policy was *Partners for Peace: Strengthening Collective Security for the 21st Century* by The United Nations Association (New York: UNA-USA, 1992).

13. Sources: United Nations Department of Peacekeeping Operations, UN Peacekeeping Internet homepage, http://www.un.org/Depts/dpko/, U.S. General Accounting Office; United Nations Department of Public Information Fact Sheet, DPI/1634/Rev.19, March 1, 2001.

14. Ibid.

15. The author interviewed Staff Sergeant John Burns, a U.S. Army Ranger who survived the October 1993 ambush, at Walter Reed Army Hospital in November 1993. Burns was shot trying to save the life of another injured ranger. He was shot a second time in an open humvee while being evacuated.

16. Sources: United Nations Department of Peacekeeping Operations, UN Peacekeeping Internet homepage, http://www.un.org/Depts/dpko/, U.S. General Accounting Office.

17. Ibid.

18. Ibid.

19. Ibid.

20. United Nations Document S/P RST 1995/9, February 22, 1995.

21. *New York Times*, June 25, 1995 p. A6.

22. *The New Republic*, October 30, 1995.

Part I

Traditional Peacekeeping

The UN Charter was not intended to protect repressive dictatorships or empires. The purpose of the Charter is not only to discourage the use of force in international affairs; it is also to promote a world order based on democratic values and practices.

—Jeane J. Kirkpatrick[1]

Chapter 2

Roosevelt's Doomed UN Vision

No balance of power, no spheres of influence, no alliances, none of the traditional forms of diplomacy will be necessary now that there is an international organization.

—Cordell Hull, 1945

[A] sure competitor for the most absurd utterance made since the invention of language.

—Abba Eban, on the above quote, 1986[2]

The elation that blossomed from the UN founding conference in San Francisco in May 1945 withered by 1946 as the UN became one of the first victims of the Cold War. Joseph Stalin's utter contempt for international law and self-determination meant that neither President Franklin Delano Roosevelt's realist UN plan nor a more idealistic scheme by his State Department stood any chance of being implemented. Indications of post-war Soviet policy surfaced in 1945 before the UN Charter had even been signed when the USSR signaled its intention to install a puppet government in Poland. While Roosevelt tried to convince Moscow to take a more cooperative path at the Yalta Conference and never gave up on his vision for a post-war world organization, he was well aware of the rocky road before the UN when he died. Indeed, the limitations of the UN became clear when it was barely a year old. Moscow began to use its Security Council veto to fend off condemnations of its territorial ambitions, effectively paralyzing the UN's collective security capabilities. The West, in response, wrote off the organization in favor of an alternative regional collective security organization to counter the USSR in Europe: the North Atlantic Treaty Organization (NATO).

THE ROOSEVELT/CHURCHILL UN PLAN

The miasma that begot the UN was a confusing mix of realism, utopianism, world federalism, and post-war euphoria. President Roosevelt conceived of a post-war world organization dominated by a great-power directorate. This idea horrified FDR's State Department, which was partial to more utopian international relations schemes.

FDR's plan for a post-war world organization was intended primarily to prevent the rise of another Nazi Germany or Imperial Japan. Although earlier in his career FDR had been a proponent of Wilsonian internationalism, he became disenchanted with the League of Nations by the mid-1930s and came to believe that only a balance of power scheme could save the world from future global wars. In FDR's "great-power directorate," each great power would impose peace in their respective spheres of influence but would unite when confronted with a recalcitrant state or alliance which threatened all of its members; a tacit collective agreement to make war on states that posed a serious threat to global peace. FDR intended the UN organization to have other elements, such as a representative General Assembly, but believed it should be a minor body that would not discuss important matters.

British Prime Minister Winston Churchill strongly agreed with the need for great-power rule to maintain peace after the war. Churchill, also a proponent of the League of Nations before the war, reluctantly agreed with Roosevelt that it was inadvisable to revise the League.[3] UN scholar Inis L. Claude, Jr. summarized their thoughts on this point as follows:

The Charter contemplates what is in essence a balance of power system. This was no doubt an unhappy choice for the founding fathers . . . The original scheme of the United Nations for the management of power on the international scene may thus be described as one which left the balance of power system intact for cases of major importance to global peace and order, and provided a collective security system to be applicable in cases of relatively minor significance. The Charter endorsed the ideal of collective security in unqualified terms, but envisaged its application in extremely limited terms.[4]

Historian Robert Dallek offered a more stark interpretation of Roosevelt's realist mindset and resistance to true multilateralism.

Though convinced that post-war affairs would operate under a system of great power control, with each of the powers holding special responsibility in their geographical spheres, Roosevelt felt compelled to obscure this idea through a United

Nations organization which would satisfy widespread demand in the United States for new idealistic or universalist arrangements for assuring the peace.[5]

Reining-in Stalin after the war became a goal of the two allied leaders for the UN by late 1944. FDR and Churchill feared that the USSR would not part with the East European lands it captured from the Axis and had its own post-war expansionist plans. The American and British leaders hoped that the UN organization would extend the wartime Big Three alliance, keeping Stalin engaged and thus discouraging him from enterprises which would endanger his membership in this exclusive club.

By early 1945, it was apparent to FDR and Churchill that simply including the USSR as a great power in a post-war organization was not going to guarantee its good behavior. Indeed, by March 1945, FDR and Churchill were actively discussing ways to use the UN *against* Moscow if it were to violate the terms of the UN Charter. This change in attitude was not lost on Stalin, who drove a hard bargain during the final negotiations on the UN because of his fear that Washington and London were planning to use the UN to stop Moscow from seizing or controlling new territory.[6]

THE LEAGUE REVIVED

FDR and Churchill painted their post-war world organization in broad general strokes. While they had in mind a grand alliance based on the wartime Big Three, neither leader gave much thought as to how to design such a plan because they were consumed with winning the war.[7] FDR and Churchill delegated the job of working out the details to the U.S. State Department and the British Foreign Office. This gave careerists in each foreign ministry—most of whom were ardent proponents of reviving the League of Nations—the opportunity to reshape the FDR/Churchill UN plan to their liking.

Thus, by mid-1945, after two years of discussions, British and American negotiators came up with a blueprint for a post-war organization that looked distinctly like the League of Nations. Shunning the FDR model, their post-war world organization stressed the equality of nations and enshrined the UN General Assembly as a global parliament. It moved further beyond the FDR realist model by giving the UN a leading role in arms control, economics, decolonization, and international legal issues. It is worth noting, however, that some of the U.S. State Department's more utopian proposals for the UN were dropped when the U.S. Congress learned about them. For example, congressional opposition forced State Department negotiators to abandon a proposal made at the Dumbarton Oaks Conference—where the UN Charter was drafted in mid-1944—to place U.S. domestic matters under the jurisdiction of the World Court.[8] The U.S. Congress raised similar objections in 2000 when Senate opposition delayed the Clinton administration from signing the Rome Treaty, creating an International Criminal Court.[9] Although Clinton eventually signed the Rome Treaty in the waning days of his presidency in December 2000, it is unlikely to be ratified by the United States due to opposition from the George W. Bush administration and the U.S. Senate.

Rapidly changing events in 1945 prevented FDR and Churchill from focusing on the revised UN blueprint, and it is unlikely that either leader had a firm understanding of the Dumbarton Oaks proposals.[10] The end of the war in Europe, defeating Japan, and Stalin's post-war territorial ambitions dominated their attention. In addition, FDR's failing health limited his ability to focus on his work. As a result, the only UN matter the two Western leaders engaged in during FDR's last days was ensuring that the Soviet Union actually joined the organization. They left the final planning of the world organization to others.

THE DEATH OF FDR AND THE BIRTH OF THE UN

Because of a conflux of momentous events, the high-water mark of the UN's popularity occurred between April 1945 and January 1946. The defeat of the Nazis and the end of the war with Japan created a global groundswell of utopian euphoria that embraced the UN as the key to post-war peace and security. The U.S. State Department encouraged popular U.S. support for the world body by running what Senator Robert Taft termed "a super propaganda campaign."[11] UN proponents portrayed the organization as the legacy of the late President Roosevelt, the allied leader who won World War II. (Franklin Delano Roosevelt died on April 12, 1945, less than two weeks before the convening of the UN's founding conference in San Francisco.) This argument was so powerful that it convinced many opponents of the UN to support the organization. This included Joseph Stalin, who was considering not joining the organization and had announced that he would send a low-level delegation to San Francisco. Stalin reversed his position after FDR's death.

The opening of the San Francisco Conference on April 25, 1945, reflected the enormous global support and sky-high hopes for the world organization. Thousands turned out to greet conference delegates in San Francisco. Doves were released into the air outside the conference center. U.S. congressional delegates to the conference received a standing ovation from their colleagues as they departed the U.S. Capitol.

The reality of the San Francisco Conference was a far cry from the pomp that surrounded its opening. The conference was dominated by heated debates and nearly collapsed several times. Small states fiercely opposed the permanent member veto and tried to abolish it. This debate became so rancorous that the United States made it clear that without the veto, there would be no UN. As Senator Thomas Connelly, a U.S. delegate to the San

Francisco Conference, put it in a speech to conference delegates: "You may go home from San Francisco . . . and report that you have defeated the veto . . . but you can also say, 'we tore up the Charter.'"[12]

While the smaller states backed down on this issue, they pushed on other fronts to expand the power and influence of the General Assembly, winning that body the right to discuss any international topic.[13]

The same arguments of fairness and democracy made by small states against the veto in 1945 were made again in 1993 due to the belief of many liberal internationalists that the veto would be abandoned or broadened to commemorate the UN's fiftieth anniversary in 1995. Third World disagreement on whom to add to the council and strong opposition by the U.S. Senate[14] to altering the council's size prevented enlargement in 1995 and likely will continue to do so for the foreseeable future. This is fortunate for the world and the United States. While critics today argue that the composition of the permanent membership is archaic, the current design of the Security Council provides it with a unique ability to work out difficult issues because of its small size and the prominent role of the world's most progressive, stable, and freedom-loving states—the United States, Britain, and France. Downtrodden minorities in Kosovo, Bosnia, Somalia, Northern Iraq, Sierra Leone, and Congo are unlikely to agree that the presence of these states as permanent Security Council members is unfair.

The biggest stumbling block at San Francisco was the USSR, which previewed the obstructionist tactics it would use in the UN over the next 40 years. The conference had barely begun when the Soviets claimed that it was unfair to have an American chairman and demanded three cochairmen, with one being a Soviet. A more serious problem arose over the use of the Security Council veto. Moscow wanted an absolute veto that could block the discussion of any issue. Washington and London insisted that the veto not be used to block free debate in the council. At one point, it appeared that this issue would scuttle the conference. This dispute was resolved when President Truman dispatched former FDR adviser Harry Hopkins to Moscow to personally appeal to Stalin, who overruled his foreign minister.[15]

SENATE REVIEW OF THE UN CHARTER AND PLACING U.S. TROOPS UNDER UN COMMAND

On June 25, 1945, the San Francisco Conference unanimously approved the UN Charter. Less than a week later, President Truman personally presented the charter to the U.S. Senate for ratification. The new world organization had overwhelming support in the U.S. Congress and only a handful of opponents. Leading the fight for the charter was Senator Arthur Vandenberg (R-MI), a former isolationist who served as a delegate to the

San Francisco Conference. In a Senate speech on July 29, 1945, Vandenberg expressed his reasons for supporting the UN:

[S]ince Pearl Harbor, World War II has put the cruel science of mass murder into
new and sinister perspective. . . . I again say that if World War III ever unhappily
arrives, it will bring new laboratories of death too horrible to contemplate. . . . We
must have collective action to stop the next war, if possible, before it starts, and
we must have collective action to crush it swiftly if it starts in spite of our organized
precautions.[16]

While overwhelmingly supportive of the UN, the July 1945 Senate debate
on the UN Charter featured reservations many senators had about U.S.
troops serving under UN command. The Truman administration argued
that once the Senate had ratified the charter, it could not place any restric-
tions on areas where American contingents of UN troops could operate.
President Truman also contended that he could deploy U.S. troops to UN
operations without consulting the Senate in accordance with his constitutional authority to use military force to protect U.S. interests *and* as the
officer charged with carrying out treaty obligations.[17]

Many U.S. senators were concerned that the UN not be used to deploy
American troops in hostile situations without the consent of the Senate,
which they believed would infringe on the Senate's constitutional power to
declare war.[18] Therefore, language was inserted into the UN Participation
Act—the enabling legislation that made the UN Charter U.S. law—authorizing the president to negotiate agreements to make U.S. military forces
available to the UN *subject to Senate approval.*[19]

President Truman believed he won this debate when the UN Charter was
ratified on July 28, 1945. Truman argued that Senate ratification obligated
the United States to place military forces at the disposal of the UN and that
the Senate had tacitly agreed that it had no right to vote on specific UN
deployments of U.S. troops. While formal agreements on how the United
States would supply troops to the UN still needed to be worked out, President Truman continued to out-maneuver the Senate. He announced that
he would submit these agreements to the whole Congress for approval by
majority vote in each house and not to the Senate for a two-thirds vote,
which is required under the U.S. Constitution for the ratification of trea-
ties.[20] Incredibly, the Senate went along with Truman, who probably was
able to get away with this unprecedented pronouncement due to widespread congressional support for the UN and fear by many senators that
isolationists in that body might have greater sway in the future when the
euphoria of the UN's founding wore off.

Under Article 43 of the UN Charter, UN members were to negotiate
agreements with the UN to place some of their troops at the disposal of
the Security Council to conduct collective security operations against ag-

gressor states. However, the negotiations to reach an Article 43 agreement in 1946 and 1947 were unsuccessful due to significant differences between the West and Moscow and the growing threat of Soviet militarism.[21]

When the Article 43 negotiations began, the United States proposed a UN force consisting of 20 divisions (over 300,000 men), 1,250 bombers, 2,250 fighters, and a large naval force deployed at UN bases worldwide. Moscow wanted a much smaller force of not more than 12 divisions and 600 bombers. The USSR also insisted on strict limits on UN forces. It called for UN troops to be stationed only on the territory of those nations which provided them, that they not be deployed to any operation for more than 90 days, and requiring all permanent members of the Security Council to provide exactly equal contributions to UN forces.

After it became clear that no UN troop contingents would be created, Congress amended the UN Participation Act in 1949 to allow the president to detail up to 1,000 troops to the UN without congressional approval.[22] The amendment permitted U.S. troops to serve as observers and guards but forbade them from combat roles. This had no practical effect during the Cold War, since U.S. participation in peacekeeping was extremely limited. However, it would become an issue 44 years later when the United States began to deploy large numbers of troops as UN peacekeepers with quasi-military mandates to expanded peacekeeping operations.

THE MICHAEL NEW CASE

How U.S. law and the Constitution relate to the expanded peacekeeping operations of the 1990s was put to the test in 1995 with the much-publicized case of U.S. Army Specialist Michael New. On October 10, 1995, Specialist New was ordered to wear a UN uniform and serve as a UN peacekeeper with the UN Preventive Deployment Force (UNPREDEP), which was deployed in Macedonia along its border with the Federal Republic of Yugoslavia.

Specialist New refused to wear a UN uniform, claiming that it violated his military oath and constituted an illegal military deployment by the president. He was consequently dishonorably discharged and court martialed. Among other things, New's attorneys argued that sending U.S. troops to UNPREDEP was illegal under the UN Participation Act, since the United States had more than 1,000 troops deployed to UN peacekeeping missions[23] and since troops were engaged in combat roles, which clearly went beyond the pacific roles for peacekeepers specified by Congress.

Specialist New attracted a great deal of support in the United States, especially from Congress. Several Congressmen introduced bills as a result of the New case to permit American troops to participate in UN peacekeeping missions only if they volunteer, although none of these bills have become law. As of early 2002, New still had legal appeals pending.

Photo 2.1: Specialist Michael New.

MOSCOW TORPEDOES THE UN

The euphoria of the UN's founding didn't last long. By the time the San Francisco Conference met, it was clear that Moscow would not honor the commitments it made at Yalta to hold free elections in Poland, not to mention the UN Charter it helped negotiate at Dumbarton Oaks. While it was possible to paper over the Poland issue at the San Francisco Conference, East-West tensions increased tremendously by the time the first UN General Assembly met in London in January 1946. Moscow repeatedly indicated that it intended to pursue policies antithetical to the ideals of the UN.

Moscow's rejection of UN principles was not lost on President Harry Truman, who was considerably more anti-Soviet than FDR and the U.S. State Department. As a result, Truman wrote off the UN by early 1946 and reassigned his pro-UN Secretary of State Edward Stettinius to the post of UN Ambassador to marginalize Stettinius and the UN. When Stettinius realized this, he resigned.[24]

Perhaps the one event that kicked off the Cold War and sealed the fate of the UN was a speech Joseph Stalin gave to a huge audience in Moscow on February 9, 1946 previewing his brutal post-war foreign policy. Reflecting his deep suspicions of the West, Stalin stated that a peaceful world order was impossible due to the capitalist-imperialist monopoly. He told his people that rearmament must take priority to developing the consumer sector of the Soviet economy. George F. Kennan, then chargé d'affairs at the American Embassy in Moscow, sent Washington a prescient analytic response to this speech, explaining the deep neuroses of the Soviet leadership and the likelihood that the USSR would go to any means necessary to infiltrate, divide, and weaken the West.[25]

The Soviets fulfilled Kennan's prophesy over the next 40 years using bloody and subversive tactics. They lent financial and arms support to North Korea and North Vietnam in wars against their southern counterparts. The USSR invaded Hungary in 1956 and Czechoslovakia in 1968 to brutally crush democratic movements. It invaded Afghanistan in 1979 to extend its influence in the region. Moscow and its East European puppet governments underwrote and funded dozens of terrorist and liberation movements to disrupt the West and overthrow pro-Western governments. Finally, the USSR kicked off a nuclear arms race that threatened to destroy the planet. Because of its behavior during the Cold War, the Soviet Union more than earned Ronald Reagan's famous description as an "evil empire."[26]

Moscow used its militarist foreign policy and harsh anti-Western rhetoric to intimidate U.S. allies in the UN and encourage other states to side with the Eastern bloc. As a result, by 1950, American statesmen were decrying the deterioration of the UN and how the United States increasingly found itself standing alone against Moscow. Former President Herbert Hoover protested this situation in a 1950 speech when he called for reorganizing the UN to oust the Soviets: "The Kremlin has reduced the United Nations to a propaganda forum for the smearing of free peoples. It [the UN] has been defeated as a preservative of peace and good will."[27] That same year, American-Soviet relations in the UN reached an historic low when the United States took advantage of a Soviet boycott of UN Security Council sessions to win Security Council authorization for military action to repel a North Korean invasion of South Korea.

THE COLD WAR SECURITY COUNCIL DEADLOCK

Moscow's contempt for international law and its expansionist ambitions caused the Security Council to deadlock during the Cold War. As Table 2.1 illustrates, from 1946 to 1970, the USSR was responsible for the vast majority of public vetoes cast, usually to block resolutions critical of Moscow or its client states.[28] The deadlock prevented the UN from fulfilling its primary purpose, promoting international peace and security.

The Council veto deadlock flip-flopped after 1970 when Moscow used the UN to promote a harsh anti-Western agenda (see Table 2.2). Security

Table 2.1
Public Security Council Vetoes, 1946–1970[29]

USSR	103
United States	1
China	1
France	4
United Kingdom	4

Table 2.2
Public Security Council Vetoes, 1971–1990[30]

USSR	11
United States	70
China	2
France	14
United Kingdom	26

Council resolutions vetoed during this period mostly condemned Israel, the United States, South Africa, and British policy toward Rhodesia. When the Cold War ended, East-West relations markedly improved and Security Council vetoes became rare.

THE FUN HOUSE

The UN's ability to advance international peace was hobbled further when Moscow and newly independent Third World states hijacked the organization and formed a large, fiercely anti-Western bloc. Most of these new states were headed by leftist revolutionaries, armed and financed by Moscow, who led rebellions against European colonial powers. This Soviet/ radical Third World bloc caused enormous damage to the UN. By 1970, UN General Assembly debates were dominated by three issues: radical proposals to redistribute Western wealth to the Third World, resolutions condemning the United States and Israel, and resolutions condemning the United States and South Africa. UN committees on trivial issues expanded at an incredible rate. Some examples: every year, the status of Pitcairn Island was debated in the decolonization committee, which in turn issued reports in six languages on the island's never-changing status. The UN spent over seven years preparing for a 1983 Conference on Peaceful Uses of Outer Space, despite the fact that one of the two space-faring powers—

the United States—refused to cooperate with the committee. Dozens of Third World dictatorships joined forces with the Soviet bloc to pass resolutions restricting news coverage of Third World nations, which they called the "New Information Order." But the worst Cold War abuse came in 1975 when the UN General Assembly passed a resolution condemning Zionism as racism. This resolution so outraged Americans that there was open talk in the United States of expelling the UN from American soil.

For all its problems, few U.S. administrations took the UN seriously enough to confront it. William F. Buckley, Jr. lamented this problem as an American delegate to the twenty-eighth UN General Assembly in 1973 when the State Department refused to clear a speech he wanted to give that would have asked states that practiced torture and refused to abide by the Universal Declaration of Human Rights to leave the chamber on the day of the declaration's twenty-fifth anniversary.[31] "Too controversial," he was told, for an organization that has so little regard for the United States. According to Buckley, American delegates to the UN at the time were barred from making any controversial statements. Any defense of the Jews in the UN, he wrote, could throw a monkey wrench into delicate U.S.-USSR-Arab negotiations. Raising freedom of emigration for Russian Jews would enrage the Russians and Arabs. In short, Buckley was told to let the UN delegates rant and make fools of themselves. UN debates did not matter to the United States, no matter how vile, no matter how many times UN members maligned the United States.

Gratuitous bashing of the United States continued until 1981 when President Ronald Reagan named Jeane J. Kirkpatrick as his UN Ambassador. Kirkpatrick made it known that there would be consequences for UN members who voted for resolutions harshly critical of the United States: she threatened to cut their U.S. foreign assistance. Kirkpatrick also attacked the UN Secretariat for its waste and inefficiency and for serving as a vehicle for Soviet propaganda and espionage. Soviet influence and U.S. bashing in the UN were reduced significantly due to Kirkpatrick's leadership.

AMBASSADOR LICHENSTEIN'S FAMOUS REBUKE

Extremely tense American-Soviet relations at the fall 1983 UN General Assembly session precipitated one of the most memorable speeches by an American UN diplomat. The Soviets shot down a South Korean civilian airliner killing 269 people shortly before the UN session opened in New York. Ambassador Kirkpatrick and her delegation to the UN responded with harsh condemnations. The states of New York and New Jersey refused to allow the Soviet UN delegation to land at New York City's civilian airports. Moscow and its allies responded by criticizing the United States for "mistreating UN delegates." Reflecting widespread American anger at the UN and the USSR at the time, Charles Lichenstein, one of Kirkpatrick's deputy ambassadors, answered the Soviet complaints with this famous rebuke:

If in the judicious determination of the members of the United Nations they feel that they are not welcome and they are not being treated with hostly consideration, then the United States strongly encourages such member states seriously to consider removing themselves and this organization from the soil of the United States. We will put no impediment in your way. The members of the U.S. mission to the UN will be down at dockside waving you a fond farewell as you sail into the sunset.[32]

UNREFORMABLE

Even for Jeane Kirkpatrick, reforming the UN system was next to impossible since the vast majority of UN members liked the system the way it was. While the Soviets agreed with the United States on keeping UN costs down, they had little interest in UN reform proposals that could remove its intelligence operatives from their UN jobs in New York. Few of America's Western allies would join Kirkpatrick on pressing UN reform, mostly because they did not want to offend the Third World. Moreover, some European powers reportedly saw UN graft as a way to redistribute wealth to developing states and thus justifiable. As a result, the system continued to grow more and more unwieldy through the 1980s.

Serious problems in the UN bureaucracy began in the mid-1960s when radical Third World states and the Soviet bloc used their large numbers to seize control of the United Nations bureaucracy. This led to notoriously poor management, including an overstaffed bureaucracy, cronyism, fiefdoms, featherbedding, and obscenely high, tax-free salaries. Regional "mafias" grabbed control of segments of the UN bureaucracy and consolidated their power through favoritism in hiring and promotions. Third World countries regularly plundered UN aid programs with little objection from UN officials. High-level UN officials received lavish gifts from member states seeking favors. The UN bureaucracy took a Luddite view toward technology, favoring labor intensive publishing methods well into the 1990s over cheaper and faster methods such as computers. Management problems were exacerbated by the tendencies of Third World countries to use UN posts abroad as sinecures for relatives and allies or for political foes who might try to organize coup attempts at home.

SPY CENTRAL

In 1948, after months of debate about where to locate the United Nations headquarters, Soviet diplomats consulted with Joseph Stalin on the issue. The Soviet diplomats told the Soviet leader of their concern that American plans to situate the UN headquarters in New York would give the United States too much influence over the organization. The diplomats preferred a neutral site such as Switzerland or Sweden. Stalin, however, stunned his diplomats by "heartily approving of New York City." The reason he gave was espionage.[33]

Stalin's decision was prophetic. The UN Headquarters in New York provided perfect cover for intelligence operations by the USSR and other nations hostile to the United States. UN diplomatic status in New York afforded foreign intelligence officers diplomatic immunity, free access to the United States, and numerous occasions for contact with foreigners. Moreover, due to the UN Headquarters agreement with the United States, Washington was forced to allow allies of Moscow—some of which did not have diplomatic relations with the United States, such as Libya and Cuba— to establish UN missions. This gave Moscow multiple sites in New York from which to base intelligence operations. The UN Secretariat provided even better intelligence opportunities. Soviets seconded to the UN staff had much wider access to foreigners and were paid high tax-free salaries in dollars, most of which was confiscated by Moscow.

The UN Headquarters library was a famous example of how Moscow used the UN system during the Cold War to its advantage. Until the mid-1980s, the UN library was operated by agents of the KGB to collect open-source information, translate it into Russian, and ship the purloined data back to Moscow—all at UN expense. Much of this data concerned U.S. technology and was obtained from expensive American on-line computer databases.[34]

Soviet espionage at the United Nations became a major scandal by the mid-1980s due to the attention given to the issue by the Reagan administration and the 1985 publication of *Breaking with Moscow* by Arkady Shevchenko, a high-ranking Soviet UN official who defected to the United States in 1978.[35] Shevchenko spelled out in great detail Moscow's intelligence operation in New York and charged that one-third of all Communist bloc nationals working for the UN were intelligence officers under the direct guidance of the KGB. These and other revelations led the Reagan administration to declare over 100 Soviet diplomats to the UN persona non grata on the grounds that they were intelligence officers and a threat to U.S. national security.[36]

An interesting question is whether Soviet exploitation of the UN for intelligence operations affected UN peacekeeping operations during the Cold War. Moscow and its allies had little ability to exploit Cold War peacekeeping efforts due to active efforts by the UN to exclude troops from the superpowers and Warsaw Pact nations. This was particularly true of UN Secretary General Dag Hammarskjöld, who routinely excluded Soviets and Warsaw Pact UN officials from important staff meetings, especially those dealing with peacekeeping missions. Parties to disputes also had vetoes on peacekeeping participants. It is not hard to imagine that Israel—which had strained relations with Moscow during much of the Cold War—had every reason to suspect that Moscow and its allies would use the plethora of UN peacekeeping missions deployed on Israel's borders during the Cold War to collect intelligence on Israel and pass such information to its enemies.

Moscow succeeded in sending a small number of Warsaw Pact troops to Cold War peacekeeping missions, aside from the handful of Soviet/Russian soldiers that have served with the UN Truce Supervision Organization in Palestine since 1948. Moscow's objections to the exclusion of Warsaw Pact nations from other peacekeeping missions led to the inclusion of Polish troops in the Second UN Emergency Force (UNEF II) in the Sinai in 1973 and UNDOF in the Golan Heights in 1974. Israel, however, harassed the Polish UNEF II and UNDOF contingents and refused to grant them freedom of movement. (Israel treated similarly a small Iranian contingent with the UN Interim Force in Lebanon in 1978.) Given extensive Soviet intelligence operations in all other areas of the UN system, it is reasonable to assume that Soviet intelligence exploited Soviet and Polish officers participating in both UN missions for intelligence purposes during the Cold War.

CONCLUSION

Between June 1945 and 1990, the UN deteriorated from a utopian collective security forum designed to promote world peace into an ineffective, corrupt platform for the Soviet Union and Third World states to pillory the United States and conduct espionage. As a result the Cold War UN was rendered incapable of playing the collective security–promoting role intended by its founders. If the organization were to make any significant contribution to international peace, it would have to be through some modest innovation acceptable to both superpowers. Peacekeeping was that innovation.

NOTES

1. Jeane J. Kirkpatrick, "Review Essay: The Use of Force in the Law of Nations," *Yale Journal of International Law* 16, no. 2 (Summer 1991), p. 594.

2. Abba Eban, "Interest and Conscience in Diplomacy," *Society* 23, no. 3 (April 1986), p. 19. Cordell Hull was U.S. secretary of state from 1933 to 1945. Abba Eban was concurrently Israeli ambassador to the United States and the UN from 1948 to 1959. Eban was Israeli foreign minister from 1966 to 1974.

3. Churchill had some significant differences with FDR on a post-war world organization. Churchill favored a regional security organization over a global organization, which he tried unsuccessfully to fold into FDR's UN scheme. Churchill also opposed Roosevelt's effort to promote decolonialization, which he rightly believed was an effort by the United States to dismantle the British empire. However, none of these issues were important enough to Churchill to upset the alliance to defeat Hitler. Churchill thus signed on to FDR's realist model for a post-war world

organization, dropping most of his reservations. Churchill was proved right in the end, of course, as Stalin's territorial ambitions rendered the UN moribund and led to the creation of NATO as an alternative regional alliance.

4. Inis L. Claude, Jr., "The Management of Power in the Changing United Nations," *International Organization* 15 (Spring 1961).

5. Robert Dallek, *Franklin D. Roosevelt and American Foreign Policy, 1932–1945* (New York: Oxford University Press, 1979), p. 536.

6. This problem may have surfaced during the Dumbarton Oaks Conference, a meeting held at an estate in Washington, D.C., during the summer of 1944, where American, British, Russian, and Chinese diplomats drafted the UN Charter. See Stanley Meisler, *The United Nations: The First Fifty Years* (New York: Atlantic Monthly Press, 1995), p. 10; Robert C. Hilderbrand, *Dumbarton Oaks: The Origins of the United Nations Search for Postwar Security* (Chapel Hill: University of North Carolina Press, 1990), pp. 248–257.

7. There also is ample evidence indicating that Churchill had no interest in discussing a post-war world organization until after he was sure the war was won. He apparently permitted the British Foreign Office to participate in negotiations on a post-war world organization only because of FDR's intense interest.

8. Thomas Campbell, *Masquerade Peace* (Tallahassee: Florida State University Press, 1973), p. 149.

9. See John R. Bolton, "Why an International Court Won't Work," *Wall Street Journal*, March 30, 1998, p. A19.

10. Campbell, *Masquerade Peace*, pp. 94–95.

11. Ibid., p. 154.

12. Thomas Connally, *My Name Is Tom Connally* (New York: Crowell, 1954), pp. 282–283.

13. Townsend Hoopes and Douglas Brinkley, *FDR and the Creation of the UN* (New Haven, CT: Yale University Press, 1997), p. 202.

14. Under Article 108 of the UN Charter, the legislatures of the five permanent powers of the Security Council must ratify any amendments to the UN Charter. This gives the U.S. Senate the ability to veto charter amendments.

15. Hopkins met with Stalin on June 2–6, 1945. The San Francisco Conference closed on June 26, 1945. Hoopes and Brinkley, *FDR and the Creation of the UN*, pp. 200–204.

16. 91 Congressional Record 7089, July 29, 1945.

17. James Reston, "Wheeler Starts Storm in Senate by Charter Speech," *New York Times*, July 24, 1945, p. 1.

18. "Troop Issue Splits Democrats," *New York Times*, July 26, 1945. See also UN, "Limitations in Leading Missions Requiring Force to Restore Peace," U.S. General Accounting Office, GAO/NSIAD-97-34 March 1997 (Washington, DC: Government Printing Office, 1997), p. 27.

19. United Nations Participation Act, Public Law 79-264, December 20, 1945.

20. James Reston, "Senate Ratifies Charter 89-2," *New York Times*, July 29, 1945, p. 1.

21. It is worth noting here that Article 43 required the United States to negotiate but not to conclude an agreement. Therefore, this attempt satisfied Washington's Article 43 obligations.

22. Amendment of United Nations Participation Act, Public Law 81-34, October 10, 1949.

23. As of December 31, 1995, the United States had 2,851 soldiers serving as UN peacekeepers. The breakdown was as follows: UNMIH (Haiti): 2,226; UN-PREDEP (Yugoslavia/Macedonia): 565; MINURSO (Western Sahara): 29; UN-IKOM (Iraq/Kuwait): 15; UNPROFOR: 1. Source: Project on the United Nations Internet web page, http://www.clw.org/pub/clw/un/troops1199.html.

24. Campbell, *Masquerade Peace*, pp. 194–195.

25. Dean Acheson, *Present at the Creation: My Years in the State Department* (New York: Norton, 1969), p. 222.

26. Liberal internationalist foreign policy experts in the West angrily condemned President Reagan's 1983 characterization of the Soviet Union as an evil empire. These experts almost uniformly ascribed to a "moral equivalency" theory that portrayed the American and Soviet political systems as morally equal and pursuing similar foreign policy goals. Such persons also refused to believe that Moscow actively supported terrorist activity against the West despite considerable evidence. CIA Director Robert Gates has written about Soviet support of terrorism against the United States and the resistance of the foreign policy establishment to accept this fact. See Robert M. Gates, *From the Shadows* (New York: Simon and Shuster, 1996), pp. 204–205, 338.

27. Russell Porter, "Hoover Proposes Reorganizing UN to Oust Russians," *New York Times*, April 28, 1950, p. 1.

28. Tables 2.1 and 2.2 do not include vetoes cast during secretary general elections, most of which are cast in secret ballots. However, the majority of these vetoes probably were cast by Moscow.

29. Source: Table of Vetoed Draft Resolutions in the United Nations Security Council, 1946–1991. International and Commonwealth Section, Research and Analysis Department, Foreign and Commonwealth Office, 1994.

30. Ibid.

31. William F. Buckley, Jr., *United Nations Journal: A Delegate's Odyssey* (New York: Anchor Books, 1977), pp. 138–140.

32. Richard Bernstein, "U.S. Aide Suggests Members Take the UN Elsewhere if Dissatisfied," *New York Times*, September 20, 1983, p. A1.

33. William Sherman, "Spies Who Came in for the Gold," *New York Daily News*, May 4, 1977, p. 4.

34. William Branigin, "As the UN Expands, So Do Its Problems," *Washington Post*, September 20, 1992, p. 1.

35. Arkady Shevchenko, *Breaking with Moscow* (New York: Knopf, 1978).

36. On March 8, 1986, the Reagan Administration ordered the expulsion of 105 Warsaw Pact personnel from UN missions in New York, accusing them of espionage against the United States and endangering U.S. national security. On September 18 of that same year, the United States expelled 25 diplomats from the Soviet mission to the UN, charging them with being senior Soviet intelligence officers.

Chapter 3

The Genesis of Peacekeeping: The UNEF Model

Peacekeeping can rightly be called the invention of the United Nations.
—Boutros Boutros-Ghali[1]

To understand traditional peacekeeping, one must study the UN Emergency Force (UNEF).* The traditional UN peacekeeping concept was born in 1956 when UNEF was created to help end the Suez Crisis, a dangerous international situation when two great powers—Great Britain and France—invaded Egypt and occupied the Suez Canal while Israel invaded the Sinai Peninsula.

The Suez Crisis deadlocked the Security Council as France and Britain used their Security Council vetoes to block council action. The UN General Assembly subsequently took up the crisis under the Uniting for Peace procedure, a process the United States invented during the Korean War to allow the General Assembly to discuss urgent matters on which the Security Council was deadlocked.[2] After several days of negotiations, the General Assembly passed a resolution calling on the UN secretary general to submit a plan for a UN force to secure and supervise a cease-fire.[3] UN Secretary General Dag Hammarskjöld and Canadian Foreign Minister Lester Pearson drew up a plan for this operation, the first modern peacekeeping force.[4] It was to be known as the UN Emergency Force (UNEF).

The secretary general submitted a preliminary report on November 5, 1956 that was immediately endorsed by the General Assembly in a reso-

*UNEF became known as the First UN Emergency Force (UNEF) in 1967 to distinguish it from its successor, the Second UN Emergency Force (UNEF II). For simplicity, this chapter uses the acronym "UNEF" to refer to UNEF I.

lution that was remarkable for the extraordinary latitude it gave the secretary general.[5] UNEF was deployed days later to the Sinai Peninsula
between Israeli and Egyptian forces and facilitated the departure of French
and British forces. In a related development, Pearson also wanted to send
a UNEF-like force to Hungary in response to a Soviet invasion of that
country that occurred six days before the Suez Crisis. This was impossible
because of Soviet opposition and underlined what would become a cardinal
rule of UN peacekeeping: it could not be deployed where the superpowers
did not want it.

LEGAL BASIS

UNEF had a unique legal justification that differs from most subsequent
peacekeeping operations. According to the UN, UNEF was a subsidiary
organ of the UN General Assembly created under Chapter IV, Article 22
of the UN Charter,[6] which permits the General Assembly to establish subsidiary bodies to help it carry out its functions. This was a rare instance
when the assembly exercised its right to discuss any issue under Articles 10
and 11 of the UN Charter as well as its right under Article 14 to make
recommendations to peacefully resolve any situation. This legal justification
was an historical anomaly. Most later peacekeeping operations were created by the Security Council. Indeed, its successor, UNEF II, was created
by the council.

At first glance, Chapter VI of the UN Charter, *Pacific Settlement of Disputes*, appears to provide the legal foundation for UNEF and subsequent
traditional peacekeeping operations. It specifies non-military solutions to
international conflicts and stipulates that disputants shall seek a solution
through negotiation, inquiry, mediation, conciliation, arbitration, judicial
settlement, resort to regional agencies or arrangements, or other peaceful
means of their own choice. Chapter VI also permits the Security Council
to recommend peaceful solutions to international disputes. Chapter VI thus
differs significantly from Chapter VII, *Action with Respect to Threats to
the Peace, Breaches of the Peace, and Acts of Aggression*, which allows the
council to mandate solutions to international conflicts, using force if necessary. However, using Chapter VI as the legal basis for peacekeeping
would conflict with Chapter I, Article 2 of the Charter, which forbids the
United Nations from intervening in the domestic matters of states except
under Chapter VII.

Dag Hammarskjöld argued in 1961 that UNEF drew its legal basis from
several areas of the UN Charter, but mainly from a notional "Chapter
VI½,"[7] which put peacekeeping's legal basis between Chapters VI and VII.
Hammarskjöld once tried to explain this duality by contending that "peacekeeping is not a job for soldiers, but only soldiers can do it."[8] While Hammarskjöld's "Chapter VI ½" interpretation gained many adherents, it

remained controversial and was debated for decades. For example, Secretary General U Thant noted in a speech in 1970 that the UN was still sharply divided over the specific provisions of the UN Charter under which peacekeeping missions were undertaken.[9] In 1993, UN Secretary General Boutros Boutros-Ghali seemed to lean toward Hammarskjöld's interpretation when he said, "peacekeeping is a missing link between Chapters VI and VII."[10]

PRINCIPLES OF THE UNEF MODEL

From November 6 to 18, 1956, Hammarskjöld conducted extensive consultations to devise ground rules for UNEF. Mission principles had to factor in the sensitive political situation and how to set up a multilateral force outside the provisions of the UN Charter and without Security Council endorsement. UNEF had to be fashioned in such a way that did not offend or threaten the parties to the dispute or the permanent members of the Security Council. (Washington, Moscow, London, and Paris all had strong views on the Sinai situation.) But it also had to be a substantial and effective operation. To achieve these goals, Hammarskjöld devised the following principles for UNEF that would form the bedrock of all traditional operations to follow it.

Consent

The most important UNEF principle was obtaining—and maintaining—the consent of the parties to the dispute. This reflected Hammarskjöld's view that because UNEF was not an enforcement action under Chapter VII of the UN Charter, it could operate in host countries only with their consent. Egypt consented to the deployment of UNEF on its territory, while Israel refused to permit UNEF troops either on its territory or behind armistice lines.[11] Egypt consented to full freedom of movement of UNEF troops and overflights of Egyptian territory by UN aircraft. Israel refused to grant these privileges. UNEF troops were therefore deployed only on Egyptian territory, with Egypt's permission. Nominal consent was obtained from Israel, which agreed to the cease-fire and cooperated with UNEF as far as it could without allowing UNEF troops to cross the armistice line. Britain and France also abided by the cease-fire and cooperated with UNEF as they withdrew from Egyptian territory. Map 3.1 illustrates how UNEF was deployed.

UNEF's consent principle largely was the result of Egyptian President Gamal Abdel Nasser's concerns that UNEF would infringe on Egyptian sovereignty. Hammarskjöld signed several bilateral agreements with Egypt addressing these concerns,[12] which were endorsed by the UN General As-

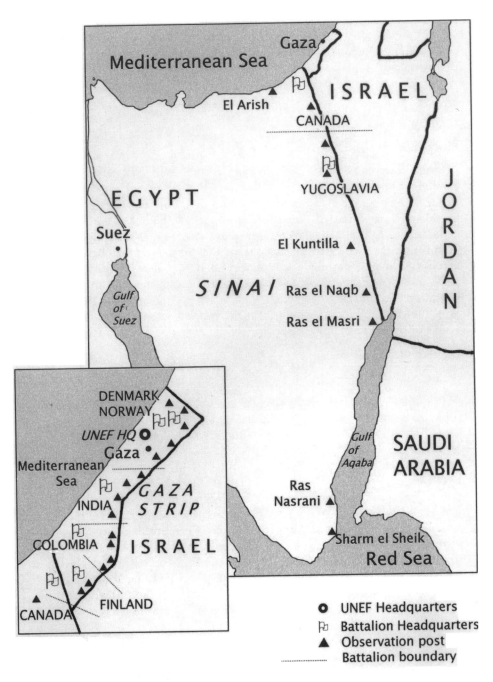

Map 3.1: UNEF I deployment, 1957. (Julie Fleitz)

sembly on November 7, 1956.[13] Essential points of the UNEF consent concept were:

- UNEF could not stay or operate in Egypt unless Egypt continued its consent.
- UNEF could not stay or operate in Egypt if consent was withdrawn.
- UNEF could not submit Egypt to external control or otherwise infringe on its sovereignty.
- UNEF was a temporary operation.[14]

Not all of these principles were carried out as intended. UNEF lasted 10 years and would have continued longer if war had not broken out. While Hammarskjöld agreed that consent was an absolute condition for the continuance of a peacekeeping force, his successor, U Thant, thought otherwise. Despite Cairo's demand for UNEF's withdrawal on May 16, 1967, Thant resisted withdrawing UNEF, even after Egyptian forces overran UN positions.

Troop Contributions

Another important UNEF principle was the use of impartial peacekeeping troops acceptable to the host government, Egypt. Since Israel refused to permit UNEF on its territory, its views on UNEF participants, while considered, were less important. Hammarskjöld believed this was an important dimension of the consent principle but resisted giving host nations an absolute veto on force participants. For example, Nasser tried to veto the participation of Canadian, Danish, and Norwegian troops because they were NATO members and British allies. Hammarskjöld objected and Nasser dropped this demand. In all likelihood, however, if Nasser had insisted that these troops not participate, Hammarskjöld probably would have acquiesced.

Despite overruling Nasser's initial objections, Hammarskjöld excluded troops from UNEF that would unduly offend Israel or Egypt. For this reason, Hammarskjöld excluded, according to the United Nations, "troops from the permanent members of the Security Council or from any country which, for geographical and other reasons, might have a special interest in the conflict."[15] To Hammarskjöld, this especially applied to Arab states and Warsaw Pact members.

Hammarskjöld also believed that impartiality could be maintained by assuring that UN peacekeeping forces had balanced geographical compositions. Hammarskjöld mandated that national contingents be roughly the same size and ensured that UNEF did not rely too heavily on any one state or region. Of several dozen offers of troops, Hammarskjöld chose 10 participants, listed in Table 3.1.

Photo 3.1: UNEF I peacekeepers on patrol, 1957. (UN photo, UN/DPI)

Self-Contained Contingents

Hammarskjöld had certain minimum requirements for UNEF contributions. He insisted that nations provide contingents capable of patrolling and taking responsibility for their own assigned zones. Contingents usually had to be self-contained and largely self-sufficient. They operated their own base camps and checkpoints. UNEF contingents were sent as a unit with their own commanders. National commanders answered to the deputy UNEF commanders who were UN officials.

The self-contained contingent principle gave some autonomy to participant units, easing administrative and management burdens on the UNEF commander, who coordinated the national contingents through his senior staff. However, it also made UNEF and subsequent traditional peacekeeping forces unwieldy and difficult to control, especially in crises. Most troubling was the tendency of national peacekeeping contingent commanders to clear orders from UN commanders with their capitals.

Use of Force

How UNEF would use military force was of great concern to Nasser. After protracted negotiations with Egypt, Hammarskjöld laid down very specific and limited conditions as to when UNEF could use force:

Table 3.1
Composition of UNEF at Peak Strength, September 1957[16]

Brazil	545
Canada	1,172
Colombia*	522
Denmark	424
Finland*	255
India	957
Indonesia*	582
Norway	498
Sweden	349
Yugoslavia	673
Total	**5,977**

*These contingents withdrew between 1957 and 1958. The rest remained until UNEF's withdrawal in 1967.

• UNEF was to use force only in self-defense.
• It would never use force in the interest of one party.

Hammarskjöld elaborated on these principles for future peacekeeping missions in a 1958 report:

A reasonable definition seems to have been established in the case of UNEF, where the rule is applied that men engaged in the operation may never take the initiative in the use of armed force, but are entitled to respond with force to an attack with arms, including attempts to use force to make them withdraw from positions which they occupy under orders from the Commander, acting under the authority of the Assembly and within the scope of its resolutions. The basic element involved is clearly the prohibition of any initiative in the use of armed force.[17]

In practical terms, UNEF was an armed presence that relied not on arms but on the good faith of disputants and the will of the international community to succeed. It was substantial enough so that warring parties could not casually move through its positions undetected. However, UNEF was also a non-threatening symbolic presence that either party could overrun if they chose to. It was able to function despite this military disadvantage because:

• UNEF did not have political objectives.
• UNEF was a neutral buffer force positioned between two parties.

• UNEF's mission was to oversee the cessation of hostilities and the withdrawal of armed forces.[18]

Command

While somewhat limited by the wishes of the great powers, contributing governments, the General Assembly, and parties to the dispute, Hammarskjöld had considerable latitude in managing and directing UNEF. The secretary general chose participating states and negotiated with Egypt and Israel on UNEF deployments. He issued rules governing the force and made other executive decisions. To assist him in these duties, Hammarskjöld relied upon informal committees of military and civilian advisors at UN Headquarters. His management of UNEF won universal support and greatly raised the stature of the UN secretary generalship.

Hammarskjöld won this autonomy to manage UNEF due to the Security Council deadlock. While UNEF had been approved by the UN General Assembly, it did not have the ability to manage a military operation. Moreover, Hammarskjöld and the West believed it was better to avoid giving UN bodies too much say over UNEF's day-to-day operations to insulate the operation from Cold War politics.

The choice of UNEF's commander was an officer neutral to the conflict and acceptable to both sides. The first commander was Canadian Lieutenant General E.L.M. Burns. General Burns was succeeded by commanders from India, Brazil, and Yugoslavia. The UNEF commander was operationally responsible for UNEF's performance and for deployment and assignment of troops. The commander appointed the officers in his command in consultation with the secretary general.

Deployment and Operations

UNEF was one of the most rapidly deployed UN forces in the history of peacekeeping. The first UNEF troops arrived on Egyptian soil on November 15, 1956—only 11 days after the secretary general was asked by the General Assembly to draw up a plan and one day after Egypt gave its consent to the force. Colombian, Danish, and Norwegian UNEF troops arrived on November 15 and 16. The target strength of 6,000 troops was reached in February 1957. Like many peacekeeping forces to follow it, UNEF was gradually reduced in size over time due to reduced tensions and financial problems. Its minimum size of 3,378 was reached in May 1967 when Cairo ordered it to withdraw.

UNEF had mobile units that could quickly respond to incidents. It manned 72 observation posts by day and conducted foot patrols along the demarcation line at night. UNEF was also greatly aided by terrain. Rough terrain, mine fields, and lack of roads greatly limited the number of infiltration points. Outside of Gaza, the few possible infiltration points were barren desert and relatively easy to monitor.

UNEF also benefited from close liaison with the two parties, especially Egypt. Concerns and incidents were thus easily defused or addressed. UNEF's efforts in the Gaza Strip succeeded because it had the full cooperation and support of the Egyptian and Palestinian police. Without this cooperation, the Palestinians in Gaza may have risen up against UN forces.

Like most of the peacekeeping operations to follow, UNEF engaged in a host of non-peacekeeping activities that earned it the good will of local citizens. These duties included civil administration, smuggling control, assistance to public utilities, and distribution of food. UNEF repaired roads and rendered other infrastructure support. The UN force also arranged exchanges of prisoners and cleared land mines.

Assessment

Hammarskjöld's strict principles governing UNEF allowed it to promote peace in the region for 11 years. Although both Israel and Egypt wanted a truce, they needed help establishing and maintaining one. UNEF filled this role well. Its principles of neutrality, consent, and limited use of force stood the test of time by forming the foundation for over two dozen subsequent operations. Most importantly, UNEF established the secretary general as an independent actor on the international stage.

UNEF typified the weaknesses and limitations of traditional peacekeeping. While UNEF's contingents were mostly competent, the operation was plagued with administrative, financial, and leadership problems. But UNEF's ability to keep the peace was unaffected, since no matter how badly the UN force was run, neither Israel nor Egypt wanted to go to war, and both parties viewed UNEF as a symbolic presence whose continuation was in their interests. UNEF was, in effect, their excuse for not fighting.

UNEF's record also was a harbinger of things to come. By most measurements, it was successful. UNEF facilitated the withdrawal of British, French, and Israeli troops from Egyptian territory. Its success in preventing illegal border crossings greatly lowered tensions between Israel and Egypt. The force also served U.S. interests by extricating two NATO allies from a difficult situation and protecting Israel—America's most valuable ally in the Middle East—from intervention by Moscow and its Arab allies.

However, the force did not succeed in several important ways. Like most traditional peacekeeping operations, UNEF was not linked to peace negotiations. Not only were no peace talks held between Israel and Egypt during this time, Israel considered Egypt still to be at war with her. As a result, the force was withdrawn in 1967 when war between Egypt and Israel broke out again.

NOTES

1. Boutros Boutros-Ghali, "An Agenda for Peace," UN Document A/47/277, June 17, 1992, p. 14.

2. Hammarskjöld won approval for UNEF I through the UN General Assembly by using the "Uniting for Peace Resolution" mechanism invented by the United States during the Korea crisis in 1950 (Resolution A/1775, November 3, 1950). This procedure allowed the General Assembly to authorize and pay for UN operations in Korea despite the Security Council veto. Considered patently illegal by many observers, this procedure went against the intentions of the UN's founders, who specifically entrusted military matters exclusively to the Security Council. However, the Uniting for Peace procedure won the support of the majority of UN members, since the operation in Korea was a UN operation in name only—the vast majority of troops were from the United States and South Korea—and because General Assembly resolutions passed under this scheme were mostly put forward to score political points against Moscow. Thus, the Korea case established the legally shaky precedent that the General Assembly can consider dire international security cases once the Security Council has been deadlocked for 24 hours.

3. UN General Assembly Resolution 998, November 4, 1956.

4. Not all experts agree that Hammarskjöld and Pearson founded peacekeeping. Some international relations analysts have posited that UNEF's origins stemmed from earlier UN peace efforts such as the UN Truce Supervision Organization (UNTSO), deployed in 1948 or the UN Special Committee on the Balkans (UNSCB), deployed in 1947. Some experts go further than this. Others have argued that modern peacekeeping is the descendent of collective security efforts attempted by the League of Nations in Upper Silesia in 1921 and Greece/Bulgaria in 1925. A few claim that peacekeeping's antecedents go back much further to the Concert of Europe, the Treaty of Westphalia, and even the ancient Greeks. The events of 1956 suggest that Hammarskjöld and Pearson operated on the fly to draw up an ad hoc plan that best fit the dire political situation of the time. The final word on this subject may come from Brian Urquhart, a former senior UN peacekeeping official who retired in 1986 after 40 years with the United Nations. Urquhart described Hammarskjöld's plan for UNEF as "a conceptual masterpiece in a completely new field, the blueprint for a non-violent, international military operation." Brian Urquhart, *A Life in Peace and War* (New York: Norton, 1987), p. 133. See also 1957 Nobel Peace Prize Presentation Speech for Lester Pearson, Nobel Committee, http://www.nobel.se/laureates/peace-1957-presentation.html and 1961 Nobel Peace Prize Presentation Speech for Dag Hammarskjöld, Nobel Committee, http://www.nobel.se/laureates/peace-1961-presentation.html; The United Nations Association, *Partners for Peace: Strengthening Collective Security for the 21st Century* (New York: UNA-USA, 1992), p. 8.

5. UN General Assembly Resolution 1000, November 5, 1956.

6. *The Blue Helmets: A Review of United Nations Peacekeeping*, 3rd ed. (New York: UN Department of Public Information, 1996), p. 43.

7. *The Blue Helmets*, 2nd ed. (New York: UN Department of Public Information, 1991), p. 5.

8. Hammarskjöld, quoted in *Nordic UN Tactical Manual*, vol. 1, Joint Nordic Committee for Military UN Matters (1992), p. 17.

9. Indar Jit Ritke, Michael Harbottle, and Bjorn Egge, *The Thin Blue Line: International Peacekeeping and Its Future* (New Haven, CT: Yale University Press, 1974), p. 3.

10. Boutros Boutros-Ghali, "Towards a New Generation of Peacekeeping Operations," *Bulletin of Arms Control* (May 1993), p. 7.

11. While it had the most powerful military in the region, the State of Israel had legitimate security concerns. The Arab world refused to make peace with it. Egyptian President Nasser remained publicly belligerent, and his anti-Israeli harangues grew more hostile through the 1960s. Israel faced restive Palestinians living within its borders and did not want to deal with UN interlopers interfering with its efforts to deal with them. Moreover, Israel already had several hundred unarmed UNTSO observers on its territory as part of the 1948 General Armistice agreements. Geography, however, was the Jewish state's most compelling concern. Composed of a narrow sliver of land no more than 60 miles wide (and less than 20 miles wide at its narrowest and most volatile area), Israel was extremely vulnerable to being overrun. It could not afford to cede any territory to a UN buffer force.

12. See UN Documents A/3375 and A/3526, November 1956.

13. UN General Assembly resolution 1001, November 7, 1956.

14. *The Blue Helmets*, 3rd ed., pp. 37–41.

15. Ibid., p. 42.

16. Source: Gabriella Rosner, *The United Nations Emergency Force* (New York: Columbia University Press, 1963), p. 122.

17. UN Document A/3943, October 9, 1958.

18. See Rosner, *The United Nations Emergency Force*, pp. 33–34 and Nils Sköld, *United Nations Peacekeeping after the Suez War: UNEF: The Swedish Involvement* (New York: St. Martin's Press, 1996), p. 18.

Chapter 4

From Prototype to Doctrine

United Nations peacekeeping may only be employed when both parties
to a conflict accept their presence. Accordingly, they may also be used
by the warring parties to avoid having a conflict escalate and, in the
event, also to have a struggle called off.
—Nobel Peace Prize statement for the 1988 Nobel
Peace Prize, awarded to UN peacekeeping forces[1]

Despite a vague definition and ambiguous legal basis, the traditional UN
peacekeeping model pioneered by Hammarskjöld became a coherent tech-
nique to address some international conflicts during the Cold War by deftly
navigating numerous political, military, and resource obstacles. Hammarskjöld's UNEF model was validated by the success of operations like
UNFICYP in Cyprus and UNTAG in Namibia—which were faithful to his
peacekeeping principles—as well as ONUC, the disastrous mission to
Congo in the 1960s, which was not. This chapter looks at how traditional
peacekeeping operations over 40 years transformed Hammarskjöld's prototype into a doctrine.

This study counts 21 UN peacekeeping missions conducted from 1947
through April 2002 as traditional operations (see Table 4.1). This selection
was made on the basis of the prerequisites for traditional peacekeeping
described in this chapter.[2] All of these missions generally honor peacekeeping guidelines delineated by Dag Hammarskjöld. Missions that go substantially beyond Hammarskjöld's guidelines are defined as expanded missions
and will be addressed in Chapters 7 and 8. UNIKOM (Iraq/Kuwait) is one
of several missions that arguably could be placed in either group. This

Table 4.1

Traditional Peacekeeping Missions[3]

	Start/End Dates	Authorized Size	Total Cost ($ millions)
UNMOGIP (India-Pakistan)	1948–	102	163
UNTSO (Palestine)	1948–	572	592
UNEF I (Sinai/Gaza Strip)	1956–1967	6,073	214
UNOGIL (Lebanon)	1958	591	4
ONUC (Congo)	1960–1964	19,828	400
UNSF (W. New Guinea)	1962–1963	1,576	26*
UNYOM (Yemen)	1963–1964	189	2*
UNFICYP (Cyprus)	1964–	1,257	980
UNIPOM (India/Pakistan)	1965–1966	96	2
UNEF II (Sinai/Suez)	1973–1979	6,973	446
UNDOF (Golan Heights)	1974–	1,454	732
UNIFIL (Lebanon)	1978–	7,000	3,240
UNIIMOG (Iran/Iraq)	1988–1991	399	190
UNGOMAP (Afghanistan/ Pakistan)	1988–1990	50	14
UNTAG (Namibia)	1989–1990	7,500	400
UNAVEM I (Angola)	1989–1991	70	16
ONUCA (Central America)	1989–1991	1,098	89
MINURSO (W. Sahara)	1991–	3,000	430
ONUMOZ (Mozambique)	1993–1995	7,100	520
UNASOG (Libya/Chad)	1994	9	0.7
UNMEE (Ethiopia/Eritrea)	2000–	4,200	180

Notes: Data as of November 2001. Cost figures are not adjusted for inflation. *Disputants bore the full costs of these operations.

analysis does not include UNIKOM as a traditional operation, since it was imposed on Iraq and relies on the threat of overwhelming force against Baghdad if it were to interfere with or attack the force. On the other hand, ONUC is included here since, although it evolved into a mission toward the end of its deployment that went considerably beyond the bounds of traditional peacekeeping, this was not ONUC's purpose.[4]

Over time, peacekeeping became understood to include both unarmed military observer missions like the UN Truce Supervision Organization (UNTSO) in Palestine and the UN Military Observer Group in India and

Pakistan (UNMOGIP) in Kashmir as well as lightly armed buffer missions permitted to use military force in self-defense, such as UNEF I, UNEF II, UNDOF (Golan Heights), UNFICYP (Cyprus), and UNIFIL (Lebanon). Observers generally were charged with monitoring cease-fire agreements, while armed peacekeepers usually patrolled demilitarized or buffer zones. A plurality of traditional peacekeeping operations (seven) has been sent to the Middle East. Israel was a party to all but one of these, the UN Yemen Observer Mission (UNYOM).

Traditional missions have not been limited to the Cold War era nor to simple observation or buffer force mandates. Nine traditional missions have been created since 1988; four in the 1990s. UNSF (West New Guinea) and UNTAG (Namibia) conducted national elections. Only one traditional mission, ONUMOZ (Mozambique), is an intrastate operation. While UNFICYP (Cyprus), UNTAG (Namibia), UNAVEM I (Angola), and ONUC also were conducted entirely within the borders of one state, they were not solely intrastate operations, since each were charged with facilitating the withdrawal of foreign forces and/or mercenaries.

DEFINITION AND LEGAL BASIS

Although the precise definition of peacekeeping has been long debated, the UN came up with one of the most widely used formulations in 1990:

As the United Nations practice has evolved over the years, a peacekeeping operation has come to be defined as an operation involving military personnel, but without enforcement powers, undertaken by the United Nations to help maintain or restore international peace and security in areas of conflict. These operations are voluntary and are based on consent and cooperation. While they involve the use of military personnel, they achieve their objectives not by force of arms, thus contrasting them with the "enforcement action" of the United Nations.[5]

Peacekeeping's legal basis remained an unresolved but dormant issue until the early 1990s when some Western academics and statesmen—mostly in the United States—began to assert that the traditional peacekeeping model is based solely on Chapter VI of the UN Charter, Pacific Settlement of Disputes. This line of argumentation was controversial. Despite pressure from the United States, the UN Security Council has never agreed to invoke or refer to Chapter VI in approving peacekeeping mandates. The reason is that the majority of UN members believe that Chapter VI refers to bona fide mediation efforts, such as good offices missions by the UN secretary general, and not peacekeeping missions. See Table 4.2 for a synopsis of UN Charter chapters and articles relevant to peacekeeping and peace enforcement.

Central to the definition and legal basis of traditional peacekeeping is

Table 4.2
The UN Charter on Peacekeeping and Peace Enforcement*

Chapter I: Introduction

Article 2, Paragraph 7	Bars UN from intervening in the domestic affairs of nation-states except under Chapter VII.

Chapter V: The Security Council

Article 25	Security Council decisions are legally binding on UN members.

Chapter VI: Pacific Settlement of Disputes

Articles 34–38	The Security Council may recommend "appropriate" procedures to resolve international disputes.

Chapter VII: Action with Respect to Threats to the Peace, Breaches of the Peace, and Acts of Aggression

Article 39	Gives the Security Council the power to determine whether a threat to the peace has occurred.
Article 40	Gives disputants a last chance to resolve a dispute before the council votes on an enforcement resolution.
Article 41	The Security Council may employ non-violent means, such as embargoes and sanctions, to restore the peace.
Article 42	Allows the Security Council to take military action to restore the peace.
Articles 48 and 49	UN members must implement Security Council enforcement measures unless exempted by the council.
Article 50	Non-disputants hurt by UN economic or military sanctions may seek recompense from the council.
Article 51	UN members may defend themselves and to come to the defense of an ally.

Chapter VIII: Regional Arrangements

Article 53	The Security Council can deputize regional organizations to conduct enforcement actions.

---

*Obsolete parts of the Charter on this subject, such as Articles 43–47, have been omitted.

the fact that traditional peacekeeping operations are *not* collective security missions which are, according to Inis L. Claude, Jr., intended to deal with *aggressive intent* (i.e., when the international community unites to combat an aggressor).[6] Peacekeeping addresses *dangerous situations* (i.e., when parties voluntarily agree to a multilateral solution to their dispute and no party is designated the aggressor by the international community). Peacekeeping forces therefore include neutral troops, require the consent and cooperation of warring parties, and use force only in self-defense.

PREREQUISITES FOR TRADITIONAL PEACEKEEPING

Through trial and error during the Cold War, the international community adapted and amended Hammarskjöld's UNEF principles into a set of minimum conditions for the deployment of a peacekeeping force. While scores of experts over the last 40 years postulated a torrent of such conditions, James H. Allen, a former Canadian peacekeeper, has compiled one of the best lists, reflecting his experience and Canada's long and proud participation in UN peacekeeping missions.[7] He posits three simple prerequisites: acceptance, impartiality, and minimum use of force.

Acceptance

Acceptance means that parties to a dispute consent to the deployment of a peacekeeping force and agree to cooperate with it. Disputants must desire a peacekeeping presence to help reduce tensions and agree to peace negotiations—that is, there must be a peace to be kept. The acceptance requirement reflects the crucial distinction of peacekeeping from peace enforcement: peacekeeping missions are not occupation forces or military interventions. They are careful not to violate or offend the sovereignty of state-parties to disputes. But traditional peacekeeping must have more than just the consent of governments; they must also have the acceptance of the local population.

Acceptance is crucial to the safety of peacekeepers. Warring parties will agree to accept a traditional peacekeeping force on its territory because it does not pose a military threat. Peacekeepers are thus lightly armed or unarmed and could easily be captured or killed by former warring parties. But because peacekeepers are deployed with the acceptance of local parties, they are generally not in danger. This arrangement worked remarkably well during the Cold War, and casualties were relatively low. Table 4.3 illustrates the relationship between acceptance and peacekeeping to casualties.

The UN Transition Assistance Group (UNTAG), deployed to Namibia from 1989 to 1990, is one of the best examples of acceptance. UNTAG was deployed to oversee Namibia's transition from a South African colony to a free and independent state. It oversaw free and fair elections, monitored a cease-fire, and verified the removal of South African forces. The operation went smoothly with only two UN fatalities from hostile action because it had the full and unconditional support of the parties to the dispute, South Africa and the South West African People's Organization (SWAPO). The support of the United States, USSR, Angola, and Cuba also illustrated how active pressure from outside parties—especially great powers—can help ensure that disputants cooperate with a peacekeeping mission. In this case, the support and pressure of the United States, which engineered the peace settlement, was the most important factor.

Table 4.3
Fatalities from Hostile Action of Selected Traditional Peacekeeping Missions[8]

	Level of Acceptance	Fatalities from Hostile Acts*
ONUMOZ (Mozambique) (1993–1995)	High	1
UNTAG (Namibia) (1989–1990)	High	2
UNDOF (Israel/Syria) (1974–)	High	7
UNFICYP (Cyprus) (1964–)	Medium	15
UNTAC (Cambodia) (1992–1993)	Medium	25
UNIFIL (Lebanon) (1978–)	Low	83
UNPROFOR (Yugoslavia) (1992–1995)	Low	74
UNOSOM II (Somalia) (1993–1995)	Low	110
ONUC (Congo) (1960–1964)	Low	135

*Excludes accidents and deaths from other causes.

Acceptance has also been a crucial factor behind the success of the UN Disengagement Force (UNDOF), a small force of only 1,000 peacekeepers deployed to the Golan Heights since 1974. UNDOF was part of a U.S.-mediated peace plan to end the Yom Kippur War that broke out when Egypt and Syria simultaneously invaded Israel on October 6, 1973. UNDOF monitors a buffer zone between Israeli-occupied Golan—which Israel seized from retreating Syrian forces during the war—and Syrian forces.

UNDOF has encountered few hostile incidents from either Israel or Syria, both of which respect the force as an impartial intermediary that keeps them from returning to war. A cease-fire has been maintained and fatalities have been low. Progress over the past three years toward a peace agreement could lead to the withdrawal of UNDOF and replacement by a non-UN force.

The UN Interim Force in Lebanon (UNIFIL) is a notorious example of the consequences when a traditional peacekeeping force is only partially accepted by warring parties. Approved by the Security Council in 1978, UNIFIL was charged with overseeing the withdrawal of Israeli forces from Lebanon, to serve as a buffer between Israel and Lebanon, and to restore Lebanese authority to southern Lebanon.

UNIFIL has long been a precarious operation because of the refusal of disputants to fully cooperate with the mission and honor its mandate. Israel refused until 2000 to withdraw completely from Lebanon and supported a Christian militia group (the "South Lebanon Army") that occupied positions in southern Lebanon in defiance of UN resolutions. These positions consisted of a "security zone" between the Israeli border and UNIFIL forces. UNIFIL has been ineffective in preventing Palestinian, Amal, and Hizballah armed elements from occupying positions within the UNIFIL area of operations and launching attacks on Israel. UNIFIL has suffered high casualties—83 fatalities from attacks—due to the lack of a meaningful cease-fire, and was almost overrun in 1982 when Israel launched a major invasion of Lebanon through UNIFIL positions.

In May 2000, as a result of an improvement in the security situation in southern Lebanon, Israel withdrew its forces and the South Lebanon Army from Lebanon. The United Nations responded by adjusting UNIFIL's area of operations to move into the former Israeli "security zone." Unfortunately, the government of Lebanon refused to deploy its military forces to southern Lebanon and Hizballah and other terrorist groups moved in instead. This caused a resumption in violence and tension in the region. Because of the new violence and the lack of cooperation of the Lebanese government, the UN announced in mid-2001 that it plans to cut the size of UNIFIL by 50 percent over the next two years. Map 4.1 illustrates the current deployment of UNIFIL.

By mid-2001 Israel-UN relations hit a low point. Already gravely concerned by new Hizballah attacks into Israel from southern Lebanon, Israelis were infuriated with United Nations officials for refusing to release an October 2000 UNIFIL videotape that reportedly showed Hizballah terrorists disguised as UN peacekeepers and driving vehicles with UN markings kidnap three Israeli soldiers. After denying the existence of the videotape for months, the UN finally acknowledged it in June 2001 but refused to release it to Israel, which wants the tape to help identify the kidnappers. Hizballah warned that if the UN released the tape, Hizballah would begin treating UNIFIL troops as spies and Israeli collaborators. The UN has proposed releasing the tape with the faces of the Hizballah kidnappers edited out, a solution Israel has rejected. Both of these developments bode poorly for UNIFIL and stability along the Israel-Lebanon border.

The UN Operation in [the Republic of] the Congo,[9] *Opération des Nations Unies au Congo* (ONUC), deployed to the Congo from 1960 to 1964, demonstrated the special problems peacekeeping operations have securing acceptance from disputants in civil wars. ONUC initially was deployed at the request of the Congo government to facilitate the removal of Belgian forces, which Brussels sent to the country after a breakdown in law and order threatened Belgian citizens and interests. Later, however, as Congo sank into a four-sided civil war, ONUC ran afoul of each of the warring parties and found itself in a situation where combatants did not want peace and viewed the UN presence as contrary to their interests. Consequently, ONUC was attacked by all sides and suffered high casualties.

The UN Peacekeeping Force in Cyprus (UNFICYP), deployed from 1964 to the present, proved that despite the ONUC tragedy, civil war peacekeeping was possible. UNFICYP contributed to the peace in Cyprus

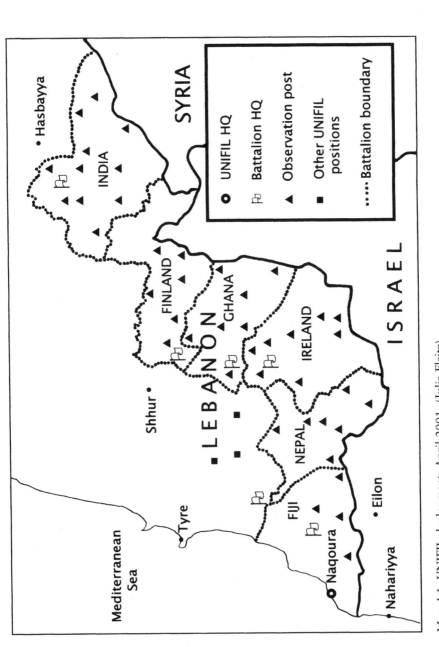

Map 4.1: UNIFIL deployment, April 2001. (Julie Fleitz)

through strict neutrality and strong pressure on parties to the dispute by the United States and the United Kingdom. Unlike ONUC, the Cyprus disputants (which included Turkey and Greece) wanted a UN presence and did not want to return to arms.

The UN Operation in Mozambique (ONUMOZ), deployed from 1993 to 1995, improved on UNFICYP's success and illustrated that the traditional peacekeeping model can still work in civil war situations after the Cold War. Linked to a strong peace agreement and a commitment from the two warring factions to cooperate, ONUMOZ succeeded in arranging national elections and was able to withdraw after fully and successfully completing its mandate. Key to the acceptance of ONUMOZ was pressure from outside parties, especially Italy, to keep former warring parties from backing out of the peace accord.

Acceptance and Withdrawal: Theory and Practice

In theory, traditional peacekeepers are sent with the consent of warring parties and must leave if a party to a dispute withdraws its consent. In practice, however, the UN has resisted withdrawing peacekeeping missions in such situations. UN Secretary General U Thant reluctantly withdrew UNEF I from the Sinai and Gaza Strip in May 1967 after ignoring both Egyptian demands for the removal of the force and Egyptian occupation of UNEF positions. When Israel invaded Lebanon in June 1982, it gave the commander of UNIFIL—which was deployed in southern Lebanon—30 minutes notice and informed him that Israel expected UNIFIL not to impede Israeli troops. UNIFIL ignored this warning and instead attempted to block the Israeli Army's advance with small obstacles.

Developments in 2000 and 2001

Three interesting peacekeeping developments occurred in 2001 involving the peacekeeping acceptance principle. In July 2000, the Security Council approved the UN Mission in Ethiopia and Eritrea (UNMEE), a 4,200-man traditional peacekeeping mission sent to monitor a buffer zone and ceasefire between these two countries. UNMEE, which has the full consent of Ethiopia and Eritrea, illustrates the useful role UN traditional peacekeeping still can play after the Cold War in resolving international disputes.

On the other hand, on March 27, 2001, the United States vetoed a French Security Council resolution that would have sent a peacekeeping observer force to the West Bank and Gaza over the objections of Israel and the United States. This proposal violated the acceptance principle, since it called for imposing a traditional peacekeeping force on the territory of a sovereign state (Israel) over that state's objections. More importantly, this resolution was one of the few calls for a peacekeeping force in the UN's history that was tabled despite strong opposition from a permanent member of the Security Council. Press reports suggested that this effort was largely a political stunt by the European Union and Russia to embarrass the United States by forcing it to cast a lone veto. A similar resolution failed to pass in December 2000 because it received only eight votes, one short of the minimum required under UN rules.[10]

Prospects for Western Sahara were not promising as of late 2001. The UN made an important decision concerning Western Sahara in May 2001 that could affect the acceptance of one party—the POLISARIO liberation group—of MINURSO, the UN peacekeeping force that has been stationed in Western Sahara since 1991. On June 29, 2001, the Security Council gave a tentative endorsement to a plan by former U.S. secretary of state and UN Special Envoy to Western Sahara James Baker to hold talks between the POLISARIO and Morocco on autonomy for the territory within Morocco, to be followed by a referendum on independence 10 years or more from now.[11] This plan was an abrupt about-face for the UN, which had been trying since 1991 to arrange a referendum based on a 1974 Spanish census of Western Sahara. This effort has been unsuccessful because of irreconcilable differences between the two sides over who is eligible to vote. The Baker Plan would allow a new census to be taken in advance of a future referendum that both sides could support. Although the POLISARIO initially indicated that it would discuss the Baker Plan, it rejected the plan in August 2001 and threatened to return to war. The Security Council on November 27, 2001 extended MINURSO's mandate for three more months to give Baker and the parties more time to negotiate a solution. It seemed unlikely as of April 2002 that a diplomatic solution would be found.

Negotiating an autonomy plan with the POLISARIO will be extremely difficult. Even if this could be accomplished, because of the high tensions between the two sides, some type of UN presence is likely to remain for many years to come.

Impartiality

Impartiality refers to the importance of traditional peacekeeping troops being acceptable to warring parties and having no stake in their dispute. Impartiality requires peacekeepers to exercise fair and unbiased treatment of parties to a dispute, to be open, and to promptly investigate complaints. Peacekeeping impartiality is crucial to promoting mutual trust and decreasing tensions. Rod Paschall, former head of the U.S. Military History Institute and drafter of the first peacekeeping doctrine for U.S. armed forces, gives a good description of how impartial peacekeepers can lower tensions: "[I]f a peacekeeper's conduct is impeccable and recognized as impartial, former warring parties will begin to register written or verbal protests about violations with peacekeepers rather than making their point with bullets or shells fired on an enemy."[12]

Confusing this issue is the erroneous belief that UN peacekeeping was invented solely to keep the superpowers out of regional conflicts. While the United States and the Soviet Union[13] sometimes were excluded from peace-keeping missions during the Cold War for this reason, many other states considered partial or politically sensitive also have been excluded from traditional peacekeeping efforts, including Bulgaria, Cuba, Israel, Romania, South Korea, Spain, Germany, and Japan.[14] Instead, neutral and "non-aligned" states such as India, Ireland, Sweden, Fiji, Nepal, and Finland were tapped for the majority of peacekeeping missions during the Cold War. Australia, Canada, and Norway are exceptions to this practice. Although close allies of the United States (Canada and Norway are also NATO members), these three nations have been able to maintain a reputation of impartiality in peacekeeping missions and have been troop contributors to most UN peacekeeping efforts.

Inis L. Claude, Jr. suggested in 1994 that the traditional peacekeeping impartiality principle still has merit when he wrote that post–Cold War peacekeeping contingents should be "voluntarily supplied by states acceptable to the parties as sufficiently evenhanded to be trustworthy."[15] John R. Bolton, U.S. Under Secretary of State for Arms Control and International Security, is a vocal proponent of this view and has argued that a Cold War "Perm Five Convention"—an informal agreement among the Security Council's veto members to avoid participating in peacekeeping missions—was key to peacekeeping successes during the Cold War because it recognized that great powers could never be viewed as truly disinterested and neutral in peacekeeping situations. Bolton believes the Perm Five Convention remains equally valid today.[16]

ONUC's difficulties did not result from a lack of impartiality, as it consisted of carefully chosen neutral contingents from African nations, Sweden, and Ireland. Troops from the Warsaw Pact, the United States, and former colonial powers were deliberately excluded to avoid offending the superpowers or parties to the dispute. ONUC also initially relied on the UNEF rules of engagement, which barred it from interfering in domestic affairs or taking sides among factions.[17] These same guidelines proved to be the force's undoing, as each faction turned on ONUC when it would not promote their interests.

For example, Hammarskjöld earned the enmity of the Congo's pro-Soviet Lumumba faction as well as the USSR when he refused to order ONUC to promote Congolese Prime Minister Patrice Lumumba's agenda—especially taking action against Möise Tshombé, leader of Congo's Katanga province, which was trying to secede. Hammarskjöld felt that ONUC should not interfere in the domestic affairs of a state and was adamant that ONUC not become a tool of Lumumba and Moscow. Lumumba's death at the hands of another faction further alienated his faction and the USSR. Moscow was so irate at Hammarskjöld's management of ONUC that Soviet Premier Nikita Khrushchev called on Hammarskjöld to resign in a Sep-

Photo 4.1: French UNIFIL Troops, 1980. (United Nations/Photo by J.K. Isaac 151005)

tember 1960 speech to the UN General Assembly. After Hammarskjöld died in a plane crash in the Congo in 1961, U Thant reluctantly sided with a new Congo government against Tshombé, ostensibly to rid Congo of foreign mercenaries. Thant's rationale for this decision, which resulted in poorly executed UN assaults on Katanga, severely undermined international confidence in peacekeeping's neutrality and limited new UN peacekeeping efforts for almost a decade.

ONUC was not the only traditional peacekeeping operation to get into trouble by running afoul of the impartiality requirement. French troops had to withdraw from UNIFIL in 1986 after they came under attack by radical Muslim elements in Lebanon. The attackers—mostly pro-Iranian Shiite Muslims—viewed the French as biased, since they supported Iraq in the Iraq-Iran War and backed the 1982 U.S.-led invasion of Beirut. Moreover, French troops demonstrated little aptitude for peacekeeping in Lebanon and other UN missions, often opting for aggressive military responses rather than negotiation when crises occurred. Although French troops have historically been among the most competent, their aggressive tactics and tendency to ignore orders from UN officials have long been a problem.

The tragic 1988 kidnapping, torture, and murder of Lieutenant Colonel William R. Higgins, USMC, by Lebanese terrorists while participating in a UN Truce Supervision Organization (UNTSO) mission in southern Lebanon illustrated the problem of using great-power troops—who rarely are seen as neutral to all parties—as peacekeepers. The Higgins tragedy stunned U.S. policymakers, most of whom were not aware that lightly armed American soldiers had been sent on patrols in southern Lebanon.[18]

The Mixed Blessings of Diversity

The UN continues to subscribe to Hammarskjöld's belief that balanced geographic representation ensures the impartiality of peacekeeping missions. In practice, however, this principle has undermined the effectiveness of peacekeeping operations. Costs are driven up by the requirement to transport and support troops from distant countries. Oftentimes, Third World troops lack adequate training or equipment. Mission diversity also has led to interoperability, cultural, and command problems.

An unexpected but mostly positive consequence of Hammarskjöld's requirement for balanced geographical participation was the development of Third World states specializing in UN peacekeeping. This phenomenon occurred out of necessity. The UN insisted on geographic diversity in peacekeeping missions despite a lack of competent and willing troops from non-Western countries. Allowing neutral Third World states to specialize in peacekeeping assured a supply of qualified Third World peacekeepers. Third World states liked this arrangement, since it provided them with an easy way to earn hard currency. Fiji, Nepal, Ghana, and India are examples of Third World countries that have specialized in UN peacekeeping and established impressive records of professionalism and accomplishment serving in UN missions.

Why Are Black African Troops Banned from UNFICYP?

The UN's long-running operation in Cyprus (UNFICYP) is an illustration of the lengths to which the United Nations sometimes will go to exclude peacekeeping contingents considered objectionable by warring parties. Since its inception, UNFICYP has excluded troops from African or Asian states and only recently accepted troops from South America. Several sources alleged that Greek Cypriots vetoed Third World troops—especially Africans—for racial reasons.[19] Other sources contend that Turkey vetoed Third World troops due to Ankara's fear that the Congo experience—which snuffed out a Third World secessionist movement—would lead Third World contingents to discriminate against the secessionist Turkish community on Cyprus.[20] Both explanations are probably true to some degree. While UN officials objected to demands to limit UNFICYP contributions—especially from the Greek Cypriots—it held that parties to disputes had a right to veto the participation of troops from any nation on sovereignty grounds. For this reason, UNFICYP troops were entirely drawn from Western Europe, Canada, Australia, and New Zealand when it was deployed in 1964. When financial problems caused the UN to look further afield for replacement troops in 1993, troops from Hungary and Argentina were chosen. Troops from Africa were not considered.

Minimum Use of Force

Another important axiom of traditional peacekeeping is the minimum use of force. Peacekeeping forces are not sent to compel parties to a dispute to work toward peace—they are deployed to facilitate peace settlements and help maintain truces. Peacekeepers are permitted to use force in self-defense, although in the case of sniper fire, they usually avoid engagement if possible for fear of being seen by parties to a dispute as a combatant, a development that would undermine the fragile trust peacekeeping forces must maintain to remain viable. Moreover, lightly armed, small forces obviously cannot rely on military force to carry out their mandates. Professor John Ruggie explains this delicate situation as follows:

> Unlike fighting forces, then, peacekeepers are not intended to create the peace they are asked to keep. They accept the balance of forces on the ground and work within it. Ironically, this military weakness may be an advantage in that it reassures all parties that the peacekeeping force cannot alter the prevailing balance to their disadvantage. In short, peacekeeping is a device to guarantee transparency, to reassure all sides that each is carrying out its promises.[21]

ONUC was the first UN mission to probe the limitations of military force by a peacekeeping operation. As the Congo situation deteriorated, ONUC took more forceful action to defend itself and keep order. Secretary General U Thant was less attached to his predecessor's conception of peacekeeping neutrality and eventually directly allied with the central Congo government and launched a military campaign to defeat Katangan secessionists. By doing so, ONUC became a combatant in the Congo conflict and undermined UN peacekeeping's reputation as a neutral arbiter.

ONUC's initial major military operations were a comedy of errors. Its first mission on September 13, 1963, to seize the town of Elizabethville in Katanga Province from Tshombé's forces was an embarrassing debacle and stalemate. UN forces failed to properly implement the attack plan because they did not understand their orders or simply refused to follow them. Indian UN troops armed with 1918 vintage rifles engaged in hand-to-hand combat with Katangan rebels. After UN forces took Elizabethville, it was bombed and strafed the next day by a lone Katangan jet fighter. A month later, better-armed UN forces again engaged Katangan rebels and positions. This attack was also uncoordinated and disorganized. The UN drove the rebels off but in the process accidentally bombed churches, missionaries, and hospitals, and killed many civilians. The resulting carnage severely damaged the UN's reputation, especially in the United States and Europe.

As a result of the ONUC debacle, UNFICYP's official stance on impartiality was revised. UN Under Secretary General Ralph Bunche believed ONUC got into trouble because it was directed to "assist" the Congolese government, and due to a misunderstanding over the meaning of the word "neutrality" in ONUC's mandate.[22] Bunche's solution was to replace "neu-

Photo 4.2: Danish armored vehicle in the UNFICYP buffer zone, 1990. (UN Photo 157787)

trality" in UNFICYP's mandate with the word "impartial" and to spell out more precisely how UNFICYP would be allowed to use force. On this point, Bunche was very clear:

As regards the principle of self-defence, it is explained that the expression "self-defence" includes the defence of United Nations posts, premises and vehicles under armed attack, as well as the support of other personnel of UNFICYP under armed attack. When acting in self-defence, the principle of minimum force shall always be applied and armed force will be used only when all peaceful means of persuasion have failed.[23]

Limits on UNFICYP's rules of engagement led it to employ a variety of pacific techniques to resolve conflict. UNFICYP has never been permitted to disarm parties or seize arms. Strict limitations on the use of force by UNFICYP made it unusually hesitant to use force even in self-defense. UNFICYP peacekeepers instead use persuasion to stop incidents like shootings across the buffer zone. To get its way, it will employ written complaints, discussions, arguments, and warnings. If these measures fail, the force will resort to interposing itself between the parties. The UNFICYP rules on the use of force have been very successful and every traditional peacekeeping operation since 1964 has employed them.

A key UNFICYP innovation was the "UN safe area."[24] On July 23, 1974, the Turkish Army was advancing across Cyprus and announced its intention to seize the Nicosia airport, which the two communities had agreed to turn over to UNFICYP. The UN feared that Turkish occupation of the airport would greatly exacerbate tensions by convincing the Greek Cypriots that the UN had betrayed them. UN Headquarters in New York therefore ordered UNFICYP Commander Lieutenant General Prem Chand to stand his ground. This was an unprecedented order for UN peacekeepers: they had been ordered to impede a military operation by a sovereign military force. Chand's solution was to surround the airport with troops from all of UNFICYP's participating nations. Britain also sent tanks from its nearby base and conducted overflights with fighter-bombers. Since this strategy would have forced Turkey to commit acts of war against a dozen friendly nations, Ankara decided the airport was more trouble than it was worth and backed off.

NON-UN TRADITIONAL PEACEKEEPING OPERATIONS

Although traditional peacekeeping missions must be multilateral, they do not have to be conducted by the UN. One of the most successful peacekeeping missions ever deployed, the Multinational Force Organization (MFO), is a non-UN multilateral operation in the Sinai Peninsula created to help verify the terms of the 1979 Israel-Egypt Camp David Accords. Another successful non-UN traditional peacekeeping effort was the 1995–1999 Military Observer Mission Ecuador-Peru (MOMEP). Two recent and successful non-UN traditional peacekeeping were initiated by Australia in 1999 and 2000 in Papua New Guinea and the Solomon Islands. This study counts the four non-UN peacekeeping efforts in Table 4.4 as traditional operations. Twelve other non-UN peacekeeping-like missions are classified as expanded peacekeeping missions and are addressed in Chapter 7.

OSCE NON-PEACEKEEPING EFFORTS

The 53-member Organization for Security and Cooperation in Europe (OSCE), a regional security organization that includes all of Europe, the former USSR, Canada, and the United States, has been involved with numerous diplomatic efforts in Europe and the former Soviet Union that are frequently and mistakenly referred to as peacekeeping missions. To date, the OSCE has sent small to medium-sized humanitarian and reconstruction operations to Kosovo, Bosnia, and Croatia and deployed "observer missions" to Georgia, Estonia, Moldova, Latvia, and Tajikistan. It also sent election monitors to Ukraine, Kazakhstan, Belarus, Croatia, Georgia, and Kyrgyzstan.

While OSCE observer missions are neutral, they do not meet minimum requirements for peacekeeping. OSCE observer missions also do not consider themselves as peacekeeping efforts.[25] For example, these missions are

Table 4.4
Non-UN Traditional Peacekeeping Operations[26]

Mission and Dates	Size	Mandate
MFO (1981–) *Multinational Force and Observers in the Sinai*	2,000	Monitors Egypt-Israel demilitarized zone in the Sinai. U.S. troops participate.
MOMEP *Military Observer Mission Ecuador/Peru*	35	Observer mission sent to monitor a cease-fire between Ecuador and Peru and the demilitarization of their border. U.S. troops participated.
PMGB (1998–) *Peace Monitoring Group in Bougainville*	262	Australian-led regional peacekeeping force tasked with monitoring a peace accord and cease-fire between the Papua New Guinea government and its secessionist province of Bougainville.
PMGSI (2000–) *Peace Monitoring Group in the Solomon Islands*	49	Australian-led regional peacekeeping force tasked with monitoring a peace agreement and a cease-fire between Guadalcanal and Malaita, feuding islands of the Solomon Islands.

Data as of June 2001.

unarmed and rely on disputants for transport and defense. Moreover, their purpose is to report back to the OSCE membership on local conditions. Deterring hostile activity is a secondary objective of most OSCE missions because of their small sizes. The OSCE mission in Kosovo may be the OSCE's most important international operation and works closely with a UN peacekeeping mission (UNMIK) and a NATO peace enforcement mission (KFOR) in helping rebuild the region and deliver humanitarian assistance.

Negotiations have been under way for almost eight years to deploy the first bona fide OSCE peacekeeping mission in Nagorno-Karabakh. This effort has been stymied by difficulties achieving a political settlement among the parties to this dispute. Future OSCE peacekeeping is likely to be limited by the politics of the OSCE, which requires votes to be taken by consensus, as well as by competition from the European Security Defense Initiative (ESDI), a proposed 50,000-man European Union military force that its sponsors (principally France and Germany) claim will have regional peacekeeping responsibilities. Table 4.5 summarizes current OSCE missions.

Table 4.5
OSCE Non-Peacekeeping Operations, July 2001[27]

	Established	Size
OSCE Mission to Estonia	1992	6
OSCE Mission to Georgia	1992	20
OSCE Activities in Latvia	1993	7
OSCE Mission to Moldova	1993	8
OSCE Mission to Tajikistan	1993	16
OSCE Assistance Mission to Chechnya	1995	6
OSCE Mission to Bosnia and Herzegovina	1995	180
OSCE Mission to Croatia	1996	98
OSCE Presence in Albania	1997	16
OSCE Spillover Monitor Mission to Skopje, Macedonia	1999	8
OSCE Mission in Kosovo	1999	586

TRADITIONAL PEACEKEEPING'S RECORD: SUCCESS IS RELATIVE

UN peacekeeping was a valuable mechanism to manage conflicts. Serving as trusted and neutral arbiters, traditional UN peacekeeping operations played a crucial role reducing tensions in dozens of conflicts around the world. Peacekeeping advanced U.S. interests on many occasions during the Cold War, especially in the Middle East, where six operations deployed between 1948 and 1978 promoted the security of Israel, one of America's closest allies. Traditional peacekeeping efforts have aided other important U.S. allies such as Turkey, Greece, Pakistan, and Morocco. Table 4.6 illustrates how several long-standing peacekeeping operations benefited U.S. interests.

However, despite its accomplishments, traditional peacekeeping has major weaknesses that define the limits of its usefulness in promoting international security. The most important is its inability to bring about negotiated settlements to disputes. The capabilities of peacekeeping forces also are at the mercy of the notoriously inefficient and corrupt UN bureaucracy.

By the early 1960s, the world came to realize that traditional peacekeeping efforts would rarely achieve their ultimate goal: bringing about final negotiated solutions to international conflicts. In fact, it became apparent that peacekeeping operations tended to *discourage* resolution of international disputes by removing the impetus for parties to negotiate with each

Table 4.6

U.S. Foreign Policy Interests Served by Long-Standing Peacekeeping Operations[28]

Operation (Year First Deployed)	U.S. Interests Served
UNTSO (Palestine) (1948)	—Contributes to Middle East stability by helping to reduce tensions between Israel and its neighbors. —Operates in areas of southern Lebanon where UNIFIL is not deployed. —Implements the remaining 1949 Arab-Israeli armistice agreements.
UNMOGIP (India/Pakistan) (1948)	—Contributes to stability in South Asia by helping to reduce tensions between India and Pakistan. —Demonstrates continued UN support for settling the Kashmir question by peaceful means.
UNFICYP (Cyprus) (1964)	—Contributes to stability in southern Europe by helping to prevent civil war on Cyprus and hostilities between Turkey and Greece. —Withdrawing UNFICYP would increase tensions and could spark a costly regional war. —Encourages continued diplomatic efforts to reunify Cyprus by peaceful means.
UNIFIL (Lebanon) (1978)	—Contributes to Middle East stability by addressing the humanitarian situation in southern Lebanon. —Withdrawing UNIFIL would likely increase the influence in southern Lebanon of Hizballah, an Iranian-supported terrorist group.
MINURSO (Western Sahara) (1991)	—Contributes to stability in North Africa by preventing a return to hostilities in Western Sahara that could involve Algeria and Morocco. —Supports Morocco, a longtime U.S. friend and ally.

other. In short, the peacekeeping force itself became the solution. As a result, few traditional UN peacekeeping operations have completely fulfilled their mandates (see Table 4.7). Five out of 15 current forces have been deployed 20 years or more. Two were first deployed in the 1940s.

By the 1960s, the international community accepted peacekeeping's limitations and the reality that peacekeeping was better suited to manage conflicts by maintaining truces than attempting to solve them. This state of affairs was not considered objectionable during the Cold War. UN members tolerated the inability of peacekeeping forces to bring about negotiated

Table 4.7
Comparison of Negotiation Requirements of Traditional Peacekeeping Missions

	Negotiation Status	Years in Place	Disposition
UNMOGIP (India/Pakistan)	None. Parties refuse to talk.	43	Indefinite deployment.
ONUC (Congo)	Limited. Civil war prevented talks.	4	Withdrew after quelling secession of Katanga and realization that its ability to stabilize the country was limited. After decades of dictatorship, civil war returned in the late 1990s. A UN new peacekeeping mission, MONUC, was sent to the Congo in 1999.
UNFICYP (Cyprus)	Little to none. Prospects for peace talks bleak.	27	Indefinite deployment. Parties continue to arm.
UNIFIL (Lebanon)	None until 2000 when Israel withdrew from southern Lebanon. UNIFIL is increasing its size to patrol this area. No final peace accord in sight.	23	Indefinite deployment.
MINURSO (Western Sahara)	Limited.	10	Efforts to negotiate peace agreement and hold national elections have been difficult. Neither side willing to accept loss in national election.
UNTAG (Namibia)	Part of peacekeeping agreement.	2	Force withdrawn after U.S.-brokered peace process led to elections and South African withdrawal.
ONUMOZ (Mozambique)	Part of peacekeeping agreement.	2	Force withdrawn after Italian-brokered peace process led to national elections and political reconciliation.

solutions because deploying these operations indefinitely was better than war, and they were comparatively inexpensive and few in number. Moreover, peacekeeping missions for many situations became ways to maintain stability for the day when it would be possible to resolve disputes through negotiations.

For example, the withdrawal of UNFICYP, which has separated Greek and Turkish forces since 1964, likely would lead to an eruption of hostilities between Greece and Turkey. In place for 25 years, the Cyprus buffer zone has caused the differences of the two Cypriot communities to harden. A generation of children has grown up on both sides hating neighbors they have never met. This prolonged separation has exacerbated ethnic differences and intolerance. It is a breach that will not be bridged easily.

NOTES

1. Nobel Peace Prize Presentation statement, 1988. The Nobel Foundation, Internet website: http://www.nobel.se/laureates/peace-1988-1-bio-html.

2. This analysis does not count a handful of other UN missions, mostly deployed in the UN's early years, as peacekeeping efforts because they were closer to UN diplomatic missions than peacekeeping efforts. Some examples include the UN Commission on the Balkans (UNSCOB), sent to Greece in 1947, and the UN Representative to the Dominican Republic (DOMREP), deployed in 1966. A more vexing problem is how to classify two UN missions sent to the Korean peninsula before the Korean War, the UN Temporary Commission on Korea and the Commission on Korea. While the former resembled a fact-finding mission, the latter operation had a mandate to "observe the actual withdrawal of the occupying forces." (See UN General Assembly Resolution 112 [II], November 14, 1947 and Resolution 195 [II], December 12, 1948.) Since these missions were not deployed with the consent of both warring parties, this analysis does not classify them as peacekeeping.

3. UN Department of Peacekeeping Operations Internet homepage, http://www.un.org/Depts/dpko/, U.S. General Accounting Office; United Nations Department of Public Information Fact Sheet, DPI/1634/Rev.19, March 1, 2001.

4. Scholars have long argued whether ONUC qualifies as a peacekeeping operation. There is no doubt that its mandate expanded over time and suffered from a phenomenon now known as "mission creep." The International Court of Justice weighed in on this question in 1962 when it found in an advisory opinion that although this mission was authorized to use force by the UN Security Council and had conducted military operations against mercenaries and Katangan separatists, it "was not an enforcement action within the compass of Chapter VII of the Charter." (See *Certain Expenses of the United Nations*, Advisory Opinion of July 20, 1962, ICJ Internet homepage: http://www.icj-cij.org.) This was because ONUC addressed a situation within a state, was initially deployed at the request of the Congolese government, and was approved by the Security Council to be a UNEF-like peacekeeping operation. This was also the contention of the Nobel Committee when it posthumously awarded the 1961 Peace Prize to UN Secretary General Hammarskjöld: "The UN force [in Congo] was to function as a noncombatant peace force;

there was to be no interference in disputes involving matters of internal policy, and arms were to be used only in self-defense." (See Gunnar Jahn, Nobel Peace Prize Presentation Speech, Nobel Lectures, 1961, Nobel Foundation, http://www.nobel.se/peace/laureates/1961/press/html.)

    5. *The Blue Helmets: A Review of United Nations Peacekeeping*, 2nd ed. (New York: UN Department of Public Information, 1991), p. 4.

    6. Inis L. Claude, Jr., *Swords into Plowshares*, 4th ed. (New York: Random House, 1971), p. 321.

    7. James H. Allen, *Peacekeeping: Outspoken Observations by a Field Officer* (Westport, CT: Praeger, 1996), pp. 137–141.

    8. The United Nations, data through May 2001.

    9. The Republic of the Congo was renamed Zaire in the mid-1960s. In 1999, it was renamed the Democratic Republic of the Congo.

    10. "U.S. Vetoes UN Observer Force for West Bank, Gaza," CNN.com, http://www.cnn.com/2001/world/meast/03/28/mideast/index/html.

    11. Security Council Resolution 1359, June 29, 2001.

    12. Rod Paschall, "U.N. Peacekeeping Tactics: The Impartial Buffer," in Barbara Benton, ed., *Soldiers for Peace* (New York: Facts on File, 1996), pp. 51–55.

    13. The United States and the USSR generally did not participate in peacekeeping operations during the Cold War after 1948. The United States and the USSR have participated in UNTSO (Palestine) since its inception in 1948 in Palestine and continue to do so. The United States also participated in UNMOGIP (Kashmir) from 1948 until the 1970s when India forced U.S. troops to withdraw because New Delhi claimed Pakistan had "allied" with the United States. One of Hammarskjöld's principles for peacekeeping, which he drew up on the basis of his experience with UNEF, was that "UN forces should not include units from any of the five permanent members of the Security Council or from any country which may be considered as having a special interest in the situation." Sydney D. Bailey, *The United Nations: A Short Political Guide* (New York: Praeger, 1964), p. 60. See also *The Blue Helmets*, 2nd ed., p. 55.

    14. Trevor Findlay, *Challenges for the New Peacekeepers* (Oxford: Oxford University Press, 1996), p. 11.

    15. Inis L. Claude, Jr., "The New International Security Order: Changing Concepts," *Naval War College Review*, 48, no. 1 (Winter 1994), p. 14.

    16. John R. Bolton, Testimony before the House of Representatives Committee on Government Affairs, February 9, 1994.

    17. See Hammarskjöld Nobel Presentation speech, 1961. The Nobel Foundation, Internet website: http://www.nobel.se/laureates/peace-1988-1-bio-html.

    18. UNTSO, an observer mission, has performed a number of missions related to the Arab/Israeli conflict since it was deployed in 1949 and has assisted the UN Interim Force in Lebanon since its inception in 1978.

    19. See Karl Th. Birgisson, "The UN Peacekeeping Force in Cyprus," in William Durch, ed., *The Evolution of UN Peacekeeping* (New York: St. Martin's Press, 1993), p. 227; Alan James, *Peacekeeping in International Politics* (New York: St. Martin's Press, 1990), p. 226.

    20. See Rosalyn Higgins, *UN Peacekeeping: Documents and Commentary*, vol. 4 (Oxford: Oxford University Press, 1981), pp. 46–49.

    21. John Gerard Ruggie, "The United Nations and the Collective Use of Force:

Whither or Whether?" in Michael Pugh, ed., *The UN, Peace, and Force* (London: Frank Cass, 1997), pp. 1–20.

22. Brian Urquhart, *Ralph Bunche: An American Life* (New York: Norton, 1993), p. 370.

23. Report by the Secretary General to the UN Security Council on Cyprus, Document S/5950, September 10, 1964.

24. This episode stands in sharp contrast to the UNPROFOR safe areas in Bosnia, which were overrun by Serb forces in 1995, despite the presence of UN troops. The differences were that (1) the Bosnian safe areas were not attacked by a national government but an ethnic/secessionist force with no diplomatic equities, and (2) the UN force guarding the safe areas was small and composed of forces mostly from one country. On the other hand, the UN Preventive Deployment Force in Macedonia (UNPREDEP), deployed in 1995, was a successful trip-wire force to dissuade Serbian forces from crossing into Macedonia. Composed around a core of U.S. peacekeepers, UNPREDEP offered a stark warning to Belgrade that defying this force was tantamount to war with the United States. See Chapter 8 for more on UN peacekeeping in Bosnia and Macedonia.

25. The author corresponded with OSCE missions in Kosovo, Croatia, Chechnya, Moldova, and Albania on this question. All of these missions claimed they were not peacekeeping efforts. Observers deployed by these missions were unarmed.

26. Sources: *The Military Balance 1999–2000* and *The Military Balance 2000–2001*, The International Institute for Strategic Studies (Oxford: Oxford University Press 1999 and 2000); Associated Press, United Press International.

27. Source: OSCE Internet website and author correspondence with OSCE missions to Kosovo, Moldova, Chechnya, Albania, Georgia, and Croatia. Mission size figures do not include locally recruited staff.

28. Adapted from United States General Accounting Office, *UN Peacekeeping: Status of Long-standing Operations and U.S. Interests in Supporting Them*, GAO/NSIAD-97-59 (Washington: Government Printing Office, April 1997), p. 26.

Chapter 5

Peacekeeping Management and Command

UN mismanagement is pervasive, deep-rooted, and apparently running out of control. This fundamental deficiency of the UN system undermines confidence in the UN's competence across the range of its activities.

—Final Report of the United States Commission
on Improving the United Nations, Minority
Statement, September 1993[1]

Severe UN administrative and chain of command problems have badly hampered traditional peacekeeping and played a role in the collapse of expanded peacekeeping operations. This chapter discusses how the UN organizes, manages, and commands peacekeeping forces. Also discussed are the UN's refusal to enact administrative and financial reform and the August 2000 Brahimi Report[2] on reforming UN peacekeeping.

Peacekeeping operations germinate from one of three types of requests: a request by a party to a dispute, a request by a third party trying to broker a settlement, or an initiative by the Security Council. The secretary general, after receiving a request for peacekeeping, usually prepares a mission outline for consideration by the Security Council. After the council approves a request for peacekeeping, it will request the secretary general to prepare a detailed implementation plan that describes estimated cost, size, and duration. The secretary general also will sound out potential troop contributing countries. For small operations, the UN chief will name only a force commander or a chief military observer. Larger operations are headed by a special representative of the secretary general (SRSG).

UN ADMINISTRATION OF PEACEKEEPING PRIOR TO 1992

From 1947 to 1993, UN peacekeeping was managed by an ad hoc, on-the-fly system plagued by waste and corruption that barely kept missions operating. The deployment of new operations routinely was subject to lengthy delays as the UN frantically rounded up troops and equipment. Logistic and supply problems created severe strains on many missions and led to withdrawals of national contingents. UN troop contingents often deployed late, were poorly trained, or arrived without supplies and equipment.

For example, despite its success in limiting hostilities, the 1956–1967 UNEF I mission in the Sinai was wracked by administrative and management problems as well as funding shortfalls. Its logistics and supply were in a permanent state of disorganization. Rarely were more than half of UNEF I's land vehicles in working order. There were serious chain of command problems, especially from national contingent commanders who refused to follow orders from UN commanders. UNEF I also tended not to report cease-fire violations to UN Headquarters to make itself look better.[3]

One problem UNEF I did not have was a dearth of competent troops. UN Secretary General Hammarskjöld was overwhelmed with troop offers for UNEF, most of which arrived on time and well equipped. This was not the case for UNIFIL, deployed to Lebanon since 1978. Rapidly slapped together, UNIFIL suffered severe strategic, logistic, and procurement difficulties and lacked coherent organization. Contingents arrived with no clear duties or areas of operation. One contingent, from Nepal, arrived with no sleeping bags or vehicles. (West Germany and the United States stepped in and provided the Nepalese troops with vehicles along with five-hour driving lessons.)[4] Worst of all, UNIFIL was totally unprepared for the hostile situation where it was deployed, the most dangerous since ONUC in 1960.

Procurement delays have been a standard problem for all UN peacekeeping missions. The commander of UNYOM (Yemen) resigned in protest in August 1963 when the UN system, which was badly overextended at the time because of the huge ongoing ONUC operation in the Congo, was unable to provide supplies. UNEF II, which successfully kept the peace between Israel and Egypt for six years until it was withdrawn in 1979, experienced extreme delays obtaining supplies and was never able to overcome a water shortage for its troops.

US troops deployed to MINURSO (Western Sahara) have described this mission as chaotic and extremely inefficient. One American MINURSO peacekeeper reported that

the root of [MINURSO's] problems rests with a UN career civilian force that has no experience working in the field and a military organization haphazardly put together. . . . [T]here are continuing battles on who controls what, which has resulted in conflicting guidelines and continual counter-orders being issued on operational as well as logistical matters.[5]

In response to such problems, a variety of ad hoc solutions have been employed. Once in place, savvy peacekeeping commanders quickly learn how to work around the UN system and UN Headquarters, a practice that has led to corruption. Important peacekeeping functions often are performed and paid for "off the books" by Western countries. The United States has frequently airlifted peacekeeping troops from poor countries to distant destinations at no cost to the UN. Developed countries such as Britain and France sometimes have equipped and trained peacekeeping troops from less developed countries.

The UN has tried to compensate for troop deployment delays by using UNTSO, its underutilized observer force in Palestine, to jump start new peacekeeping operations. This practice allowed UN officials to send small contingents of experienced UN troops to conflict areas with only a few hours notice. UNTSO has played this role over a dozen times since 1947, including deployments to Congo (1960), Yemen (1963), Mozambique (1992), and Yugoslavia (1992).

TRADITIONAL PEACEKEEPING BUREAUCRACY

From 1947 until 1992, UN peacekeeping forces were generally small and simple operations overseen by a staff of a couple dozen in the UN Department of Special Political Affairs. A particular problem during this period was the Field Operations Division, which was located in a separate UN department, making it difficult to coordinate finances and logistics with peacekeeping mission planning. Figure 5.1 illustrates peacekeeping decision making and chain of command until 1992.

Although small and understaffed, the UN's pre-1992 peacekeeping staff at UN Headquarters worked adequately for the small number of missions it needed to direct. Especially advantageous was the leading role played by the two UN under secretaries general (USGs) for special political affairs and their staffs. While both USGs managed and planned peacekeeping missions on behalf of the secretary general, one of these posts, first held by American Ralph Bunche, came to be the de facto head of UN peacekeeping. Bunche, appointed to this post in 1960, was succeeded by Britons Brian Urquhart in 1971 and Marrack Goulding in 1985. These Western UN officials used quiet leadership and informal arrangements to bypass the UN's troubled bureaucracy to manage operations, find qualified personnel, and limit Soviet influence over peacekeeping.

The UN peacekeeping staff headed up by Urquhart and Goulding was efficient but still had major problems. Strapped for resources and personnel,

Figure 5.1
Peacekeeping Chain of Command Prior to 1992

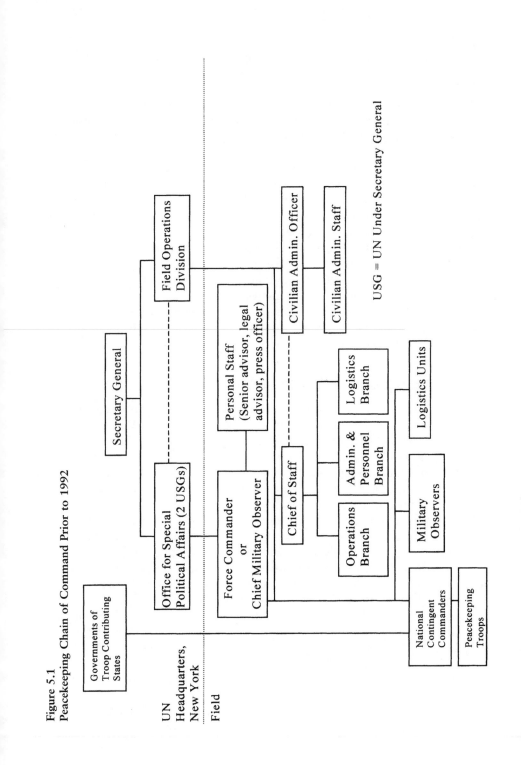

it muddled through as best it could. Urquhart described his staff as "simple, extremely small, and improvised." However, he takes pride in the accomplishments of his peacekeeping staff, which was able to deploy peacekeepers to the Suez in seven days in 1956 and the first 10,000 troops to Congo in ten days in 1960.[6] Moreover, implementation of the missions that Urquhart and Goulding oversaw usually went fairly smoothly because there was unity of purpose between negotiators and operational personnel, since they were the same people.

FUNDING

Funding problems have hampered all UN peacekeeping operations since the 1950s. Older missions found that as international interest waned, UN member payments would arrive late, if at all. The first peacekeeping funding crisis occurred in the early 1960s when France and the USSR refused to pay their UN dues for UNEF I and ONUC.[7] This precipitated a UN financial crisis in the early 1960s that almost bankrupted the organization. A settlement was reached in 1965 when Moscow and Paris agreed to pay future peacekeeping assessments and the General Assembly gave them an "exemption" for their ONUC and UNEF peacekeeping arrears, which amounted to almost $73 million (in 1965 dollars). U.S. Ambassador to the United Nations Arthur Goldberg opposed this deal and said at the time that if UN members could assert a right not to pay for UN activities they opposed, the United States someday might do the same.

The most discussed UN peacekeeping financial issue in 2000 was the question of U.S. peacekeeping arrears. Although it was popular in the halls of the UN to attack the United States for UN debts that supposedly crippled UN peacekeeping, the astronomic rise in the number of peacekeeping missions since 1993 made this claim questionable. Most U.S. withholding of UN peacekeeping funds was linked to efforts to force the United Nations to enact real reforms to reduce waste and corruption, which the UN to this day has resisted. Some U.S. withholding of UN payments has been in response to poor decision making by UN peacekeeping officials. For example, the 2000 UN debacle in Sierra Leone—when 500 UN peacekeepers were taken hostage—led the U.S. Congress in August 2000 to cut off funding for a similar poorly designed peacekeeping mission proposed for the Democratic Republic of the Congo and for other regions without stable ceasefires or where combatants refused to negotiate in good faith.

On the other hand, there is ample evidence, including a compelling 1996 U.S. General Accounting Office report,[8] that the United States historically has supplied hundreds of millions of dollars of gratis support to peacekeeping operations. For this reason, the U.S. Congress responded to gratuitous attacks on the United States for its peacekeeping debts by calling for U.S. peacekeeping assessments to be lowered. Some members of Con-

gress have gone further. For example, U.S. Congressman Roscoe Bartlett
(R-MD) submitted a bill in 1997 entitled "The UN Erroneous Payment
Act." If it had been enacted, this bill would have forced the U.S. Department of State to seek $3.5 billion that Congressman Bartlett and 53 other
members of Congress calculated that the United Nations owed the United
States in 1997 for unreimbursed services Washington had provided to UN
peacekeeping operations. This was in contrast to the $1.3 billion the UN
claimed the United States owed in peacekeeping arrears as of January 1,
1997. In December 2000, the United States and the UN reached an accord
on Washington's UN arrears that included lowering America's UN assessments. A key aspect of this deal was an agreement by American billionaire
Ted Turner to pay a large portion of America's UN debts.

Peacekeeping debts became a major issue at the UN in the 1990s, since
several billion-dollar operations were deployed simultaneously. Continued
profligate UN spending and new efforts in 1999 and 2000 to deploy five
large UN peacekeeping missions was evidence that the alleged crippling
effect of America's UN arrears on peacekeeping has been exaggerated.

THE 1992–1993 RESTRUCTURING

In 1992 and 1993, the UN restructured its peacekeeping bureaucracy in
an attempt to better manage a proliferation of new peacekeeping efforts.
A close examination of these reforms suggests that they were actually minor
changes that papered over the UN's inability to plan and command offensive military operations. While solving this problem was probably impossible, a serious attempt to do so would have entailed creating a large and
competent UN military command staff. The 1992–1993 reforms fell far
short of this. Moreover, whatever good these changes accomplished was
eviscerated over time as they fell victim to the corruption and bureaucracy
that permeates the UN system.

The most significant reform was the 1992 restructuring of the UN headquarters staff. The Department of Special Political Affairs, which previously
managed peacekeeping missions, was abolished. In its place, three new Departments were created: the Department of Peacekeeping Operations
(DPKO), the Department of Humanitarian Affairs, and the Department of
Political Affairs. DPKO was made the primary department for planning
and administering peacekeeping missions. To ease the logistics and financial
problems of prior peacekeeping missions, the Field Operations Division
(FOD) was moved into DPKO and renamed the Field Administration and
Logistics Division (FALD).

The 1992–1993 restructuring significantly increased the number of UN
peacekeeping administrators. Only about two dozen UN staffers handled
UN peacekeeping in the Department of Special Political Affairs in 1989.
By 1996, that number had grown to 400 in DPKO alone. A 24-hour watch

center, known as the Situation Center, was created at the urging of the United States in 1993 to improve communications between UN headquarters and the field. The center was also given an intelligence branch, which was to receive contributions of intelligence from UN members. A database also was established to track troops offered on a stand-by basis by UN members for peacekeeping missions.

Finding competent personnel to man DPKO was a significant problem. Managing the new and more complex peacekeeping efforts deployed in the 1990s was far beyond the capabilities of most UN career staffers, many of whom owed their jobs to the UN personnel system's exacting national quota requirements and cronyism. The UN solved this problem with "gratis military officers"—military officers sent to work in peacekeeping offices at UN Headquarters for short periods at no cost to the UN. Most of the gratis officers were seconded by the West. These experienced officers comprised about a quarter of DPKO and made monumental changes to peacekeeping mission planning, communications, training, and overall management. Without the gratis officers, it is unlikely that any of the complex peacekeeping missions the UN deployed in 1993 and 1994 would have got off the ground. Despite their accomplishments, these officers were few in number and could not save UN peacekeeping by themselves, nor could they prevent most expanded peacekeeping missions from eventually collapsing.

A BUREAUCRATIC NIGHTMARE

The UN's capacity to support, manage, and command peacekeeping missions—which was barely functional during the Cold War—broke down in 1993 due to the deployment of seven new peacekeeping missions costing over $4 billion and utilizing over 70,000 troops, a 16-fold increase in cost over 1988. Casualties occurred in Somalia when some peacekeeping contingents refused to follow orders given by UN commanders without first consulting with their capitals.[9] Peacekeeping troops often could not work together due to interoperability, training, language, and competency problems. Despite pressure by the United States on the UN to initiate reforms to address these problems, a State Department Inspector General Study determined in March 1997 that the UN's peacekeeping department still lacked a modern command and control system, sufficient competent civilian administrators, and a responsible procurement system.[10]

Unchecked by oversight measures, the massive 1993 explosion of peacekeeping budgets yielded massive mismanagement and corruption. During the UNTAC mission in Cambodia from 1991 to 1993, UN officials and contractors committed "outright thievery" by stealing millions of dollars through phantom payrolls and work never performed, according to a 1993 *60 Minutes* investigation.[11] The 1993–1995 UNOSOM II mission in Somalia spurred similar reports, including the theft of $3.9 million, $76,000 in cash destroyed by mildew, and millions of dollars in contracts for vastly overpriced supplies and unnecessary contracts.[12] UNOSOM II mismanagement and corruption was so bad that U.S. Ambassador Daniel Simpson derided it in 1994 as "the world cash cow."[13]

Recruitment of competent troops, administrators, and civilian personnel became a serious problem by late 1993 and worsened over time. Three operations in place simultaneously in September 1993, UNOSOM II in Somalia, UNTAC in Cambodia, and UNPROFOR, required over 70,000 troops. Since the UN continued to mandate regional quotas for peacekeeping troops, it was forced to dramatically lower its standards to find peacekeepers. As a result, many nations sent grossly unqualified and ill-equipped soldiers. One actually emptied its prisons and dispatched criminals.[14] Troop shortages led to long delays before missions could deploy. Deployment of ONUMOZ to help end the civil war in Mozambique, for example, was postponed more than six months.

As expanded peacekeeping missions faltered and peacekeeping funds diminished, good quality peacekeeping troops became even harder to find. In addition, some sources claim that two UN contingents sent to Sierra Leone were well-trained elite troops who went to collect their UN paychecks and were told they would not have to fight.[15] Whatever the truth to this story is, it is clear that such troops were poor choices for the volatile Sierra Leone situation.

A similar problem plagued peacekeeping administrators. UNTAC Special Representative of the Secretary General Yashusi Akashi, a notoriously inept Japanese UN official, would have doomed the UNTAC mission in Cambodia if it had not been for the leadership of Force Commander John Sanderson, an Australian general who took control of the operation and managed it behind the scenes. Unfortunately, the UN credited Akashi with Sanderson's accomplishments and rewarded the Japanese UN official by making him SRSG to UNPROFOR in Yugoslavia, where his incompetence contributed to that mission's collapse.[16]

Bickering among the UNAMSIL commanders in Sierra Leone exacerbated this mission's problems. Already considered a fiasco because of hostage taking of UN troops by Revolutionary United Front (RUF) rebels, the *Washington Post* reported on September 10, 2000 that UNAMSIL had become paralyzed by infighting by its top commanders.[17] In a May 2000 memo that he leaked to the press, UNAMSIL Commander Major General Vijay K. Jetley of India accused his deputy commander, General Mohammed Garba, and SRSG Oluyemi Adeniji, both Nigerians, of collaborating with the RUF and accused Nigeria of involvement in blackmarket diamond trade with the RUF and Liberia. Jetley also accused Nigeria of placing "stooges" in the UN system to assist its blackmarket diamond racket. The UN reacted to these charges on September 12, 2000 by announcing that Jetley would be replaced.[18] This episode was painful for the UN because it led to the withdrawal of the Indian contingent, UNAMSIL's most competent troops.

THE UN BUREAUCRATS RETURN

Problems with civilian peacekeeping support staffs became a serious issue by early 2000. Irritated that the gratis military officers were denying them high-paying and important jobs in DPKO, the Third World forced the UN to release most gratis officers from DPKO by early 1999. The UN civil career service then proceeded to claim DPKO billets and fill them with less competent career UN bureaucrats. This severely undermined DPKO's ability to plan and administer new peacekeeping operations and contributed to the hostage-taking disasters that befell UNAMSIL in May 2000. The quality and quantity of UN civilian personnel in the field have also decreased in recent years, since these jobs are not seen as career enhancing by the UN personnel system.[19] Making matters worse is a scheme by senior UN officials to use civilian peacekeeping field jobs as a dumping ground for problem UN employees and as part of a paper shuffling exercise to retain personnel and positions that the UN has falsely told Western states it has cut as part of as part of budgetary and administrative reforms.[20] As a result of this "shell game," UN civilian staffs supporting expanded peacekeeping missions in Bosnia and Kosovo have high numbers of vacancies and jobs filled by incompetent UN careerists.[21] By mid-2000, DPKO and peacekeeping field operations were in such bad shape that there was open talk at the UN of another major reorganization.

The UN situation and intelligence centers also were not the successes hoped for in 1993. Because of financial and management problems, the UN Situation Center in 2001 was more a communications facility that takes and relays telephone calls than a modern command and control center. The UN intelligence center has come under heavy criticism by the U.S. Congress for poor security and compromising sensitive U.S. intelligence. Problems with the security of the center led all but a handful of nations to refuse to cooperate with it.[22]

It was apparent by late 1993 that recent reforms were inadequate for managing a large number of operations, some of which closely resembled military interventions rather than traditional peacekeeping missions. Some reforms actually undermined peacekeeping management by spreading decision-making power among competing bureaucracies and creating a thicket of new peacekeeping components in New York. A particular problem has been a disconnect between the Department of Political Affairs, which handles mediation and negotiation, and DPKO, which implements peacekeeping agreements. Poor communication between the two departments has led to numerous misunderstandings as to what disputants have agreed to, when operations will deploy, funding, and logistics.

Photo 5.1: UN Situation Center, 2000. Photo taken by author during visit to UN Headquarters, August 2000. Standing is Italian UN officer Francesco Manca, Acting Chief of the Situation Center. Seated are regional analysts from Russia and Sierra Leone at their watch desks.

Post–Cold War peacekeeping efforts continue to lack basic military competence. According to John Hillen, who has written one of the best recent books on peacekeeping:

the UN is inherently anti-professional in the military sense; at best it is suited for managing only quasi-military and very limited operations. . . . The recent steps taken to professionalize UN military operations have failed because the military capability of the UN cannot be separated from its political nature, from political characteristics that purposely limit and constrain its forays into the functional management of military force.[23]

Hillen's observations were confirmed to the author by senior Clinton administration officials in late 2000 at the Departments of State and Defense, who contended that this situation worsened significantly in 2000 because of the departure of the gratis military officers from DPKO.

Despite the consolidation of the Field Administration and Logistics Division (FALD) into DPKO, logistics and budget matters are still not streamlined. Peacekeeping commanders do not have control of their field logistics and can be vetoed by the FALD representative to their missions. UN peacekeeping logistics networks have not improved and typically take two to three months to set up. Procurement can take up to four to six months to obtain vital supplies. Figure 5.2 illustrates the post-1993 UN bureaucracy in New York. Figure 5.3 shows how the New York bureaucracy relates to the field.

Peacekeeping procurement has long been a quagmire and remains so today. During the UNTAC operation in Cambodia, U.S. automotive firms were irate over the UN's rigged bidding procedures that prevented U.S. firms from bidding on lucrative UNTAC orders for all-terrain vehicles. UN officials routinely direct peacekeeping contracts to their home countries or to their friends. The author has heard claims from several credible sources of UN peacekeeping missions overpaying for unsafe or decommissioned aircraft, including helicopters. Brian Boquist, president of a U.S. firm that has provided air transport and logistics to several UN peacekeeping missions, confirmed these claims in an August 2000 interview with the author. Boquist claims to have seen UN helicopters in Sierra Leone with tail numbers "that did not exist anymore" indicating that they had been decommissioned and should have been destroyed or cannibalized. Boquist also reports seeing 14 UN helicopters in Sierra Leone in mid-2000 that could not fly. Boquist describes the UN procurement system as "absolutely corrupt" and "a social welfare operation to enrich UN officials."

Boquist's allegations about corrupt UN aircraft procurement were bolstered by a March 2001 United Nations announcement requesting bids to charter "a six-seater high speed jet aircraft . . . for use throughout the Sierra Leone mission area" (probably a Learjet or Citation jet costing $3,000 per hour and $120,000 a month).[24] Given that Sierra Leone only has one airport that could accommodate this aircraft and the fact that the country is controlled by rebels outside the capital, it is difficult to imagine why UN officials in Sierra Leone would want to secure such expensive transportation. In light of past abuses of resources by high-level UN officials and the aforementioned allegations by Indian Major General Jetley in late 2000 of corruption by UNAMSIL's Nigerian commanders, there is a strong possibility this jet was requisitioned for non-operational reasons, possibly for shopping trips to Europe by senior UNAMSIL officials.[25]

UN REFORM, 1998–2000: MIXED RESULTS

The election of Kofi Annan as secretary general in late 1996 was billed by U.S. officials as an opportunity to clean up the UN system. Annan was a U.S.-educated Ghanaian with close ties to the United States. Unfortunately, he was also a 25-year UN veteran with no appetite for UN reform. Annan's initial proposals to cut waste and abuse were mostly cynical gestures, such as slashing 1,000 vacant positions, and promising to cut expenses while drastically increasing UN spending. These actions infuriated the U.S. Congress and made it more reluctant to pay America's large UN "debts."[26]

Figure 5.2
UN Peacekeeping Headquarters Bureaucracy, 1993–2000

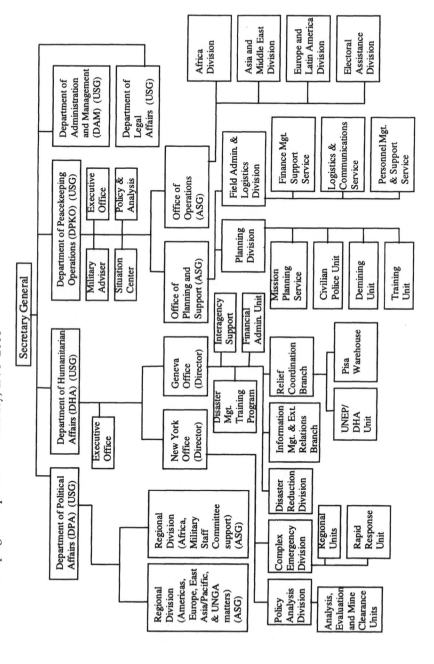

Figure 5.3
Peacekeeping Chain of Command, 1993–2000

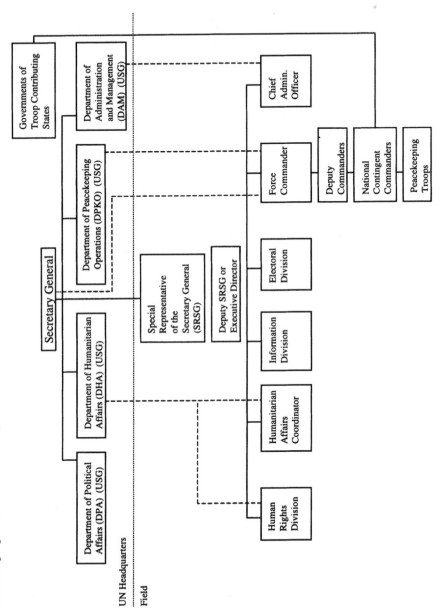

However, in 1998, according to a May 2000 U.S. General Accounting Office report,[27] Annan initiated some serious reforms. The UN began to better structure its bureaucracy and adopted some accountable personnel standards. The U.S. Congress enthusiastically greeted the GAO report as the first good news about UN management in over 20 years.

Unfortunately, these reforms have had little if any effect on the parts of the UN bureaucracy that administer peacekeeping. DPKO refuses to submit to an independent audit or enact personnel reforms initiated in the rest of the United Nations and, as stated earlier, UN officials continue to use peacekeeping as part of a "shell game" to evade personnel reforms.[28] Moreover, reports circulating at the UN in August 2000 that the world organization planned to spend almost $1 billion to renovate UN headquarters and add 11 additional floors to the Secretariat building suggested that the United Nations was planning significant staff increases. Some engineers believe the proposed addition of more floors to the Secretariat building could cause it to collapse.[29]

THE BRAHIMI REPORT'S PROPOSALS TO REFORM UN PEACEKEEPING BUREAUCRACY: MUCH ADO ABOUT NOTHING

A great deal of excitement was generated in the media over a report issued in August 2000 by a blue-ribbon commission named by Secretary General Kofi Annan to make recommendations on reforming UN peacekeeping, *Report of the Comprehensive Review of the Whole Question of Peacekeeping Operations in All Their Respects*, commonly known as the *Brahimi Report* after its chairman, former Foreign Minister of Algeria Lakhdar Brahimi. The report made notable recommendations on the use of force by UN peacekeepers (which will be discussed in Chapter 8) and peacekeeping management. The Brahimi Report was widely endorsed by UN officials and member states.[30]

Unfortunately, the Brahimi Report contained few substantive recommendations to improve peacekeeping management, ignored UN peacekeeping's most serious problems, and made some dubious recommendations that would worsen peacekeeping management. The report scored points with some UN watchers by openly attacking the political process that has led to the appointment of blatantly incompetent SRSGs.[31] It also confirmed allegations reported in this chapter that the UN personnel system discourages competent and qualified UN staff from taking assignments with peacekeeping civilian field staffs.[32] The report repeated a number of previously proposed reform initiatives, such as having UN members place troops on "stand-by" for peacekeeping duty and mandating that peacekeepers answer solely to UN commanders and not separately to their home capitals. However, rather than simplify the thicket of bureaus supporting operations in the field, the report called for the creation of a new layer of bureaucracy between the field and headquarters. It also had no serious proposals on reforming procurement and omitted mentioning that UN procurement is rife with corruption. A senior U.S. Department of Defense official told the author in September 2000 that procurement fraud and abuse was considered "too controversial for the high-level panel to address." The report includes numerous other proposals to increase UN spending and hire more staff.

The first indications that the Brahimi Report was losing its luster came at a September 20, 2000 U.S. House of Representative subcommittee hearing when witnesses and members of Congress strongly questioned the content of the report.[33] It is likely to attract further criticism from the George W. Bush administration.

THE SECRETARY GENERAL'S ROLE IN MANAGING PEACEKEEPING

In November 1956, the UN General Assembly[34] gave the secretary general wide-ranging powers to set up UNEF I in the Sinai. This was the beginning of a controversial outgrowth of UN peacekeeping: the emergence of the UN secretary general as an independent actor.

The secretary general was intended by the UN's founders to be a principal administrator, not a world leader deploying and managing UN forces on his own authority to resolve international conflicts.[35] The secretary general has only implied peacemaking powers under Article 99 of the UN Charter, which gives him the power to bring any dispute to the attention to the Security Council that in his opinion threatens international peace and security. Table 5.1 summarizes the UN Charter's provisions concerning the secretary general and their meaning.

UN Secretary General Dag Hammarskjöld built on his successful efforts to end the 1956 Suez Crisis to increase significantly the power and prestige of the secretary generalship. In 1958, he sent, without the authorization of the Security Council, his own representative to monitor the situation in Jordan. In 1959, he unilaterally sent his own representative to Laos. In 1960, Hammarskjöld used his authority under Article 99 of the UN Charter to convene a Security Council meeting to discuss the situation in the Congo. Hammarskjöld was so successful in building up the power and influence of his office that he openly defied Soviet demands in 1960 that he resign and made it impossible for the Security Council to micromanage him.

Other UN secretaries general followed in Hammarskjöld's footsteps. In 1988, Secretary General Perez de Cuellar deployed troops of the UNGO-MAP peacekeeping force to Afghanistan on his own initiative before obtaining the agreement of the Security Council (the Council did, however, retroactively endorse Perez de Cuellar's action). Secretary General Perez de

Table 5.1
The UN Charter and the Secretary General

The UN Charter provides for the UN head to be an administrator and not a world leader or diplomat. It gives the secretary general no discretion except for the right to bring matters to the Security Council. The expanded powers that UN secretaries general have exercised stem from the Security Council's lack of an executive capacity and necessity.

Chapter XV: The Secretariat

Article 97. *The Secretariat shall comprise a Secretary General and such staff as the Organization may require. The Secretary General shall be appointed by the General Assembly upon the recommendation of the Security Council. He shall be the chief administrative officer of the Organization.*	Specifies limited role of the secretary general. "Such staff as the Organization shall require" was used on several occasions to deploy UN police to conflict areas in lieu of peacekeepers.
Article 98. *The Secretary General shall act in that capacity in all meetings of the General Assembly, of the Security Council. . . . The Secretary General shall make an annual report to the General Assembly on the work of the Organization.*	The secretary general has used reports to the General Assembly and Security Council to lay out his own agenda and criticize UN members.
Article 99. *The Secretary General may bring to the attention of the Security Council any matter which in his opinion may threaten the maintenance of international peace and security.*	The basis for independent action by the secretary general.

Cuellar made a bolder move in 1991 when he deployed 500 "UN Guards" to Northern Iraq. This force, the UN Guard Contingent in Iraq (UNGCI), was first composed of UN Headquarters' security guards and was justified under Article 97 of the charter. Perez de Cuellar had no specific Security Council mandate to deploy what were essentially peacekeepers, although Security Council Resolution 688 (April 5, 1991) "requested" him to "use all resources at his disposal" to help the Kurdish refugees in northern Iraq. A peacekeeping force was not authorized and UNGCI has never been counted by the UN as a peacekeeping mission due to the opposition of China, which would not allow the Security Council to endorse what it viewed as an intervention into the internal affairs of a nation-state. Like secretaries general before him, Perez de Cuellar acted to fill a void created by a Security Council deadlock. Given UNGCI's mandate and the fact that it lacks the consent of Iraq, it probably qualifies as an expanded peace-keeping mission.

UN secretaries general assumed operational control of peacekeeping forces by default during the Cold War, since the superpower deadlock in the Security Council made it difficult to decide questions concerning international security. Tensions in the UN were often so bad that for many years the council seldom met at all. Secretary general command of peacekeeping missions kept their day-to-day operations out of Cold War politics.

Although the secretary general's control of UNEF irritated France and the USSR, military prerogatives of this office became truly controversial during the 1960–1964 UN peacekeeping mission in the Congo (ONUC) when the Soviets objected to the direction of the operation and withdrew their support. In 1974, both states again raised objections to the legality of UNFICYP, which had to be restructured from an observer force deployed throughout the island to a buffer force separating the Turkish and Greek communities. To get around Soviet and French objections on UN-FICYP and to avoid allowing them an opportunity to manipulate troop deployment decisions, Secretary General Kurt Waldheim, the United States, and Britain treated the radical 1974 changes to UNFICYP's mandate as a redeployment—which did not require a Security Council vote—rather than a new mission (which it really was). Since the troops were already on the ground, there was nothing Moscow or Paris could do about this.

Criticism of the UN secretary general intensified in the mid-1990s. There are a number of reasons for this. Most would agree that part of the problem was the personality of Secretary General Boutros Boutros-Ghali, who was imperious, stubborn, and sometimes manipulated UN members. It also is clear that Boutros-Ghali wanted to increase his power and influence as a peacemaker and commander of UN troops. Many observers thought he saw himself as another Hammarskjöld.[36] The problem was that with the end of the Cold War, Security Council members wanted to play an active role in managing (some would say *micromanaging*) UN forces and no longer wanted or needed to deputize the secretary general to perform this role.

But the main reason for intensified criticism of Boutros-Ghali stemmed from the need of Western states to find a scapegoat for failed UN peacekeeping missions they initiated from 1993 to 1995. This is not to say that Western criticism of Boutros-Ghali's management and refusal to reform the UN was completely misplaced. But Boutros-Ghali was no less a reformer than his predecessors. It is worth repeating here that while Boutros-Ghali reportedly supported and may have advocated some aggressive actions by UN peacekeepers in 1993, such as the effort to arrest Somali warlord Aideed, by September 1993, peacekeeping setbacks led him to change his position and argue that peacekeepers must be limited to traditional mandates and tasks. Boutros-Ghali made this argument concerning Bosnia,

Photo 5.2: UN Secretary General Boutros Boutros-Ghali meeting with UNPROFOR troops in Bosnia, 1992. (UN Photo, 182513 by A. Morvan, DOC 1018L)

where he felt UN troops had been given inappropriate and dangerous mandates that put peacekeepers at unnecessary risk.

Given Boutros-Ghali's tentative support for expanded peacekeeping and his reluctance to go along with most of the questionable peacekeeping decisions of the 1990s that resulted in fiascoes, how did he get blamed for these failed missions? *Los Angeles Times* writer and UN analyst Stanley Meisler tried to explain this in a 1996 article:

UN Ambassador Madeleine Albright had come to New York espousing a doctrine of "assertive multilateralism," in which the United States would strengthen the UN while asserting leadership over it. The UN's Somalia mission—tailored to American specifications and run by a retired American Admiral—was the model. But the mission soon crumbled into a fiasco. In panic, the Clinton Administration not only abandoned assertive multilateralism but swiftly branded the UN the sole culprit in Somalia. Having used the UN as a scapegoat once, the Clinton Administration soon found that the world organization could be used as a convenient shield to hide American failure to come up with a coherent policy for Bosnia.[37]

Kofi Annan, Boutros-Ghali's successor, has had a record that differs little from Boutros-Ghali, with the possible exception that he is more polite. He has been just as reluctant to reform the UN system, often promotes missions the United States opposes, and is trying to carve out a role for himself in which he could command international troops in crises. Annan was re-elected UN secretary general in June 2001 by a unanimous vote and with no opposition. The Ghanian UN leader has been lionized in the U.S. press for his successful "reforms" of the UN system and for attracting bipartisan support from American elected officials. In truth, what reforms Annan promoted have been fairly minor. While many U.S. officials strongly oppose Annan's views on UN peacekeeping, the United States probably supported his reelection out of recognition that Annan is not anti-American and may be the best leader America can expect at the UN. Moreover, Washington learned in 1996 the high cost of being the lone opponent to a popular Third World secretary general candidate when UN Ambassador Madeleine Albright spearheaded a campaign to deny Secretary General Boutros-Ghali a second term.

UN MANAGEMENT: A MAJOR LIMITATION ON PEACEKEEPING

Poor UN administration hurt peacekeeping by limiting the organization's ability to carry out peacekeeping missions. Traditional peacekeeping missions were able to function despite UN administrative problems because they usually had simple mandates and the cooperation of warring parties. Thus such missions could still function even if they deployed late, lacked working equipment, and consisted of poor troops.

Traditional peacekeeping during the Cold War had some management advantages over expanded peacekeeping operations. Although the peacekeeping staff at headquarters during the Cold War was undermanned, it generally was efficient. UN secretaries general, granted effective "command" of peacekeeping missions by default due to the Cold War, used their authority to create workable mandates and outmaneuver Moscow and other states from politicizing or damaging operations. While they had their share of problems, most peacekeeping efforts during the Cold War were lean but effective.

But the fact remains that peacekeeping barely got by during the Cold War. When large, expanded peacekeeping missions were hurled at the UN in the 1990s, the organization's antiquated and understaffed bureaucracy could not handle them and contributed to the failure of several of these operations.

To date, there have been no serious efforts by the UN nor Western states to reform UN peacekeeping management. This includes the Brahimi Report. Moreover, there still are numerous signs that the UN system is as determined as ever to resist reform. Without massive reform of the UN and its peacekeeping bureaucracy, deploying large and complex UN peacekeeping missions will continue to be expensive acts of futility.

NOTES

1. *Defining Purpose: The UN and the Health of Nations, Final Report of the United States Commission on Improving the United Nations: Minority Statement,* September 1993. This statement was signed by Commissioners Edwin J. Feulner, Jr., Alan L. Keyes, Jeane J. Kirkpatrick, Charles M. Lichenstein, Reverend Richard John Neuhaus, and Jose S. Sorzano.

2. *Report of the Comprehensive Review of the Whole Question of Peacekeeping Operations in All Their Respects,* UN document A/55/305– S/2000/809, August 21, 2000. Hereafter referred to as the "Brahimi Report."

3. Brian Urquhart, *Ralph Bunche: An American Life* (New York: Norton, 1993), p. 296.

4. Mona Ghali, "United Nations Interim Force in Lebanon," in William J. Durch, ed., *The Evolution of Peacekeeping* (New York: St. Martin's Press, 1993), p. 192.

5. After action report of a U.S. MINURSO peacekeeping soldier, December 15, 1992.

6. Author interview of Sir Brian Urquhart, September 6, 2000.

7. Moscow refused to pay for UNEF because of its concern that the organization was promoting Western interests. The USSR stopped paying for ONUC because it disagreed with the direction of this mission and believed it was controlled by the United States, the United Kingdom, and France. Preoccupied with its status as a major power, France refused to pay for UNEF because the operation was approved by the General Assembly, which Paris viewed as an affront to its permanent membership on the Security Council. Paris also had sovereignty concerns that stemmed from its effort to hold on to Algeria. It refused to pay for Congo mostly because the assessments were levied by the General Assembly.

8. See *Peace Operations: U.S. Costs in Support of Haiti, Former Yugoslavia, Somalia, and Rwanda,* GAO/NSIAD-96-38 (Washington, DC: Government Printing Office, March 1996).

9. U.S. General Accounting Office, *United Nations Limitations in Leading Missions Requiring Force to Restore Peace,* GAO/NSIAD-97-34 (Washington, DC: Government Printing Office, March 1997), p. 19.

10. U.S. Department of State, Office of Inspector General, *Report of Audit: Peace Operations Reform: Implementation of PDD-25 and Related Issues,* 7-CI-003 (Washington, DC: U.S. Department of State, March 1997), pp. 20, 33–35.

11. CBS News program *60 Minutes,* originally aired September 19, 1993.

12. Jack Anderson and Michael Binstein, "Somali Heist Followed UN Carelessness," *Washington Post,* October 19, 1995, p. B23.

13. Julia Preston, "Waste in Somalia Typifies Failings of UN Management," *Washington Post,* January 3, 1995, p. A11.

14. About 30 percent of the peacekeepers sent by Bulgaria in 1992 to the UNTAC peacekeeping mission in Cambodia were convicts sent to make prison space available. Sheila McNulty, "Some UN Peacekeepers Put Profits Before Mission," *Washington Times,* December 13, 1993, p. 12.

15. Author interview with Brian Boquist, president, ICI, August 14, 2000.

16. Former Australian Prime Minister Gareth Evans, in a July 11, 2000 interview

with the author, confirmed this characterization of Akashi, describing his performance in Yugoslavia and Cambodia as "an unmitigated disaster."

17. Douglas Farah, "Internal Disputes Mar UN Mission," *Washington Post*, September 10, 2000, p. 1.

18. James Bone, "Head of UN Force to Be Replaced after Leak," *London Times*, September 12, 2000, p. 9.

19. Author interview of senior U.S. Department of State official, June 29, 2000. See also the Brahimi Report, paragraphs 133–140.

20. Author interview of senior U.S. Department of State official, June 29, 2000.

21. Ibid.

22. For more details on problems with U.S. intelligence sharing with the UN see Joseph G. Hays III, "Oversight of U.S. Intelligence Support to UN Peacekeeping Operations," in Perry L. Pickert, ed., *Intelligence for Multilateral Decision and Action* (Washington, DC: Joint Military Intelligence College, 1997), pp. 433–472. Also see Bill Gertz, "Administration Playing Down Leaks of U.S. Secrets by UN," *Washington Times*, January 20, 1995; "Snowe Accuses UN of Breaches," *Washington Times*, March 22, 1995.

23. John Hillen, "Peace(keeping) in Our Time: The UN as a Professional Military Manager," *Parameters* (Autumn 1996), pp. 17–34.

24. UN bid announcement RSQN-6486/VMS, http://www.un.org/Depts/ptd/airchrt.htm.

25. A U.S. diplomat assigned to the U.S. Mission to the U.N. in New York told the author in October 2001 that the U.S. Mission was aware of UNAMSIL's effort to acquire a corporate jet and that the United States was blocking this request.

26. "US Politicos' Malaise Seen as Risk for UN Existence," *Diplomatic World Bulletin*, March 3–24, 1997, p. 1; Ben Barber, "UN Cuts Not Likely to be Deep or Painful," *Washington Times*, May 12, 1997, p. 1.

27. U.S. General Accounting Office, *United Nations: Reform Initiatives Have Strengthened Operations, but Overall Objectives Have Not Yet Been Achieved*, GAO/NSIAD-00-150 (Washington, DC: Government Printing Office, May 2000).

28. Author interview of senior Department of State official, June 29, 2000.

29. Michael Littlejohns, "The $964 Million Plan for Rebuilding HQ," *The Earth Times* 9, no. 18 (August 2000), p. 16.

30. See UN Security Council Resolution 1318, September 7, 2000.

31. Brahimi Report, paragraphs 92–102.

32. Brahimi Report, paragraphs 133–135.

33. U.S. House of Representatives Subcommittee on International Organizations and Human Rights, Hearing on the Millennium Summit and Current United States Policy on United Nations Peacekeeping, September 20, 2000.

34. UN General Assembly Resolution 998 (ES-I), November 4, 1956.

35. Article 97 of the UN Charter defined the secretary general as the organization's "chief administrative officer." Given that the secretary general of the League of Nations never assumed important responsibilities and the FDR/Churchill plan for the United Nations to be run by a great-power directorate, no one in 1945 desired the UN chief to become an important independent actor in world affairs.

36. Sir Brian Urquhart told the author during a September 6, 2000 interview that he believes Boutros-Ghali saw himself as another Hammarskjöld. David Rieff

wrote about Boutros-Ghali's imperious nature in August 1996. See Rieff, "The Bill Clinton of the UN," *The New Republic*, August 5, 1996, pp. 16–20.

37. Stanley Meisler, "From Hope to Scapegoat," *The Washington Monthly*, July–August 1996, p. 31.

Chapter 6

Iraq and the UN "Renaissance"

SHADES OF KOREA

The 1991 Persian Gulf War (Operation Desert Storm) brought about a universal realization that the Cold War had indeed ended and the world had entered a new era. Greatly improved relations between the United States and Russia and the collapse of the Nonaligned Movement—which lost its ostensible raison d'être as a neutral bloc between East and West—created unprecedented opportunities for global cooperation.

Operation Desert Storm, like the 1950–1953 Korean War, was a UN-sanctioned peace enforcement operation. In the Korean War, the United States took advantage of a Soviet boycott[1] of Security Council sessions to win approval for a resolution calling on all UN members to support a U.S.-led coalition to defend South Korea and repel an invasion by North Korean forces sponsored, if not instigated, by Moscow. While the U.S.-led Korean operation was ostensibly a "UN force," of the 60 nations who were UN members in 1950, just 16 sent troops. Only the United States, the United Kingdom, Canada, and Turkey sent more than token forces, and more than 90 percent of this "UN force" was from the United States and South Korea. UN Charter procedures for collective security operations, such as management by the UN Military Staff Committee and oversight by the Security Council, were absent during the Korean operation. The operation was, however, conducted under the UN flag. Inis L. Claude, Jr. gave this explanation as to why Washington did not employ the conflict resolution formula for the Korean conflict provided for by the UN's founders in the UN Charter:

[T]he role of the United Nations in the Korean case is more accurately characterized as the collective legitimization of collective self-defense than as the initiation and management of a collective security operation. Moreover, it is clear that the United States conceived the plan as a device whereby it might invoke the moral support of the United Nations for such resorts to force as it might find necessary and desirable in the course of its cold war struggles. In proposing the scheme, the United States did not purport to expose itself to new and more rigorous obligations to aid victims of aggression. American policy has consistently failed to develop the capacity of international agencies to decree that the United States must or must not engage in military action.[2]

In 1991, the Security Council again bypassed the charter and deputized the United States to conduct Operation Desert Storm against Iraq. This decision flowed in part from the Bush administration's* mistrust of the UN's competence to manage military operations. Like the Korea operation 40 years earlier, execution of the Gulf War was at the discretion of the United States, and Washington prevented the UN from playing any meaningful operational role. The UN Security Council did not even meet from November 29, 1990 to February 16, 1991, the period of maximum violence in Iraq. America's effort to use the UN as a figleaf for Operation Desert Storm offended many at the UN, especially Secretary General Javier Perez de Cuellar. Determined not to permit the UN to be used in the way it was during the Korean War, Perez de Cuellar turned down a request by President Bush to allow the anti-Iraq coalition to fight under the UN flag.[3]

The UN Security Council passed 25 resolutions on the Iraq-Kuwait conflict in 1990 and 1991. The importance of these resolutions to the Desert Storm operation has been widely misunderstood. While they were sought by Bush officials to give the U.S.-led operation the veneer of international law to assuage apprehensions by Arab states and for domestic political reasons, the United States would have conducted this operation with or without the support of the council.[4] Yet these resolutions would have a profound effect on later peacekeeping operations. The first resolution on Iraq passed by the Security Council, Resolution 660 (August 2, 1990), called for Iraq's unconditional withdrawal from Kuwait and defined Baghdad's invasion of Kuwait as a violation of international peace and security under Article 39 of the UN Charter. This resolution was unprecedented, since never before had all five permanent members of the council agreed on a condemnation of a breach of the peace.

The second significant resolution, 678 (November 29, 1990), approved the use of military force to dispel Iraqi forces from Kuwait under a U.S.-led coalition. This was a remarkable moment when China and Russia did something they never would have done only a year earlier: condone a mil-

---

*"Bush administration" in this chapter refers to President George H. W. Bush, president of the United States from 1989 to 1993.

itary operation by the United States against a Third World state. Despite dissimilarity from the UN founders' concept of collective security, 678 was heralded by many UN proponents as evidence that the UN had begun to play the assertive international role envisioned at the San Francisco Conference in 1945.

The most revolutionary resolution passed in connection with the Gulf War was Security Council Resolution 688 (April 5, 1991). Resolution 688 ostensibly authorized the UN to protect and give humanitarian aid to Iraqi Kurds by declaring Baghdad's attacks on them a threat to international peace and security. But this was not its actual purpose. While 688 did reflect the concern of the United States and UN Secretary General Perez de Cuellar with respect to the appalling conditions of the Iraqi Kurds in northern Iraq, the United States also hoped that this resolution would strengthen an irredentist movement in the area that could challenge Saddam Hussein's hold on power.

Passing 688 was not easy. China, uncomfortable with prior U.S.-orchestrated initiatives at the UN related to Desert Storm, would not go along with the proposed multinational operation in northern Iraq, which the United States and Perez de Cuellar were describing as a peacekeeping mission. Therefore, the specifics of this mission were left vague. As explained in the previous chapter, Perez de Cuellar initiated this effort by deploying guards from UN headquarters as ersatz peacekeepers. It was understood by Washington and Perez de Cuellar that the United States would assume control and responsibility for this mission, which it did shortly thereafter.

In July 1992, the Bush administration used the precedent of Resolution 688 to send UNOSOM I, a UN observer force, to facilitate the delivery of humanitarian aid to Somalia, which was hard-hit by drought, starvation, civil war, and anarchy. When this operation failed, the Security Council passed Resolution 794 (December 3, 1992) approving the deployment of the Unified Task Force (UNITAF), a U.S.-led peace enforcement mission.[5] Resolution 794 further expanded the 688 precedent by explicitly citing Chapter VII, thus stretching the bounds of UN collective security to humanitarian disasters within sovereign states. This heavily-armed peace enforcement operation, which was for all intents and purposes a military occupation, provided security to Somalia for a brief period, allowing the delivery of food and medicine.

UN FEVER

It did not matter to UN proponents that President George H. W. Bush used the UN as a shill to facilitate U.S. policy in the Persian Gulf. They were grateful for the resulting public relations boon that caused UN euphoria to break out again in the United States as it had in 1945. This new

American love affair with the UN was especially strong with the media and stemmed from the fact that the public did not understand the UN's limited role in Desert Storm and mistakenly gave the UN much of the credit for that operation's success. In addition, Desert Storm came on the heels of the successful UNTAG operation in Namibia, other small peacekeeping successes, and the awarding of the Nobel Peace Prize to UN peacekeeping forces. As a result, the world organization's reputation soared.

Reacting to the post–Cold War UN fever, President George H. W. Bush chaired an historic UN Security Council head of state summit in January 1992. The summit recognized the potential role that the UN could play to promote international security and tasked UN Secretary General Boutros-Ghali to prepare recommendations on ways to strengthen and improve preventive diplomacy, peacemaking, and peacekeeping. On June 17, 1992, Secretary General Boutros-Ghali complied with a report entitled *An Agenda for Peace: Preventive Diplomacy, Peacemaking, and Peacekeeping.*[6]

HITHERTO TROUBLE

Summarizing the meaning of *An Agenda for Peace* is difficult, since it has several vastly different interpretations. Boutros-Ghali appeared to intend the document to serve as the foundation for a new type of UN operation capable of using force to carry out UN mandates, which he termed "enforcement actions." A sentence in *An Agenda for Peace* that peacekeeping forces had been deployed *hitherto* only with the consent of warring parties was read by many observers as implying that the secretary general favored dropping the consent of disputants requirement as a peacekeeping prerequisite.

An Agenda for Peace was a cautious document. Boutros-Ghali actually endorsed the traditional peacekeeping concept and wanted separate military forces to conduct coercive enforcement actions. This was consistent with his frequent opposition to Western efforts to give combat mandates to traditional peacekeeping efforts. Boutros-Ghali also called for the UN to strike agreements with UN members on troops they would maintain on standby for use by the UN. The only novel proposal by the secretary general was his call for preventive deployment of peacekeepers to prevent conflicts from breaking out. This idea was the basis for the successful UNPREDEP peacekeeping force along the Macedonia/Serbia border.

While the first Bush administration essentially tasked Boutros-Ghali with crafting *An Agenda for Peace*, the document had little effect on its foreign policy or view of the UN. Bush officials had little real interest in UN missions much more ambitious than traditional peacekeeping efforts, although they were amenable to permitting U.S. troops to serve as traditional peacekeepers in limited circumstances. For example, Washington agreed to send U.S. troops to the UN peacekeeping mission to Western Sahara in 1991 because Morocco's King Hassan would not cooperate with the UN effort without participation by the United States. The Bush administration reluctantly agreed to send a small contingent of U.S. troops to Cambodia in 1992 to demonstrate American support for the peace process. However, these troops were assigned observer duties and kept out of harm's way. UNTAC also was strictly neutral and avoided provocative actions.

Boutros-Ghali retreated from the tentative endorsement he gave to significantly expanding peacekeeping by mid-1993—*before* major peacekeeping debacles occurred in Somalia, Haiti, and Yugoslavia. He wrote in a summer 1993 *Orbis* article:

The UN cannot keep peace when there is no peace to keep. The UN can serve as a catalyst, framework, and support mechanism for parties to seek peace and can help when hostile factions are prepared to work towards this common goal. But viable political structures cannot be imposed from the outside.[7]

Boutros-Ghali retreated further from *An Agenda for Peace* in 1996 when he wrote:

Effective UN peacekeeping requires the full consent and cooperation of the parties; UN peacekeepers must maintain their neutrality; they must have a clear and practicable mandate; and member states must support them with the necessary human and financial resources.[8]

On the other hand, the Clinton administration and other Western governments took an opposite view of *An Agenda for Peace* and used it to push a utopian UN program that went far beyond what Boutros-Ghali proposed. These leaders used the document as a blueprint to entrust the UN with unprecedented power to address international problems, including intrastate disputes such as civil wars and humanitarian disasters. This effort was driven by internationalist idealism as well as a deliberate effort by some Western leaders to dump intractable problems on the UN. The Clinton peacekeeping policy and its main policy document—Presidential Decision Directive 25—are discussed in detail in Chapter 8.

In summary, the end of the Cold War and the successful Gulf War led to new cooperation in the UN that encouraged many to believe that the world organization would finally assume the leading international role intended by the UN's founders. Some believed this to be the UN's rebirth. These same people regarded the first Bush administration's praise for the UN and Boutros-Ghali's *An Agenda for Peace* as compelling evidence that a new internationalist era had begun. Unfortunately, these were the factors that set the stage for one of the most disastrous initiatives ever conducted by the UN: expanded peacekeeping operations.

NOTES

1. Russia was boycotting Security Council sessions in 1950 to protest the refusal of the council to give the UN seat held by the Republic of China (Taiwan) to the People's Republic of China.

2. Inis L. Claude, Jr., *Swords Into Plowshares*, 4th ed. (New York: Random House, 1971), pp. 269–270.

3. Stanley Meisler, *The United Nations: The First Fifty Years* (New York: Atlantic Monthly Press, 1995), p. 268.

4. The United States also could have justified coming to Kuwait's aid under Article 51 of the UN Charter, which allows UN members to come to the defense of another member.

5. UN Security Council Resolution 794, December 3, 1992.

6. UN document A/47/277, June 17, 1992

7. Boutros Boutros-Ghali, "An Agenda for Peace: One Year Later," *Orbis* 37, no. 3 (Summer 1993), pp. 323–332.

8. Introduction to *The Blue Helmets: A Review of United Nations Peacekeeping*, 3rd ed. (New York: UN Department of Public Information, 1996), p. 5.

Part II

The Post–Cold War
Peacekeeping Train Wreck

At a lecture at Oxford University last week, Mr. Goulding, until recently the UN's top peacekeeping official, also explained that the force's
[UNPROFOR's] task was not really peacekeeping at all but "cease-fire
enforcement," meaning that "it could open fire in situations other than
self-defense—e.g., to silence guns that persisted in violating the cease-
fire."

—*New York Times*, March 8, 1993[1]

Chapter 7

Expanded Peacekeeping: Theory and Reality

The United Nations has entered a domain of military activity—a vaguely defined no-man's land lying somewhere between traditional peacekeeping and enforcement—for which it lacks any guiding operational concept. It has merely ratcheted up the traditional peacekeeping mechanism in an attempt to respond to wholly new security challenges. The result is that the majority of the nearly 70,000 blue-helmeted peacekeepers now in the field serve in contexts for which peacekeeping was not intended.

—John Gerard Ruggie, November 1993[2]

Expanded peacekeeping, a concept coined by former UN Secretary General Boutros-Ghali in 1993[3] (and the best of many terms for peacekeeping-like missions deployed in the 1990s), describes some three dozen UN peacekeeping efforts undertaken after the Cold War. By abandoning the strict prerequisites governing the deployment of traditional peacekeeping operations, expanded peacekeeping caused the number of UN forces to explode from 13 to 48 between 1988 and 1998, and the number of peacekeepers to grow to a record 78,000 in December 1994, compared with only 11,000 in 1988.[4] Most of these UN missions were driven by U.S. policy and occurred during the Clinton administration, although a few were deployed during the tenure of President George H. W. Bush.* While Bush and Clinton policies toward the UN differed significantly, peacekeeping operations deployed during both administrations shared several characteristics:

---

*"Bush administration" in this chapter refers to President George H. W. Bush, president of the United States from 1989 to 1993.

- They were deployed to areas formerly denied to UN peacekeepers due to the East/West conflict.
- They were given more ambitious mandates.
- They had at least limited participation by troops from the permanent members of the Security Council.

This study counts 35 UN peacekeeping missions conducted from 1991 through December 2000 as expanded peacekeeping operations (see Table 7.1). Operations are included in this group if they substantially deviate from the prerequisites for traditional peacekeeping explained earlier, especially the consent requirement.

Expanded peacekeeping missions have been deployed only since 1991. Most are operations that have or are prepared to use force to compel a combatant to abide by a Security Council mandate, have the consent of only one warring party, and/or are deployed primarily to perform non-peacekeeping duties, such as nation building.

Eight expanded peacekeeping operations were deployed in 1993, the largest number of UN forces ever created in one year. Because of the difficulties many encountered, the pace of new missions slowed significantly until fall 1999, when four new expanded peacekeeping operations were created. A plurality of expanded peacekeeping missions were deployed to Africa (11). Fourteen expanded peacekeeping missions were sent to disputes involving just two countries; eight were sent to address the conflicts to which Serbia was a party; six others were sent to Haiti.

BUSH'S CAUTIOUS PEACEKEEPING EXPERIMENTS

Of the 35 expanded peacekeeping missions deployed to date, seven were deployed at the behest of the first Bush administration: ONUSAL (El Salvador), UNAVEM II (Angola), UNPROFOR (Yugoslavia), UNAMIC (Cambodia), UNTAC (Cambodia), UNIKOM (Iraq/Kuwait), and UNOSOM I (Somalia). These UN missions broke with the traditional model by their emphasis on formerly ancillary peacekeeping functions such as election monitoring and civil administration. Several were deployed to intrastate conflicts. As stated in the previous chapter, Washington supported limited participation in these operations by American troops and for soldiers from the other permanent Security Council members. In most respects, however, UN peacekeeping missions deployed during the Bush administration honored traditional peacekeeping prerequisites, including a stable cease-fire, cooperation of warring parties, and neutrality of peacekeepers.

The first Bush administration only partially endorsed a conflict resolution role for peacekeeping. While many of the UN operations it advocated, such as ONUSAL (El Salvador), UNAVEM II (Angola), and UNTAC (Cambo-

Table 7.1
Expanded Peacekeeping Missions[5, 6]

	Start/End Dates	Authorized Size	Total Cost ($ millions)
ONUSAL (El Salvador)	1991–1995	1,108	107
UNIKOM (Iraq-Kuwait)	1991–	1,100	496*
UNAVEM II (Angola)	1991–1995	655	175
UNAMIC (Cambodia)	1991–1992	1,504	†
UNTAC (Cambodia)	1992–1993	22,000	1,600
UNPROFOR (Yugoslavia)	1992–1995	45,000	4,600
UNOSOM I (Somalia)	1992–1993	4,270	43
UNOSOM II (Somalia)	1993–1995	28,000	1,600
UNOMUR (Rwanda)	1993–1994	81	15
UNOMIG (Georgia)	1993–	136	250
UNMIH (Haiti)	1993–1996	6,800	316
MICIVIH (Haiti)‡	1993–1996	100	?
UNOMIL (Liberia)	1993–1997	400	85
UNAMIR (Rwanda)	1993–1996	5,500	437
UNMLT (Cambodia)	1993–1994	20	5
UNMOT (Tajikistan)	1994–2000	120	30
UNAVEM III (Angola)	1995–1997	4,220	890
UNPREDEP (Macedonia)	1995–1999	1,106	570
UNCRO (Croatia)	1995–1996	7,000	300
UNMIBH (Bosnia)	1995–	2,900	810
UNTAES (Croatia)	1996–1998	5,177	350
UNMOP (Croatia)	1996–	28	26
UNSMIH (Haiti)	1996–1997	1,500	56
MONUA (Angola)	1997–1999	3,575	293
MINUGUA (Guatemala)	1997	155	5
UNTMIH (Haiti)	1997	250	20
MIPONUH (Haiti)	1997–2000	300	40
UNPSG (Croatia)	1998	233	70
MINURCA (Central African Republic)	1998–2000	1,360	73
UNOMSIL (Sierra Leone)	1998–1999	250	40
UNMIK (Kosovo)	1999–	6,000	1,200
UNAMSIL (Sierra Leone)	1999–	17,500	1,300
UNTAET (East Timor)	1999–	10,790	1,300
MONUC (Congo)	1999–	5,537	450
MICAH (Haiti)	2000–2001	100	10

Notes: Data as of November 2001. Cost figures are not adjusted for inflation. *Since 1993, the Government of Kuwait has paid two-thirds of the costs of this mission. †The cost of this operation was included in UNTAC. ‡Joint UN/OAS operation.

dia), tried to lay the foundation for a lasting peace and rebuild societies, these goals were pursued with the consent of local parties.

UNIKOM (UN Iraq/Kuwait Observer Mission) was a major departure from the peacekeeping consent requirement. This operation, deployed along the Iraq/Kuwait border on Kuwaiti territory without Iraq's consent, was designed by the United States to be a "permanent" peacekeeping mission. It can be withdrawn only by an affirmative vote of the Security Council; if a vote is ever taken to withdraw UNIKOM, the United States can exercise its veto. Moreover, unlike other peacekeeping missions, UNIKOM does not have to be periodically reauthorized. Although UNIKOM is lightly armed, mans a buffer zone, and has not been challenged by either Iraq or Kuwait, its lack of full consent by both parties makes it an expanded peacekeeping mission.

CLINTON'S EXPANDED PEACEKEEPING CAMPAIGN

The Clinton administration launched an ambitious plan in 1993 known as "assertive multilateralism" to use UN peacekeeping as a means to address post–Cold War regional conflicts. This strategy, which was readily endorsed by the UN and America's Western allies, gave UN peacekeeping operations much more ambitious mandates, including engaging in battle with disputants, calling in air strikes, running governments, delivering humanitarian aid, attacking warlords, and conducting elections. Despite their ambitious mandates, these forces looked like traditional operations. Instead of being heavily armed, they relied on the moral authority of the UN, in the belief that combatants would defer to them as combatants historically had deferred to traditional missions.

Assertive multilateralism caused numerous major peacekeeping failures and forced the Clinton administration to cease using this term by early 1994. Details of this policy and how it impacted specific 1990s expanded peacekeeping missions are provided in the next chapter.

DEFINING EXPANDED PEACEKEEPING

Analyzing expanded peacekeeping is challenging because of two divergent schools of thought on the subject and a wide range of conflicting definitions. Conservative foreign policy analysts tend to regard expanded peacekeeping operations as unreasonable enlargements of traditional peacekeeping haphazardly thrown together by the West to serve as a UN dumping ground for intractable international problems.[7] Liberal internationalist analysts, on the other hand, view expanded peacekeeping as a natural evolution in conflict resolution. They have devised many names for these new operations, including "next generation," "second generation," "enhanced," and "aggravated" peacekeeping.[8] Some of these same analysts have been deliberately ambiguous about peacekeeping definitions and openly endorse several definitions and descriptors, claiming that the UN Charter is a flexible, living document that must change with the times. Ambiguous peacekeeping definitions allowed government and UN planners in the 1990s the ability to fashion UN peacekeeping forces to address almost any type of international crisis. This has led to considerable confusion over definitions and mandates of new peacekeeping-like efforts, as Table 7.2 illustrates.

Many American statesmen and foreign policy experts in the late 1990s used the catch-all terms "peace operations" or "complex contingency operations" to refer to traditional peacekeeping, expanded peacekeeping, and NATO-led peace enforcement campaigns. This replaced a practice by liberal internationalists in 1993 and 1994 of using the term "peacekeeping" to refer to all multilateral military operations short of war. Some American statesmen in the early 1990s tried to go further, even referring to Operation Desert Storm as a peacekeeping operation. Joseph Jockel wrote in 1994 how the blurring of these multilateral conflict resolution typologies was not limited to American officials.

Defense policy discussions in Canada have not been immune to attempts to stretch the term [peacekeeping] to cover a wide range of military activities. Pushed to the limit, any Canadian action in the service of peace, including deterring or punishing aggressors, can be called "peacekeeping." War, in other words, can be seen as a form of peacekeeping.[9]

Alex Morrison, president of Canada's Pearson Peacekeeping Center, indicated that Canada still favored broad and vague definitions of peacekeeping when he told the author during a July 2000 interview that he considered peacekeeping to be a "broad umbrella term" incorporating peacekeeping, peace enforcement, traditional peacekeeping, "humanitarian intervention," and other types of multilateral missions.

The Clinton administration tried unsuccessfully in 1999 and 2000 to convince NATO to endorse the "peace operation" and "complex operations" concepts as vague new terms for a wide spectrum of multilateral operations. This effort was unsuccessful due to opposition from the British and French, who favored more exact terms.[10]

British objections were driven by a foreign policy that defines the difference between peacekeeping and peace enforcement as not the level of violence but simply consent.[11] In the early 1990s, the British considered giving peacekeeping troops offensive missions, describing such efforts as "gray area" or "wider peacekeeping." However, chastened by its bad experience participating in the 1992–1995 UN force in the former Yugoslavia (UNPROFOR), London rejected this concept in 1995 as "spurious historically [and] dangerous doctrinally"[12] and adjusted its wider peacekeeping doc-

Table 7.2
Comparison of Expanded Peacekeeping Terms and Definitions

Term	Proposed By	Definition
Second Generation Peacekeeping	John Mackinlay and Jarat Chopra, Brown University, 1993	"A range of contingencies sometimes erroneously described as peacekeeping . . . does not necessarily have consent of all warring parties . . . may take rigorous steps to achieve its goals, possibly including heavy weapons, airstrikes, and warships."[13]
"Chapter VII" Peacekeeping	Clinton administration, 1993	"Actions involving the use of the threat of force to preserve, maintain, or restore international peace and security or address breaches of the peace or acts of aggression. Such operations do not require the consent of the state(s) involved or other parties to the conflict."[14]
Multidimensional Peacekeeping	Henry Stimson Center, 1995	"[P]rimarily involves the settlement of internal conflicts . . . usually has the full consent of local parties, although may be authorized to use force against local elements."[15]
Second Generation Peacekeeping	U.S. Ambassador Edward Marks, 1996	"A multi-dimensional activity combining traditional peacekeeping with extensive civilian responsibilities."[16]
Peace Support Operations	John Mackinlay, Brown University, 1996	"[O]perations and activities of all civil and military organizations deployed to restore peace and/or relieve human suffering. Peace support operations may include more forceful military actions required to establish peaceful conditions."[17]
Aggravated Peacekeeping	U.S. Department of Defense, 1997	"[O]perations undertaken with nominal consent, but which are complicated by intransigence, banditry, or anarchy."[18]
Peace Restoration and Conflict Management Operation	UN Department of Peacekeeping Operations, 1997	"New and tentative concept for operations which are forced by realities in the field to turn into Chapter VII operations, such as when humanitarian convoys need to be defended by force of arms or exclusion zones by airstrikes."[19]

trine to define two types of UN operations: peacekeeping and peace enforcement, the latter term defined as a subset of combat operations.

Another popular term for the expanded peacekeeping model is "multidimensional peacekeeping." Liberal internationalist proponents of this term believe it best describes post–Cold War UN missions, since they contend that most 1990s operations included a host of non-peacekeeping functions, such as distributing aid and monitoring elections. However, an examination of traditional peacekeeping operations indicates that this rationale is erroneous. As explained earlier in Chapter 1, UNFICYP, deployed in Cyprus since 1964, established a humanitarian and economics branch to provide emergency humanitarian assistance. UNIFIL, deployed in Lebanon since 1978, has long been engaged in civilian administration, humanitarian activities, and rebuilding infrastructure. UNIFIL also operates a hospital for the local population in southern Lebanon. UNSF, deployed in west New Guinea from 1962 to 1963, built a police force, performed civilian administration, and helped organize civilian elections.[20]

LEGAL ISSUES

Establishing a sound legal basis for expanded peacekeeping was considered unnecessary by most expanded peacekeeping proponents because they did not want future expanded peacekeeping efforts to be limited by legalisms. However, as explained in Chapter 4, some academics and statesmen—mostly in the United States—began in the early 1990s to assert that the traditional peacekeeping model is based solely on Chapter VI of the UN Charter. Many also frequently referred to expanded peacekeeping forces and peace enforcement efforts as "Chapter VII" missions.

This line of argumentation was controversial. Despite pressure from the United States, the UN Security Council has refused to invoke or refer to Chapter VI in approving peacekeeping mandates, a practice that appears to reflect the preference of the majority of UN members to reserve the legal description of Chapter VI actions for bona fide mediation efforts, such as good offices missions by the UN secretary general. Chapter VII peacekeeping is a contradiction in terms, as will be explained later in this chapter.

NON-UN EXPANDED PEACEKEEPING EFFORTS

Eight non-UN expanded peacekeeping missions have been launched since 1993 (see Table 7.3). All were conducted in Africa. Most were brief, poorly run, and, except for the ECOMOG missions to Sierra Leone and Liberia, inconsequential.

OMIB in Rwanda and MISAB in the Central African Republic were unsuccessful regional peacekeeping efforts set up by France to allow French forces to withdraw from these countries. They were poorly run and even-

Table 7.3
Non-UN Expanded Peacekeeping Forces, 1990–2001[21]

Mission and Dates	Size	Mandate
ECOMOG-Liberia (1990–1997) *Economic Community of West African States Cease-Fire Monitoring Group in Liberia*	12,000	Nigerian-led military "peacekeeping" force sent to Liberia by regional states to attempt to restore order in Liberia.
ECOMOG-Sierra Leone (1990–1997) *Economic Community of West African States Cease-Fire Monitoring Group in Sierra Leone*	12,000	Nigerian-led military "peacekeeping" force sent to Sierra Leone after Liberian insurgents crossed into that country to seize diamond mines and foment instability.
NMOG I (1992–1993) *Neutral Military Observer Group*	50	Force deployed by the OAU to promote order in Rwanda.
NMOG II (1993)	130	Continuation of NMOG I.
OMIB (1993) *Operation for African Unity Mission in Burundi*	67	Observe cease-fire and protect the capital from insurgents.
ECOMOG-Guinea-Bissau (1997–1999) *Economic Community of West African States Cease-Fire Monitoring Group in Guinea-Bissau*	710	Buffer force sent to monitor a cease-fire between rebel forces and the Guinea-Bissau government, facilitate the withdrawal of foreign troops, and protect the Guinea-Bissau president.
MISAB (1997) *Mission Interafricaine de Surveillance des Accords de Bangui (MISAB)*	1,600	African peacekeeping force backed by France to serve as a buffer between rebel forces and the Central African Republic government.
Operation Maulti (1999—)	300	South African/Botswana observer force to monitor situation in Lesotho.

Data as of July 2001.

tually were replaced by UN missions. Operation Maulti is actually a South Africa-Botswana operation to prop up the Lesotho government.

The most significant non-UN expanded peacekeeping operations were conducted by the Economic Community of West African States in Liberia, Sierra Leone, and Guinea-Bissau. Known as the Economic Community of West African States Cease-Fire Monitoring Group (ECOMOG), these missions attempted to restore order in countries divided by civil war. In general, they were only able to operate in national capitals and were undermined by corruption and poor performance. The ECOMOG force in Guinea-Bissau was deployed to monitor a cease-fire between rebel forces and the Guinea-Bissau government, facilitate the withdrawal of Senegalese and Guinean troops (who invaded Guinea-Bissau on behalf of the government), and provide security to Guinea-Bissau President Vieira. It was withdrawn when Vieira was overthrown. ECOMOG missions in Liberia and Sierra Leone restored some order where they were deployed but suffered from organizational problems, lack of funding and supplies, and corruption. These missions are discussed in detail in Chapter 8.

WHY EXPANDED PEACEKEEPING COLLAPSED

In 1993, conventional wisdom held that the expansion of peacekeeping mandates and missions were evolutionary improvements in UN peacekeeping. By 1995, it became apparent that they were a disastrous experiment. UNOSOM II's ambitious efforts to build a nation out of chaos and disarm Somali clans led to dozens of UN casualties, thousands of Somali fatalities, and drew the UN into a war. In Yugoslavia, a four-year, $5 billion peacekeeping mission culminated in the execution of thousands of Muslim civilians and POWs in areas supposedly under the protection of the UN. The peace bought by the $2 billion UNTAC mission in Cambodia fell apart two years later.

How could the many great minds who devised expanded peacekeeping have been so wrong? Why did this elegant strategy yield such disasters?

The answer is simple. Expanded peacekeeping collapsed because its promoters put their idealistic and political aspirations ahead of operational realities. Little consideration was given to developing a solid conceptual foundation for new peacekeeping models, establishing sound mandates, and, as discussed in Chapter 5, initiating substantial UN reform to give the organization the ability to manage large and complex peacekeeping operations. Instead, expanded peacekeeping missions were based almost solely on good intentions and rosy assumptions. Regrettably, the post–Cold War world has proven to be messy and unpredictable . . . and the road to Hell is paved with good intentions.

CONCEPTUAL PROBLEMS

A raft of faulty assumptions doomed expanded peacekeeping missions before they were deployed. One principal assumption was that fundamental changes in the international system due to the end of the Cold War would enable the UN's long-dormant collective security ideals finally to be enacted. Unfortunately, while the world was transformed in many respects when the Cold War ended, some aspects of international relations did not change as much as experts predicted.

National sovereignty, for example, has proved to be an important Cold War/post–Cold War constant. Expanded peacekeeping required nation-states to cede at least some sovereignty to the UN The trouble was, the nation-state system was still intact after the Cold War. Indeed, there have been no signs of its demise. On the contrary, an outbreak of civil wars and secessions in the early 1990s suggested that the world actually had moved *away* from global integration and interdependence. The number of UN members has *increased* by 28 countries, or 17 percent, since 1992; 19 are new nation-states formed due to secessions. Unlike many Western leaders and foreign policy experts, most Third World leaders in the 1990s did not see the dawning of a millennial and multilateral age and had no intention of deferring to the UN or cooperating with multilateral operations on their territory unless such missions advanced their interests.

Expanded peacekeeping proponents contended that Cold War notions of state sovereignty should be revised to protect human rights. The ability of totalitarian regimes with abysmal human rights records to hide behind UN Charter's "nonintervention" provisions (UN Charter, Article 2) barring the organization from intervening in the domestic affairs of a state had long irritated liberal internationalists. During the Cold War little could be done about this, since the USSR and the Third World were stalwart supporters of absolute state sovereignty.

The rash of civil wars and ethnic conflicts that broke out in the early 1990s gave liberal internationalists an opportunity to change the UN's Cold War prohibition on nonintervention in the domestic affairs of a state by arguing that this policy should not apply to "failed" states; that is, states like Somalia, which were in anarchy, or states rent by civil and ethnic conflict, like Yugoslavia. This thinking was readily accepted in the West, which was bombarded by scenes of killing and misery from Somalia and Yugoslavia on the evening news. The Third World, China, and Russia, however, continued to maintain that this rationale violated the charter and reluctantly went along with Western-backed Security Council resolutions authorizing interventions in UN member states on humanitarian grounds on a case-by-case basis without endorsing this new Western justification for UN intervention.

Many UN members, especially Third World states participating in peacekeeping missions, resisted fully supporting expanded peacekeeping missions that they believed violated the UN's nonintervention policy for fear of creating precedents that might someday encroach on their national sovereignty. This contributed to severe command and control problems as many Third World peacekeeping contingents refused to follow UN orders or arrived in the field with numerous conditions on how they could be used or deployed.

Conceptual problems also stemmed from a poor understanding of traditional peacekeeping by expanded peacekeeping proponents. Their misreading of earlier peacekeeping deployments as limited solely by the constraints of the Cold War led them to the erroneous conclusion that once freed from these constraints, peacekeeping could be used in a far wider range of conflicts and capacities. These assumptions proved fallacious because they did not recognize the importance of obtaining the consent of combatants, the paramount principle for the success and survival of traditional peacekeeping missions.

For example, UNFICYP on Cyprus, UNDOF in the Golan Heights, UNTAG in Namibia, and the UNEF missions in the Sinai were able to keep the peace by constituting themselves as effective and neutral forces. Their primary purpose was conflict avoidance in regions where inhabitants did not want conflict. Stable cease-fires were in place before these missions were deployed and continued throughout their tenures. Because they had the consent and cooperation of warring parties, traditional peacekeeping efforts did not need to be heavily armed and usually resolved incidents that could threaten the peace using quiet diplomacy and persuasion. Conversely, traditional peacekeeping operations like ONUC in the Congo and UNIFIL in Lebanon lacked stable cease-fires and experienced serious difficulties promoting peace, were attacked by local parties, and suffered high casualties.

Another significant mistaken assumption made by expanded peacekeeping proponents was to assume that the deference and respect disputants accorded traditional peacekeeping forces like UNFICYP and UNTAG would be extended to expanded peacekeeping troops deployed with little or no consent and with mandates to use force against disputants. Several of these missions such as UNOSOM II (Somalia), UNPROFOR (Yugoslavia), and UNTAC (Cambodia) instead emphasized building infrastructure and holding democratic elections and paid little attention to gaining the consent of warring parties, promoting stable cease-fires, or preventing minor incidents that could snowball into open warfare. Predictably, warring parties refused to cooperate or defer to these missions, resulting in high casualties, increased instability, and the collapse of most expanded peacekeeping operations.

Expanded peacekeeping proponents' mistaken assumption concerning consent flowed from their belief that traditional missions deployed for decades without resolving international disputes were failures they could improve upon. Unfortunately, this belief did not take into account the relative successes achieved by long-term traditional peacekeeping efforts or the complex factors that made them the only diplomatic vehicle capable of addressing certain conflicts.

Expanded peacekeeping theory did not anticipate other practical problems. When conducting national elections in Cambodia and Angola, expanded peacekeeping mission mandates did not provide for assuring a smooth transfer of power where losing parties would peacefully accept the results of democratic elections. It did not plan how to deal with parties that refused to participate in elections. Expanded peacekeeping theory also failed to ensure that government bureaucracies were neutral before and during national elections. While expanded peacekeeping personnel often arrested individuals for violating cease-fires, attacking UN personnel, or committing other crimes, such persons usually were not tried, since the UN did not have such authority and the justice systems of the host countries were either deeply flawed or nonexistent. The failure of expanded peacekeeping forces to rebuild justice systems before they withdrew was one of several obstacles preventing states such as Cambodia from completing their transition to democracy.

Another important shortcoming of expanded peacekeeping theory was failing to recognize the need to provide for a continuing peacekeeping presence after UN-conducted elections. In Cambodia, for example, the international community treated the 1993 national elections as the end of the UNTAC peacekeeping mission and quickly withdrew the force. While this gave the West a public relations boost, since this large UN force appeared to be leaving on a high note, UN and Western leaders failed to provide for a post-election force in Cambodia to ensure that the seeds of democracy planted by the UN took root. The next chapter describes the catastrophic consequences of this failure.

UN civilian police posed special problems that expanded peacekeeping planners did not anticipate. Also known as UNCIVPOL, UN civilian police is not a new concept and was part of traditional peacekeeping efforts in Congo, Cyprus, and West New Guinea. UN police sent to traditional peacekeeping situations played a confidence-building role and relied on the consent and cooperation of warring parties. Usually unarmed, UN police serve in local security roles inappropriate for military forces. These forces rely to a significant degree on the consent and cooperation of local parties and are not capable of coping with terrorists or significant disorder.

Expanded peacekeeping CIVPOL units tried to address an "enforcement gap"—local disorder and crime that peacekeeping troops had difficulty addressing—that tended to plague UN missions sent to "failed states" and ethnic conflicts. In Bosnia and Haiti, for example, CIVPOL officers were charged with restoring order in towns and villages and monitoring local police forces. It was hoped by UN planners that CIVPOL units could keep order on the civilian level, thus avoiding the appearance of martial law imposed by UN peacekeeping troops. Unfortunately, instability and violence in most expanded peacekeeping situations were beyond the capability of UN police and often required the intervention of peacekeeping troops.

Finally, it is clear today that conceptual problems of expanded peacekeeping forces stemmed from Western policies that were more political than idealistic. Flaws in the design and direction of peacekeeping forces in Cambodia, Haiti, Somalia, Rwanda, former Yugoslavia, and Angola in part resulted from an effort by Western states—especially the United States—to use peacekeeping missions to pursue political agendas that had little to do with bringing peace and stability to these regions. In Angola, the major objective was to obliterate UNITA, a political party despised by the American left. In Haiti, the objective was to install a mentally unbalanced former priest as president because he was a favorite of the American left. Most of these factors had a "denial of reality" air about them that made already dubious expanded peacekeeping initiatives even more incoherent and less likely to succeed.

Peace Enforcement: Anti-Peacekeeping

Peace enforcement is an important concept distinct from peacekeeping and expanded peacekeeping. In 1994, NATO agreed to a concise definition of peace enforcement as missions that "generally employ conventional combat operations to achieve their objectives" and stated that "the classic peace enforcement operations have been the Korean and Gulf Wars."[22] Peace enforcement generally is understood to be a conflict resolution model consistent with the intentions of the founders of the United Nations to address threats to international security through the use of military action against a recalcitrant state that has breached the peace. It is therefore the antithesis of peacekeeping, not a variation of it. See Table 7.4 for details on peace enforcement missions deployed since 1945.

The peace enforcement concept was expanded in the mid-1990s to include two long-term NATO-led missions within a state, the Bosnia Stabilization Force (SFOR) and the Kosovo Force (KFOR). SFOR retains an intrusive mandate that acts as a check on the Bosnian Serb and Bosnian Federation governments. KFOR has even more wide-ranging powers in Kosovo, which does not have a functional government. In February 1999, SFOR replaced the elected president of the Bosnian Serb Republic because of his anti-Muslim and anti-SFOR views. In April 1999, SFOR blocked the Bosnian Serb parliament from meeting to prevent it from interfering with the NATO bombing campaign against Kosovo. Such actions, although appropriate and justifiable, disqualify SFOR and KFOR as peacekeeping operations and place them squarely within the definition of a long-term peace

Table 7.4
Peace Enforcement Operations, 1945–2001[23]

Operation and Dates	Size	Mandate
Korean War (1950–1953)	780,000	Expel invading North Korean forces from South Korea.
Indian Peacekeeping Forces (IPKF) (Sri Lanka) (1987–1990)	50,000	Indian peace enforcement operation to combat Tamil secessionists in Sri Lanka.
Operation Desert Storm (Iraq/Kuwait) (1991)	500,000	U.S.-led operation to expel Iraqi forces from Kuwait.
Unified Task Force (UNITAF) (Somalia) (1992–1993)	40,000	U.S.-led operation to deliver humanitarian assistance.
Operation Turquoise (Rwanda) (1994)	2,800	French force with UN mandate in response to genocide.
Operation Restore Democracy (Haiti) (1994)	22,000	Drive out military junta and install elected president.
Operation Deliberate Force (Bosnia) (1995)	*	U.S.-led NATO air campaign to end Serb ethnic cleansing and violence in Bosnia.
Implementation Force (IFOR) (Bosnia) (1995–1996)	60,000	NATO-led mission charged with maintaining order in Bosnia. Also includes Russian and other non-NATO European troops.
Stabilization Force (SFOR) (Bosnia) (1996–)	23,000	Succeeded IFOR. NATO-led mission of long duration charged with maintaining order in Bosnia.
Multinational Protection Force (Operation Alba) (Albania) (1997–)	6,300	NATO operation in Albania deployed after breakdown in Albanian government.
Operation Boleas (Lesotho) (1998)	3,800	South Africa/Botswana mission to defend Lesotho from insurgents/restore order.
Operation Allied Force (Kosovo) (1999)	*	NATO air campaign to end Serbian persecution of ethnic Albanians in Kosovo.
Kosovo Force (KFOR) (1999–)	50,000	NATO-led mission of long duration charged with maintaining order and administering Kosovo. Also includes Russian and other non-NATO European troops.
International Force East Timor (INTERFET) (1999)	11,300	Australian-led mission with UN mandate to expel Indonesian irregulars from East Timor and restore order.

*These operations were NATO air campaigns. They did not involve ground troops.

Table 7.5
CIS/Russian "Peacekeeping" Operations[24]

Moldova (1992)	2,500
Georgia/Abkhazia (1992–)	6,000
Georgia/South Ossetia (1992–)	1,500
Tajikistan (1992–)	8,200

Data as of July 2001.

enforcement mission within a state. Such missions could be reasonably considered international occupations.

Humanitarian Intervention

Although often portrayed as a distinct type of international operation, humanitarian intervention actually is a dimension of some expanded peacekeeping and peace enforcement operations. Humanitarian intervention has been used to justify multilateral military operations within a sovereign state without obtaining its consent, deployed on the basis of a supposed "right" of the international community to intervene. Humanitarian intervention is hence a rationalization for action and not a separate type of operation per se. Expanded peacekeeping missions such as UNOSOM I and II (Somalia) and UNPROFOR (Yugoslavia) as well as peace enforcement missions like UNITAF (Somalia) were based, at least in part, on the humanitarian intervention rationale.

Commonwealth of Independent States (CIS)/Russian Operations

Since 1993, Russia has described several operations it has conducted within the borders of the former Soviet Union as "CIS peacekeeping missions" (see Table 7.5). These operations are more accurately described as Russian peace enforcement operations. Some have had token participation by troops from other former USSR states. Others have been "collective peacekeeping" efforts with participation by Russia and the military forces of warring parties. Russian-led "peacekeeping" efforts within the former USSR have always been heavily armed.[25]

CIS "peacekeeping" missions have been viewed with suspicion by Western peacekeeping experts, most of whom consider them to be fig leafs or pretexts for Russian military operations. While some of these operations may have pursued laudable goals, they have not been neutral and have been deployed to promote the security objectives of Russia. Terry McNeill expressed this view when he wrote in the *International Political Science Review* in 1997 that Russian peacekeeping missions were "[i]nterventions, disguised as peacekeeping missions to safeguard the lives of vulnerable ethnic Russians living outside the Russian Federation."[26]

MANDATE PROBLEMS

Expanded peacekeeping troops faced mandate problems unknown to traditional peacekeepers. UN troops in Somalia, Yugoslavia, Rwanda, Angola, and Sierra Leone often did not know why they were deployed and were uncertain how much force they were permitted to use. Expanded peacekeeping missions often had ambiguous mandates because UN members could not agree on coherent strategies to address the conflicts these missions were sent to address. Many missions also had unstated political objectives that contradicted official mission mandates and goals. Moreover, the Security Council regularly added additional tasks to expanded peacekeeping operations but not the means to carry them out.

Many mandate problems stemmed from a controversial practice begun in 1993 of passing large numbers of expanded peacekeeping mandate resolutions in the Security Council containing references to Chapter VII of the UN Charter. As explained earlier, Chapter VII allows the Security Council to employ legally binding economic sanctions or authorize military action against a nation-state that poses a dire threat to international security, such as Iraq in 1990 and 1991. Before 1990, Chapter VII resolutions were rare and passed on only three occasions: Southern Rhodesia (1966 and 1968) and apartheid in South Africa (1977).[27] Each of these resolutions approved only economic or arms embargoes, and not military action.

The explosion in the number of Chapter VII Security Council resolutions can be traced to the 1990–1991 Iraq-Kuwait crisis. Of the 25 resolutions passed in connection with this situation, 20 cited Chapter VII. While some of these Chapter VII references were general, their meaning was clear. They pressured Iraq first with economic sanctions and then with an unambiguous threat of overwhelming military force. The most important anti-Iraq Security Council resolution, 678 (November 29, 1990), gave a U.S.-led coalition the UN's blessing to use overwhelming military force to expel Iraqi forces from Kuwait. The meaning and seriousness of this resolution could not have been clearer. The Security Council's Iraq resolutions passed in 1991 and 1992 after the war ended were just as clear and carried the implication that Baghdad's failures to comply with council directives would result in a military response. (Regrettably, Western resolve against Iraq weakened beginning in 1993, a development that goes beyond the scope of this book.)

As stated earlier, also important to the 1993 explosion in Chapter VII peacekeeping mandates was Security Council Resolution 794 (December 3, 1992), which invoked Chapter VII and Chapter VIII (under which the Security Council can deputize regional organizations to conduct enforcement actions) to call upon UN members to use whatever means necessary to restore order to Somalia and facilitate the distribution of humanitarian aid. This resolution represented a major precedent, since it was the first time that the UN Security Council declared a humanitarian disaster a threat to international peace requiring a Chapter VII mandate. But Resolution 794 had a concise and direct purpose similar to Resolution 678: it provided legal justification for a well-armed, temporary, and U.S.-led intervention to restore order.

UNPROFOR and UNOSOM II were different stories. From 1993 to 1995, long-standing precedents on peacekeeping mandates were abandoned as the Security Council passed 52 Chapter VII resolutions on these two conflicts, most of which were exceedingly vague and did not provide for the use of military force. For both operations, references to Chapter VII in authorizing Security Council resolutions had no clear meaning. In some of these resolutions, Chapter VII references concerned embargoes. However, most Chapter VII references in Yugoslavia and Somalia Security Council resolutions passed during this period constituted a vague threat of future military action against recalcitrant parties.[28] None of the UNPROFOR or UNOSOM II resolutions passed between 1993 and 1995 gave UN troops actual enforcement mandates or the ability to defend themselves if their so-called Chapter VII mandates got them into a war with local parties. Thus, UN soldiers were placed in the impossible situation of being incapable of fighting a war while at the same time unable to make peace. This created confusing mandates for peacekeeping forces, as UN Secretary General Boutros-Ghali explained in a May 1995 report to the Security Council: "UNPROFOR is not a peace enforcement operation and some confusion has arisen as a result of references to Chapter VII in some Security Council resolutions relating to its mandate, particularly as regards the use of force other than in self-defence."[29]

Table 7.6 illustrates the large number of resolutions passed on the Somalia and Yugoslavia situations through 1995. The situation in the former Yugoslavia has generated more Security Council resolutions than any other single conflict. Moreover, unable to pass as many resolutions as it wished on this conflict in the mid-1990s, the council established a practice of approving large numbers of "presidential statements" on the Balkans situation. Presidential statements are one- or two-page documents expressing the council's views on an international issue. They require unanimity, are not legally binding, and were seldom used before 1993.

The proliferation of Security Council resolutions, Chapter VII references in these resolutions, and presidential statements weakened the credibility of the UN and the international community during the 1990s, especially with regard to the Balkans. Security Council pronouncements became so voluminous and routine that they were no longer credible. The Security

Table 7.6

Comparison of Security Council Resolutions and Presidential Statements during Conflicts in Iraq, Somalia, and the Former Yugoslavia[30]

Iraq (1990–1991) (Operation Desert Storm)	1990	1991			
Total number of Resolutions passed	13	12			
Number of Chapter VII Resolutions	9	11			
Presidential Statements	0	4			
Somalia (1992–1995) **(UNOSOM I and II)**	1992	1993	1994	1995	
Total number of Resolutions passed	6	6	7	0	
Number of Chapter VII Resolutions	2	4	3	0	
Presidential Statements	0	0	1	1	
Former Yugoslavia (1991–1995) **(UNPROFOR and related missions)**	1991	1992	1993	1994	1995
Total number of Resolutions passed	3	22	22	13	28
Number of Chapter VII Resolutions	2	5	14	9	21
Presidential Statements	0	8	26	17	27

Council passed so many Chapter VII resolutions on the Balkan situation without backing them up with force that the Bosnian Serbs realized that they could ignore them without suffering any consequences. This emboldened the Bosnian Serbs to such a degree that in 1995 they openly threatened to kill peacekeepers and took 370 UN troops hostage. UNPROFOR Commander General Michael Rose commented in December 1993 that he had stopped reading the plethora of Security Council resolutions on the Balkans because of "a fantastic gap between the resolutions of the Security Council, the will to execute these resolutions, and the means available to commanders in the field."[31]

A key problem with expanded peacekeeping mandates is that UN troops claimed to be neutral but attacked warring parties and sometimes engaged in extremely provocative actions such as calling in airstrikes. At the same time, expanded peacekeeping troops were given the same pacific rules of engagement and light equipment as traditional peacekeepers. Boutros Ghali explained this dilemma as follows in 1995:

Nothing is more dangerous for a peacekeeping operation than to ask it to use force when its composition, armament, logistic support, and deployment deny it the capacity to do so. The logic of peacekeeping flows from political and military premises that are quite different from enforcement; and the dynamics of the latter are incompatible with the political process that peacekeeping is intended to facilitate. To blur the distinction between the two can undermine the viability of the peacekeeping operation and endanger its personnel.[32]

Unlike traditional peacekeeping missions, which due to their small numbers and size could be deployed indefinitely, expanded peacekeeping missions often were complex operations that did not have the luxury of time. Many were huge and expensive propositions that UN members would not agree to maintain indefinitely. Expanded peacekeeping missions therefore needed to fulfill their already-impossible mandates quickly and withdraw. Moreover, provisions were not made to address or compensate for UN inefficiency, corruption, and command and control problems. As a result, incompetent, undermanned, and chronically late peacekeeping contingents proved to be far more serious problems for expanded peacekeeping forces than they were for previous efforts. Trying to deploy these hastily formed, poorly equipped, and overly ambitious expanded peacekeeping missions to civil wars and ethnic conflicts proved to be a recipe for disaster.

Peacekeeping "Atrocities"

A small number of UN contingents deployed to expanded peacekeeping missions have been accused of committing "atrocities" against civilians. Upon examination, most of these allegations proved to be propaganda spread by recalcitrant parties hoping to discredit UN peacekeepers. However, some of these reported incidents may be a consequence of sending international troops to participate in poorly designed peacekeeping missions with impossible mandates, especially combining pacific peacekeeping mandates with combat mandates. True or not, these allegations hurt peacekeeping and damaged the reputations of key peacekeeping states. Some of these allegations include:

- *Belgium* tried two soldiers in 1997 for torturing two children, including allegedly trying to roast a child over a fire in Somalia, probably in 1994. Both children survived.
- *Italian* newspapers published photos in 1997 of an Italian peacekeeper applying electrodes to the hands and genitals of a Somali, probably in 1994.
- *Canada* prosecuted Canadian peacekeepers in 1996 for murdering a Somali teenager and photographing themselves next to the corpse.
- UN peacekeepers in Cambodia—especially the *Bulgarian* contingent—were accused of engaging in numerous acts of criminal activity, including black marketeering, rape, and running brothels.[33]

CONCLUSION

Utopian optimism stemming from the end of the Cold War made anything seem possible at the UN in 1992 and early 1993. A product of this optimism was expanded peacekeeping. Unfortunately, by mid-1995, it was clear that expanded peacekeeping efforts were more wishful thinking than reasoned policy. Disputants tended not to cooperate with these missions and often attacked them. This wasn't supposed to matter, since good intentions and the high rhetoric of the new world order were expected to carry the day. Not surprisingly, they did not.

NOTES

1. Paul Lewis, "UN Force May Compel Bosnia Peace Pact," *New York Times*, March 8, 1993, p. A3.

2. John Gerard Ruggie, "Wandering in the Void: Charting the UN's New Strategic Role," *Foreign Affairs* (November–December 1993), pp. 26–31.

3. Boutros Boutros-Ghali, "An Agenda for Peace: One Year Later," *Orbis* (Summer 1993), p. 323.

4. *The Blue Helmets: A Review of United Nations Peacekeeping*, 3rd ed. (New York: UN Department of Public Information, 1996), p. 4.

5. Sources: Project on Peacekeeping and the United Nations, U.S. General Accounting Office, United Nations Department of Peacekeeping Operations.

6. This chart excludes the UN Guard Contingent in Iraq (UNGCI) that has been deployed in northern Iraq since 1991 to discourage Iraqi attacks on Iraqi Kurds. While this mission theoretically may qualify as an expanded peacekeeping mission, the United States and the United Nations agreed in 1991 not to count it as a peacekeeping effort. See Chapter 5 for details.

7. For example, see Charles Krauthammer, "Let Peacekeeping Rest in Peace," *Washington Post*, June 2, 2000, p. A33.

8. Boutros-Ghali and some UN scholars have also discussed other UN missions such as "peace building" and "preventive diplomacy," which they believe are separate missions from peacekeeping. For the purposes of this book, these missions are considered part of expanded peacekeeping.

9. Joseph T. Jockel. *Canada and International Peacekeeping*, CSIS Significant Issues Series 16, no. 3 (1994).

10. Source: Author meeting with U.S. Army War College Peacekeeping Institute staff, August 14, 2000.

11. *Joint Warfare Publication 3.50: Peace Support Operations* (Northwood: UK Ministry of Defence, 1998).

12. Ibid.

13. John Mackinlay and Jarat Chopra, *A Draft Concept of Second Generation Multilateral Operations, 1993* (Providence, RI: Thomas J. Watson Institute for International Studies, 1993), p. 4.

14. PDD-25 (Clinton administration policy on UN peacekeeping), cited in George Mason University Peacekeeping Center Internet homepage, http://ralph. gmu.edu.cfpa/peace/definitions/a_g/html, August 1997.

15. William J. Durch, ed., *UN Peacekeeping, American Policy, and the Uncivil Wars of the 1990s* (New York: St. Martin's Press, 1996), p. 4.

16. Edward Marks, *Complex Emergencies: Bureaucratic Arrangements in the UN Secretariat* (Washington, DC: National Defense University Press, 1996), p. 9.

17. John Mackinlay, *A Guide to Peace Support Operations* (Providence, RI: Thomas J. Watson Institute for International Studies, 1996), p. 2.

18. U.S. Department of Defense Joint Publication 3-0, cited in George Mason University Peacekeeping Center Internet homepage, http://ralph.gmu.edu.cfpa/ peace/definitions/a_g/html, August 1997.

19. United Nations Department of Peacekeeping Operations, UN Peacekeeping Internet homepage, http://www.un.org/Depts/dpko/glossary/html, August 1997.

20. *The Blue Helmets: A Review of United Nations Peacekeeping*, 2nd ed. (New York: UN Department of Public Information, 1991), pp. 134, 175–185, 263–277.

21. Sources: *The Military Balance 1999–2000* and *The Military Balance 2000– 2001*, The International Institute for Strategic Studies (Oxford: Oxford University Press, 1999 and 2000); Associated Press, United Press International.

22. *NATO, Peacekeeping, and the United Nations* (London: British-American Security Information Council, 1994), p. 35.

23. Some have attempted to extend the definition of peace enforcement to include the Vietnam War, the 1983 U.S. military operation to liberate Grenada, and the 1982 U.S. operations to restore order in Beirut. A case can be made that these missions had a lot in common with the Korean War and Operation Desert Storm and therefore should be included. The author excluded these missions and others like them by using the 1994 NATO definition of peace enforcement, which requires such operations be truly multilateral *and* have some sort of international sanction, such as a UN authorizing resolution. The Indian Peacekeeping Forces in Sri Lanka and Operation Boleas were deployed in response to bilateral agreements and may not qualify as peace enforcement operations.

24. *The Military Balance 1999–2000* and *The Military Balance 2000–2001*; author correspondence with OSCE missions.

25. Source: Lally Weymouth, "Yalta II," *Washington Times*, July 24, 1994, p. C7; *The Military Balance 1999–2000* and *The Military Balance 2000–2001*; author correspondence with OSCE missions.

26. Terry McNeill, "Humanitarian Intervention and Peacekeeping in the Former Soviet Union and Eastern Europe," *International Political Science Review* 18, no. 1 (1997), pp. 95–113.

27. Before 1990, the Security Council passed resolutions with the phrase "acting under Chapter VII" twice, concerning Southern Rhodesia, Resolution 253 (May 29, 1968) and South Africa, Resolution 417 (October 31, 1977). In 1966, the council passed Resolution 232 (December 16, 1966) on the Southern Rhodesia situation, which invoked two Chapter VII articles: Article 39, which spelled out that there had been a breach of the peace, and Article 41, which supported the imposition of economic sanctions.

28. Despite some assertions to the contrary in the media, Chapter VII references in Security Council resolutions do not signify that such resolutions are legally binding. Article 25 of the charter specifies that all Security Council resolutions are binding on UN members.

29. United Nations, *Report of the Secretary General Pursuant to Security Council Resolutions 982 and 987*, UN document S/1995/444 (May 30, 1995).

30. Source: UN Department of Public Information, *Yearbook of the United Nations, Volumes 45–49* (Dordrecht: Martinus Nijhoff, 1991–1995).

31. Kurt Schork, "UN Commander in Bosnia Slams SC, EC," Reuters, December 30, 1993.

32. UN, *Report of the Secretary General Pursuant to Security Council Resolutions 982 and 987.*

33. Sources: Evelyn Leopold, "UN Chief Outraged at Somali Atrocities," Reuters, June 23, 1997; Jennifer Gould, "Belgian Soldiers Go on Trial for Torture," *Washington Times*, June 23, 1997, p. A1.

Chapter 8

Expanded Peacekeeping Fiascoes

Sending lightly armed peacekeepers where there is no peace to keep has
brought international discredit to the UN system.

—Abba Eban, 1995[1]

This chapter provides an overview of the seven major peacekeeping fiascoes
of the 1990s and a summary of four expanded peacekeeping missions deployed since 1999. Emphasis is placed on why expanded peacekeeping missions failed and the consequences of their failures. Attention is also paid
to the "cumulative" effect of failed expanded peacekeeping missions: a phenomenon where disputants in some expanded peacekeeping missions foiled
UN operations deployed to their regions by learning from earlier expanded
peacekeeping fiascoes. Finally, the role of Western policy—especially by the
Clinton administration—as a complicating factor is considered.

CAMBODIA

Despite the fact that Cambodia today is fraught with repression and
corruption, many foreign policy experts maintain that the UN Transitional
Authority in Cambodia (UNTAC), a $1.6 billion, 22,000-man expanded
peacekeeping force deployed from March 1992 until September 1993, was
a great success. Such a conclusion is sophistic and can be drawn only by
exaggerating UNTAC's limited and mostly ephemeral accomplishments. As
a lightly armed peacekeeping force, UNTAC did not have the armament
nor the mandate to compel warring parties to abide by crucial elements of

its mandate. As a result, UNTAC's "accomplishments" began to wither soon after it withdrew.

The UN-sponsored Paris Agreements were intended to end decades of conflict and mayhem in Cambodia. From 1975 to 1979, Cambodia was ruled by the murderous Khmer Rouge, a Maoist totalitarian regime led by Pol Pot that killed an estimated 1 million Cambodians. Due to Khmer Rouge incursions into Vietnam and rising tensions between the two countries, Vietnam invaded Cambodia in 1979, installed a puppet communist government, the Cambodian People's Party (CPP), and drove the Khmer Rouge into the mountains of western Cambodia.

Vietnam's 1979 invasion destabilized the region. The CPP committed atrocities and forced hundreds of thousands to flee the country. China and Thailand felt threatened by Vietnam's control of Cambodia. Aside from Vietnam and the Soviet bloc, the world refused to recognize the CPP government. In 1982, the Khmer Rouge forged an alliance with two non-communist Cambodian parties, the royalist FUNCINPEC party, led by Prince Norodom Sihanouk, and the Kampuchean National Liberation Front (KPNLF), led by a former Cambodian prime minister. This alliance won substantial international support and held Cambodia's UN seat from 1982 until the signing of the Paris Agreements.

UNTAC was deployed in 1992 as part of the 1991 Paris Agreements. It had the complex mission of overseeing a cease-fire among four disputants, conducting national elections, repatriating refugees, and ensuring that the power of the Cambodian government was used in a neutral fashion before and during the elections.

UNTAC succeeded in some areas, especially repatriating Cambodian refugees. It rebuilt infrastructure and conducted a national election. However, as a lightly armed peacekeeping force, UNTAC could not compel parties to cooperate fully with the peacekeeping agreement. The Khmer Rouge did not disarm and refused to allow UN troops into their areas. The CPP also did not fully disarm and refused to work with the UN to assure that the Cambodian government bureaucracy was neutral before and during the election.

Because of administrative problems and poor planning, UNTAC was unable to supervise the Cambodian government in 1992, when the CPP appeared to be willing to work with the UN. By the time UNTAC was finally prepared to assume this role, the CPP refused to cooperate. Nevertheless, UNTAC succeeded in conducting an investigation in early 1993 confirming reports that the CPP was using the government bureaucracy to foment violence against the opposition and intimidate voters. CPP violence became so severe in early 1993 that FUNCINPEC threatened to cease cooperating with UNTAC.

The CPP's well-publicized efforts to manipulate the peace process were used by the Khmer Rouge to further limit its cooperation. As a result, by early 1993, both the Khmer Rouge and CPP were moving away from the peace process and the UNTAC operation was in danger of collapsing. UN officials, believing that UNTAC would break up by the end of 1993, arranged for national elections to be hurriedly conducted in May of that year. UNTAC was successful in conducting a nationwide voter registration drive and took a number of steps to frustrate CPP efforts to intimidate or kill FUNCINPEC parliamentary candidates. The election was a tribute to the Cambodian people and their desire for democracy. Over 90 percent of the voting population—4.2 million people—risked possible attacks from the CPP and the Khmer Rouge and stood in long lines to vote. Fortunately, these attacks never materialized.

FUNCINPEC won the national elections, but the CPP threatened civil war if it was not given a share of power. Rather than insisting that the CPP honor the results of the democratic elections, the UN and the international community—led by the United States—pressured Prince Sihanouk to form a coalition government with the CPP. Prince Norodom Ranariddh, Sihanouk's son, was named first prime minister and CPP leader Hun Sen became second prime minister. Sihanouk was elected king and head of state by a royal council.

Shortly after UNTAC withdrew in early 1994, its achievements began to unravel. UNTAC's inability to disarm the Khmer Rouge and the CPP guaranteed that armed conflict and instability would resume when UN forces withdrew. The UN also failed to dislodge CPP personnel from civil administration in the period leading up to the elections and most refused to leave their positions when their party was defeated or to answer to Prince Ranariddh. The CPP used the coalition to build its political power, isolate FUNCINPEC, and recruit Khmer Rouge irregulars and leaders. The CPP staged a violent coup in July 1997 that drove Ranariddh out of the country and killed his top aides. This action spurred the *New York Times* to sharply condemn the Clinton administration's Cambodia policy in a July 10, 1997 editorial.

Washington is still searching for a diplomatic euphemism to describe this week's military ouster of Cambodia's First Prime Minister, Norodom Ranariddh, by his coalition partner and longtime rival, Second Prime Minister Hun Sen. Simply calling it a coup would bring an automatic suspension of American aid to the country. The Clinton Administration fears such instant disengagement would reduce rather than increase United States leverage.

Whatever label Washington applies, Mr. Hun Sen's bloody seizure of power is an affront to democracy and a violation of the 1991 Paris agreement that ended the Cambodian civil war. Most of all, it is a disaster for Cambodia.[2]

In 1998, the first national elections were held since UNTAC's withdrawal. The elections, in which the CPP won a plurality, were conducted entirely by CPP personnel and were widely condemned in the Western media. Former UNTAC Commander John Sanderson and Michael Maley, an UNTAC official who helped organize the 1993 elections, contended in a damning article that the 1998 elections were not free and fair and that Cambodia is essentially an authoritarian state where governmental authority comes from the barrel of a gun.[3] Sanderson and Maley alleged that the CPP used systematic violence, blackmail, torture, and political killings to stay in power. They cited one allegation that some Cambodian civilians were asked to drink a glass of water with a bullet in it after promising to vote for the CPP; the implication being that those who did not vote for the CPP would be killed.[4]

Cambodia today is a more peaceful place than it was before UNTAC deployed in 1992. Prince Ranariddh reluctantly agreed to return to Cambodia and serve as second prime minister in a CPP/FUNCINPEC coalition government. Violence in the countryside has dropped sharply. The Khmer Rouge imploded between 1998 and 2001 because of defections to the CPP and purges. Pol Pot is dead. Most remaining Khmer Rouge leaders are aged, sickly, and facing war crimes trials. Those who defected to the CPP will not be prosecuted.

But beneath a seemingly tranquil surface, Cambodian politics have not changed. CPP leader Hun Sen is a despot who dominates Cambodian politics because the CPP is more united and by doing whatever it takes, including violence, to keep its principal opponent, FUNCINPEC, off balance. At the same time, FUNCINPEC lost much of the influence it had in the early to mid-1990s because of internal political squabbling. However, the biggest factor that undermined FUNCINPEC was the implosion of the Khmer Rouge, which had been functioning as its military arm. Without the Khmer Rouge military threat, FUNCINPEC was much easier for the CPP to push around. The CPP is also more media savvy and has learned how to manipulate FUNCINPEC in subtle behind-the-scene ways, avoiding negative publicity that could jeopardize international development assistance. This outcome is hardly the result that the international community sought when it agreed to spend over $1 billion on a Cambodian peacekeeping mission. However, it is clear that the CPP's strategy in the late 1990s was based on the reality that UN and Clinton administration officials would ignore a significant amount of CPP mischief in order to maintain the fiction that UNTAC and their Cambodia policies were a success.

The UNTAC mission had serious conceptual problems. It relied on the assumption that all parties would fully cooperate with it, as disputants usually did with earlier traditional peacekeeping efforts. While UNTAC had the consent of disputants to deploy, the CPP never had any intention of relinquishing power and took steps to make sure that this did not happen. The Khmer Rouge apparently had no intention of fully cooperating with UNTAC and did not participate in national elections. (The refusal of the

CPP to fully cooperate influenced the Khmer Rouge's non-cooperation with UNTAC, although it may not have cooperated in any event.) One wise decision UNTAC made was honoring the traditional peacekeeping rule that peacekeepers should not use force to compel parties to comply with peace agreements, a decision that prevented the intransigence of the Khmer Rouge from turning UNTAC into another Cambodian combatant and limited UN casualties. UNTAC also had the foresight to limit the role of certain peace-keeping troops, especially Americans and Japanese, that might provoke warring parties. The 49 American soldiers who served in UNTAC were limited to observer roles in secure areas. Japan's 605 troops were restricted to observer missions in peaceful areas and building roads.

UNTAC also had significant mandate problems. Although its reliance on influential outside powers—Russia, China, the United States, France, Thailand, and Indonesia—brought the Cambodian disputants to the bargaining table and helped ensure a modicum of cooperation, this influence proved to be a mixed blessing when dealing with parties that refused to fully cooperate. For example, increased pressure on the CPP would cause Moscow to protest. Similarly, Beijing was protective of the Khmer Rouge and would not countenance UN military action against its Cambodian ally.

UNTAC's most serious mandate problem concerned its ultimate purpose. Was it simply to facilitate peace, conduct national elections, and promptly withdraw; or did it have a responsibility to maintain a longer-term presence and see through Cambodia's transition to democracy? This question was not addressed in advance by UNTAC's planners, who underestimated the difficulty of this operation and assumed elections would be uneventful and all parties would fully cooperate. While UN and Clinton officials did not contemplate a rapid UNTAC withdrawal, they did not have an exit strategy, either.

UNTAC's precipitous withdrawal in late 1993 was influenced by the Clinton administration, which knew that the force was collapsing and viewed the possible failure of such a large and expensive peacekeeping mission as a public relations disaster that would doom its ambitious UN-based foreign policy. Therefore, elections were held despite the fact that UNTAC had not met most of its mandate. It was then quickly withdrawn to give the UN and the United States the opportunity to declare victory before chaos returned. This was an unfortunate policy decision, since there was a chance that if UNTAC remained through 1994 it might have been able to finish what it started and increased the prospects for democratic government. This was a mistake Clinton officials tried not to make several years later when they helped design what are essentially occupation forces to address civil and ethnic crises in Bosnia, Kosovo, and East Timor.

Administrative and chain of command problems also plagued UNTAC, undermining its effectiveness and reputation. UNTAC was the most expensive and most ambitious operation the UN ever attempted. It had no coherent plan to manage such a large undertaking. As explained in Chapter 5, the conflict-adverse UN official who helped negotiate the power sharing plan—Yasushi Akashi—was lauded for his success in Cambodia and later was sent as the UN envoy to Bosnia, where he vetoed NATO airstrikes against the Bosnian Serbs even as Sarajeavans were blown to bits by Serb artillery and was accused of coddling the Serbs. Akashi was criticized during his tenure for suspicious deals UNTAC struck with Japanese automotive firms to purchase vehicles for UNTAC that American firms claimed they were not given an opportunity to bid on. As explained in Chapter 5, UNTAC survived Akashi's incompetence only because UNTAC Commander General John Sanderson effectively ran the military portion of the operation.

UNTAC suffered from significant chain of command problems. Fortunately, these snafus resulted in few casualties because of UNTAC's pacific mandate and the decision by warring parties to avoid armed confrontations with UN personnel. However, French and Dutch troops on numerous occasions exceeded their orders in using armed force against the Khmer Rouge. France also refused to deploy its troops where UNTAC directed.

Finally, as explained in Chapter 5, criminal activity by UNTAC troops, especially black marketeering and prostitution, hurt UNTAC and the UN's reputation. UNTAC troops frequenting prostitutes introduced AIDS to remote areas of Cambodia. Some UNTAC troops operated brothels and gambling halls.

In conclusion, UNTAC fared better than some expanded peacekeeping missions. It brought peace to Cambodia for a time, helped refugees and displaced persons return, and created more stable conditions that saved lives. The major mistake made by UNTAC planners was underestimating the task at hand. If UNTAC planners had a better conception of the political situation in Cambodia and a more realistic view of how to build democracy, this $1 billion–plus expanded peacekeeping effort might have left a fledgling democracy in its place instead of a corrupt autocracy that stays in power by terrorizing the population and its political opponents.

SOMALIA

The collapse of UN peacekeeping in Somalia was stark evidence of the danger of downplaying the requirement that peacekeepers obtain and maintain the consent of local parties. The UN's first Somalia mission, UNOSOM I, began in mid-1992 to relieve mass starvation in a country plagued by anarchy. Since there was no central government, obtaining consent of warring parties for the deployment of an international force was impossible. UNOSOM I sidestepped adverse consequences of its lack of local consent through a limited neutral mandate restricting the use of force and avoiding provocative actions. While this mandate kept UNOSOM I casualties low and enabled it to achieve some success in delivering humanitarian aid, it also neutered the operation, since Somali warlords refused to fully cooperate and prevented UNOSOM I troops from leaving the vicinity of the Mogadishu Airport. As a result, the UN deployed only 500 of the 3,500 troops approved for UNOSOM I by the Security Council.

In December 1992, when the failure of UNOSOM I was obvious and with the humanitarian situation worsening, the United States won Security Council approval for the Unified Task Force (UNITAF), a large, U.S.-led peace enforcement operation.[5] This mission was sent by the outgoing Bush administration with the support of President-elect Clinton. UNITAF's mandate was to establish a secure environment to allow the delivery of humanitarian aid. While UNITAF challenged and disarmed some clans thought to be a threat to security, it generally avoided provocative actions. For example, UNITAF did not attempt to disarm civilians on the street as long as they did not openly carry weapons. As a military intervention, UNITAF did not need local consent to carry out its mission. UNITAF was tolerated by Somali warlords, since it did not threaten the political balance in the country, was a heavily armed and well-organized force, and was deployed for a fixed amount of time.

In March 1993, UNITAF withdrew and was replaced by UNOSOM II, which tried to implement a more ambitious mandate despite having troops fewer in number and lower in quality. UNOSOM II tried to restore order to Somalia, disarm Somalis, and rebuild the country's economy and political institutions.[6] The force conducted raids against Somali clans and tried to arrest the leading Somali warlord, Mohammed Farrah Hassan Aideed. These extremely provocative actions deeply antagonized the local population. Former UN Under Secretary General for Political Affairs Brian Urquhart had this take on UNOSOM II's mandate:

Both the rhetoric and the action on this occasion were a radical departure from the cautious and carefully calibrated approach to peacekeeping crises in the past, when it had been considered both improper and unwise to risk intense popular hostility by attacking local leaders, however obnoxious. Traditional peacekeeping forces were not supposed to have enemies. There was no caution on this occasion, and Aideed was officially proclaimed the enemy.[7]

Because UNOSOM II planners had assumed that Somalis would defer to the UN flag and not fire on international troops, UNOSOM II was not nearly as formidable as UNITAF. UNOSOM II and supporting U.S. troops were configured as traditional peacekeepers: they were lightly armed and lacked the proper equipment for civil war situations, notably armored cars, armored personnel carriers, and tanks. This proved to be a fatal miscalculation. By June 1993, UN and American forces were at war with Somali parties and the mission suffered high casualties, including 25 Pakistanis

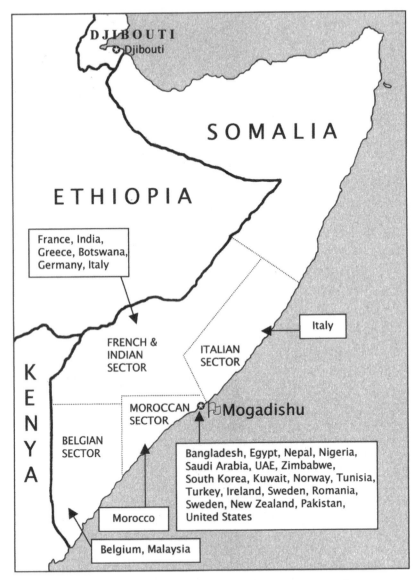

Map 8.1: UNOSOM II deployment, November 1993. (Julie Fleitz)

killed in an ambush on June 5, 1993. In response to the massacre of Pakistani peacekeepers, American and UN officials directed UN and American forces in Somalia to capture Somali warlord Aideed. This decision greatly increased tensions and was reversed in October 1993 after 18 American troops were killed in an ambush.

Two unforeseen consequences of UNOSOM II's aggressive mandate further exacerbated violence against UN and American forces. First, restoring order and rebuilding Somalia proved not to be in the interests of Somali warlords, many of whom were profiting from the anarchy in the country. Second, the UN had failed to anticipate that the delivery of humanitarian aid was not a neutral act in a nation at war with itself. UN aid deliveries often bolstered isolated and beleaguered combatants, strengthening them for another round of combat. Aid also was diverted and sold for weapons by Somali clans. Warring parties attacked UN aid convoys to enrich themselves or to keep aid out of the hands of their enemies.

On October 3, 1993, Somalis fired two rocket-propelled grenades at a UH-60 U.S. Army helicopter, forcing it to crash land. A separate attack downed another U.S. helicopter. These attacks were followed by an orgy of violence over the next 36 hours which left 18 U.S. soldiers and over 500 Somalis dead. This fiasco rocked the U.S. government and forced the Clinton administration to withdraw American troops by March 1994. The situation in Somalia continued to deteriorate after U.S. troops withdrew and caused the UN to terminate UNOSOM II and withdraw all peacekeepers by March 1995. Somalia returned to the chaotic state it was in mid-1992 and remains so today.

UNOSOM II was undermined by the same conceptual and mandate problems that affected UNTAC. The difference was that UNOSOM II had a mandate that required UN troops to go to war. While the refusal of Cambodian disputants to cooperate caused UNTAC's mandate to be unsuccessful only after it departed, in Somalia, resistance of local parties to UN forces led to violent confrontations and casualties.

Poor management exacerbated UNOSOM II's problems. The force had enormous difficulty controlling its troops because contingent commanders insisted on checking with their capitals before accepting orders from UN commanders. Often, they would not follow UN orders or would refuse to deploy to certain areas. Italian troops refused to follow UN orders and cut side deals with Somali clans at war with the UN to protect Italian troops. Waste and corruption by UNOSOM II became legendary, earning it U.S. Ambassador Daniel Simpson's nickname, "the world cash cow."[8]

UNOSOM II was an operation that attempted to carry out a nation building mandate that was considerably beyond its capabilities. The result was a catastrophe for the UN and for American foreign policy that influenced events far beyond Somalia. The disaster in Somalia—especially the

October 1993 ambush that killed 18 U.S. troops—still haunts peacekeeping planners and is often referred to as "the Mogadishu Syndrome."

HAITI

The six peacekeeping efforts deployed to Haiti since 1993 were a comedy of tragic errors because of a conceptual vacuum and an especially incoherent policy that included restoring a veritable madman to power and trying to build democracy and a free market economy in a Fourth World country. While Western statesmen tried to claim that this nation building effort was successful, in reality it was propped up by the United States and accomplished little. After spending billions of dollars on peacekeeping and an American-led peace enforcement mission, Haiti today is a violent society ruled by a despot earning millions of dollars from the drug trade.

The first Haitian peacekeeping mission, the UN Mission in Haiti (UN-MIH), was tasked with helping implement the Governor's Island Agreement of July 1993. This agreement called for democratic elections in Haiti, modernizing the country's armed forces, and creating a professional police force. The United States and the UN were dealt an embarrassing setback in October 1993 when armed thugs on the docks of Port-au-Prince turned back the first group of UNMIH troops onboard the *USS Harlan County*. As a result, UNMIH was put on hold. *Wall Street Journal* columnist George Melloan offered this analysis of the October 1993 UNMIH debacle:

In last week's episode vis-à-vis Haiti, the intention seemed to be to insert troops bearing only sidearms into a dangerous situation to act as "advisers." It was no doubt fortunate that the Haitians on the shore made such a ruckus that this foolish mission was aborted before the Americans and Canadians suffered casualties.[9]

UNMIH was completely inappropriate for the Haitian situation in October 1993. Its ostensible mandate at that time was "to assist the modernizing of the armed forces and establishing a new police force."[10] However, the Haitian government led by President Raoul Cédras believed that the actual purpose of the mission was to restore to power Jean-Bertrand Aristide, the democratically elected president of Haiti whom Cédras had deposed in a military coup d'état in September 1991. It therefore was not about to cooperate with UNMIH and knew it could easily prevent lightly armed peacekeeping troops from deploying. Haiti's thug leaders had no intention of deferring to UNMIH troops simply because they wore blue helmets.

Reeling from twin peacekeeping fiascoes in late 1993 in Haiti and Somalia, the United States regrouped in 1994 and planned a military invasion of Haiti. American diplomats attempted to justify this action by arguing that the Haitian situation was a significant American foreign policy concern

Photo 8.1: Violence in Haiti keeps out UN peacekeepers, October 11, 1993. These demonstrators at the docks of Port-au-Prince, shown here attacking a car that carried the U.S. chargé d'affaires, prevented UNMIH peacekeeping contingents from the United States and Canada on board the *USS Harlan County* from deploying. (AFP)

and a threat to international security. As part of this justification, U.S. Ambassador to the UN Madeleine Albright convinced the Security Council to pass a resolution on July 31, 1994 defining the Haiti situation as a threat to international peace and security and authorizing the use of all necessary means to restore democracy. Even the pro-Clinton *New York Times* rejected this argument and criticized the Security Council's imprimatur for the Haiti operation as "circular logic" and "a strained interpretation of the UN Charter."[11] The council's blessing was undermined further by rumors that Russia agreed to vote with the United States on the Haiti operation only in exchange for a free hand in the former Soviet Republic of Georgia.[12]

UNMIH successfully deployed after the United States led a UN-sanctioned intervention into Haiti, Operation Restore Democracy, in September 1994 and restored Aristide to power. This was a controversial move, especially in the United States, because of concerns that Aristide was not truly committed to democracy and reportedly was mentally unbalanced.[13] The U.S.-led force did not actually invade Haiti or fight its way in; the Cédras government resigned hours before the invasion was to begin, after its members were assured of amnesty. UNMIH and Operation Restore

Democracy conducted presidential elections in December 1995. Aristide agreed not to run in the elections and turned over power to the election victor, René Préval, Aristide's prime minister and candidate of the Aristide-controlled Lavalas Party.

UNMIH was charged with promoting security and stability in Haiti, assisting the development of democratic institutions, training national police, and holding national elections. Unfortunately, American and UN efforts brought neither democracy nor stability to Haiti. UN and Western leaders overlooked reports of corruption by Aristide and clear indications that he continued to run the country from behind the scenes after he stepped down in early 1996. Aristide and Lavalas obstructed the creation of democratic government and the establishment of a free market economy. Mary Anastasia O'Grady, a *Wall Street Journal* columnist, summed up the sorry state of the Haitian situation in January 2001 when she wrote that "economic deterioration, drug trafficking, and political assassinations have defined Aristide's Haiti."[14] The *San Diego Union-Tribune* stated in a February 12, 2001 editorial that cocaine shipped to the United States from Colombia had become Haiti's major industry.

With its mandate in shambles and violence increasing, American and UN forces quietly withdrew from Haiti in March 2000. A small token UN mission, the International Civilian Support Mission (MICAH), remained to monitor the Haitian situation and serve as a forward-deployed staff that could form the nucleus of a future UN mission to rebuild Haiti when and if conditions improved. Aristide was reelected president in November 2000 in elections marked by violence and massive corruption. Because of an increase of violence that coincided with the election and Aristide's return to power, the UN withdrew MICAH on February 6, 2001.

Like UNTAC and UNOSOM II, the UN Haiti missions were ill-equipped to address civil conflict and anarchy. The United States and the UN tried to build Western-style democratic and economic institutions in a Fourth World country that was not ready for such innovations. Local parties had no inclination to cooperate with the UN and neither the UN nor the United States were prepared to do anything to compel them to do so.

The American and UN Haiti missions were especially ineffective compared to UNOSOM II or UNTAC because they were from the start the product of a Clinton administration effort to achieve a political end. Deposed Haitian President Aristide was restored to power due to his support among certain elite liberal internationalist circles in the United States and not due to his fitness for office or his support for democracy and a free market economy. Mary Anastasia O'Grady wrote in July 2001 that only Aristide and his liberal American allies appear to have benefited from the billions spent on international operations sent to Haiti since 1994.

The U.S. has already spent $3 billion on Mr. Aristide, first to reinstall him as president and later to "reform" his police department. Yet Haiti's institution building is no further along than it was in the days of post-coup President Raoul Cédras. And it's not uncommon to hear Haitians to pine for the good old days of the Duvalier dictatorship. Six years of placating Mr. Aristide have advanced few but him, and possibly his telephone company associates Joseph P. Kennedy II, former Democratic Party finance man Marvin Rosen, and Clinton pal Thomas "Mack" McLarty.[15]

The *Wall Street Journal* ran an editorial in May 2001 with a much harsher condemnation of U.S. officials who allegedly entered into shady business deals with Aristide.

For people connected with the Clinton-Presidency-cum-political machine to attach themselves like pilot fish to the bleeding ruin of Haiti under Jean-Bertrand Aristide, in the wake of an enormous commitment of American prestige and money on behalf of Haiti's people, doesn't pass any conceivable smell test.[16]

Politicization of the international operations to save Haiti skewed further an already incoherent and irrational policy. Not surprisingly, when Aristide refused to promote democracy as his American backers said he would, the Clinton administration looked the other way. In short, while sending peacekeepers to Haiti probably was destined to be a debacle, political manipulation by the United States ensured this outcome and magnified its size.

FORMER YUGOSLAVIA: UNPROFOR AND RELATED MISSIONS

Like other expanded peacekeeping missions, former Yugoslavia operations in Croatia and Bosnia were seriously undermined by conceptual, mandate, and administrative problems, and may have done the most cumulative damage to the reputations of the UN and peacekeeping. This effort consisted of seven peacekeeping missions deployed between 1992 and 2000 to Croatia, Bosnia-Herzegovina, and Macedonia. Since 1999, the UN also has been conducting an expanded peacekeeping mission in Kosovo. This mission differs significantly from other UN operations in the Balkans and is addressed separately at the end of this chapter.

The Security Council first deployed UN peacekeepers to the Balkan region in February 1992 to help implement the Vance Plan to end fighting in Croatia between Croatian and Serbian forces.[17] This mission was called the UN Protection Force (UNPROFOR). In mid-1992, UNPROFOR's mandate was expanded to address fighting in Bosnia between Bosnian Serbs (supported by Serbia), Bosnian Croats (supported by Croatia), and Bosnian Muslims. In December 1992, UNPROFOR troops were deployed along the

Macedonia-Serbia border (on the Macedonian side) as a "preventive" operation to discourage incidents that could threaten peace in the region or the fragile Macedonian government. In March 1995, the UN restructured its Balkans peacekeeping effort by making missions outside of Bosnia separate operations and limiting UNPROFOR's mandate to Bosnia.[18]

Croatia

UNPROFOR initially was sent to several zones in Croatia designated "UN Protected Areas" (UNPAs), large swaths of territory where most of the fighting between Serbia and Croatia took place. The UNPAs had Serb majorities or large Serb minorities, and were known as the Krajina Serbs. UNPROFOR's Croatia mandate was to verify the withdrawal of the Yugoslav Army, demilitarize the UNPAs, facilitate the return of displaced persons, and protect persons living in the UNPAs until a diplomatic solution could be reached on their final political status.

The UN force sent to Croatia in February 1992 was based on the risky—some would say dubious—proposition that a traditional peacekeeping force could succeed without the consent of disputants in a conflict with ethnic, civil, and international dimensions. UNPROFOR was asked to promote order not by using or threatening the use of military force, but through agreements with disputants. Secretary General Boutros Boutros-Ghali acknowledged this operation's bleak prospects at the outset, making it clear that it would fail unless there was "a working cease-fire . . . clear and unconditional acceptance of the [peace] plan by all concerned, with equally clear assurances of their readiness to cooperate in its implementation."[19] The secretary general advocated the deployment of UNPROFOR despite his skepticism that these requirements would ever be met to take advantage of a lull in the fighting between Serbian and Croatian forces and to forestall further fighting between the two nations. Only on this last point can it be said that UN forces in Croatia succeeded.

UNPROFOR, configured as a traditional peacekeeping operation, was ill-suited to perform its Croatian mandate. From the beginning it was clear that neither the Croatians nor the Krajina Serbs planned to cooperate with the UN force. The UNPAs were not demilitarized, there was never a stable cease-fire, few displaced persons were able to return, and lawlessness prevailed. Moreover, the UNPAs destabilized the region by serving as launching pads for armed incursions into Bosnia. The Krajina Serbs saw UNPROFOR, and its successor, UNCRO (UN Confidence Restoration Operation in Croatia), as helping them set up their own independent state. Croatia, on the other hand, regarded the UN presence as an opportunity to build up arms to take the UNPAs by force.

In 1995, Croatia seized three of the four UNPAs. In May 1995, it overran UNPA Sector West in what Croatia claimed was a limited police action responding to a Serb provocation. In August 1995, Croatia seized Sectors North and South in an aggressive campaign during which Croatia took UNCRO peacekeepers hostage and overran UN observer posts. Croatia escaped international opprobrium for this campaign because the world was preoccupied by the dire situation in Bosnia and the Krajina Serbs were diplomatically isolated.

UNCRO was beefed up after the August 1995 Croatian offensive to prevent the Croatians from seizing the last remaining UNPA, Sector East, which would have been highly destabilizing to the region, since this UNPA bordered Serbia. In 1996, UNCRO was renamed the UN Transitional Administration for Eastern Slavonia, Baranja, and Western Sirium (UNTAES) and given an even stronger mandate. Composed of up to 5,000 high-quality troops from Russia, Pakistan, Poland, Belgium, and other countries under a U.S. commander, UNTAES came to resemble a peace enforcement mission and successfully kept the peace. UNTAES was replaced in 1998 by an Organization for Security and Cooperation in Europe (OSCE) operation that remains in place today. OSCE maintains that its Croatia mission is diplomatic in nature and is not a peacekeeping effort.[20]

In hindsight, it is clear that the situation in Croatia required a well-armed peace enforcement operation capable of occupying territory and engaging in combat, if necessary. Peacekeeping clearly had no role to play. The failure of UNPROFOR in Croatia resulted in substantial losses of Croat and Serb lives and tens of thousands of displaced persons.

Bosnia-Herzegovina

The consequences of the UN's failure in Bosnia were far more grave for the local population and the UN. Once again, UN troops were sent to a region beset by civil and ethnic warfare. Armed as traditional peacekeepers, these troops were unable to keep order in Bosnia and were manipulated by disputants. The Bosnian Serbs illustrated the utter folly of the expanded peacekeeping concept when they took 370 UN peacekeepers hostage to use as "human shields." Worst of all, UNPROFOR troops were unable to stop the Bosnian Serbs from committing ethnic cleansing and genocide.

UNPROFOR's initial responsibility in Bosnia was to protect the Sarajevo airport after warfare broke out between the three ethnic communities, the Bosnian Muslims, the Bosnian Serbs, and the Bosnian Croats. This was a near-impossible task because of the lack of cooperation of the Bosnian Serbs, who had surrounded Sarajevo with snipers and heavy weapons. Over time, the Security Council added additional duties to the UNPROFOR mission in Bosnia, including escorting humanitarian aid convoys and guaranteeing the safety of so-called UN "safe areas."[21] By 1995, UNPROFOR's Bosnian mandate had been expanded substantially beyond the capabilities of a peacekeeping force.[22]

At the root of the failure of UN peacekeeping in Bosnia was an unworkable and contradictory mandate. UNPROFOR troops in Bosnia were given a so-called "Chapter VII" mandate but were equipped as traditional peacekeepers. They were authorized by the Security Council to use force to perform parts of their humanitarian missions but relied on the permission of warring parties to move about the country. UN officials feared using offensive military force against the main protagonist—the Bosnian Serbs—for fear that they would retaliate. UNPROFOR Commander General Lewis MacKenzie described this problem in February 1993:

The fact is that the moment Western war planes are in the air shooting down local aircraft, or the moment some military installation is bombed, all UN forces on the ground would be associated—rightly or wrongly—with those committing the attacks and thus would be subject to attacks themselves. The UN troops would not be able to fight back because they are only lightly equipped and staffed to protect the delivery of food and humanitarian supplies, and to protect themselves.[23]

UNPROFOR was authorized to call in NATO airstrikes to compel warring parties to comply with Security Council resolutions. However, both UN and Western officials were reluctant to use air power. For this reason, a "dual key" system was devised that required NATO and the UN official in Bosnia to approve airstrikes. The man who held this position from 1993 to 1995 was senior Japanese UN Secretariat official Yasushi Akashi. Akashi had no stomach for using military force and approved little more than "pinprick" air strikes against the Bosnian Serbs. Stanley Meisler has characterized Akashi's veto of Bosnian airstrikes as a convenient cover by Western states for not acting militarily.[24] Many observers believed at the time that Clinton administration officials opposed airstrikes in 1993 and 1994 and deliberately agreed to a command arrangement with the UN knowing full well that the UN would be extremely hesitant to approve the use of military force in Bosnia.[25]

Like UNOSOM II in Somalia, UNPROFOR's humanitarian mandate became a dimension of the Bosnia conflict. UN aid convoys changed the power dynamics of the Bosnian conflict by sustaining parties under siege, usually the Bosnian Muslims. All parties enriched themselves by selling Western humanitarian supplies to buy weapons.

However, Bosnia differed from Somalia in an important way—sophisticated efforts by disputants to manipulate the UN to gain military or public relations advantages. The Bosnian Serbs, learning from prior peacekeeping missions in Somalia and Haiti that the UN and the West were extremely reluctant to use military force to back up peacekeepers, obstructed or ignored UNPROFOR at every turn. The Serbs employed a system of roadblocks designed to limit the effectiveness of UNPROFOR and slow down the delivery of humanitarian aid. The Serbs also shrewdly used cease-fire negotiations with the UN as cover to carry out military offensives. Although the Serbs signed numerous agreements to stop shelling Sarajevo, an average of 1,000 Serb shells landed in Sarajevo per day from April 1992 until August 1995, when NATO launched massive air strikes (Operation Deliberate Force) that ended the war in Bosnia and the shelling of Sarajevo.

The Bosnian Muslims were just as astute in their manipulation of UN-PROFOR and were far from innocent victims who did everything they could to cooperate with the international community to improve their situation and save lives. Throughout the conflict, Bosnian Muslim officials were highly uncooperative with UNPROFOR and engaged in numerous actions that increased instability and encouraged the Serbs to commit more vicious atrocities. For example, part of the arrangement the UN struck with the Bosnian Serbs on the creation of the Srebrenica safe area in 1993 was that Srebrenica would be demilitarized and the inhabitants would hand over their weapons to UNPROFOR. The Bosnian Muslims defied this order and turned over only non-serviceable weapons.[26] Former UNPROFOR Commander Sir Michael Rose said that he had "the utmost contempt for them [Bosnian Muslim leaders] because they were knowingly subjecting their populations to further war in order to protect their own interests. Most of them seem to be driven by a need to line their own pockets as much as anyone else."[27] In a 1994 report, Secretary General Boutros-Ghali criticized the Bosnian Muslims for using safe areas as "locations in which its troops can rest, train, and equip themselves as well as fire at Serb positions, thereby provoking Serb retaliation."[28] Bosnian Muslim leaders resisted and eventually halted UN efforts to evacuate Srebrenica because they did not want to cede political and military advantages to the Bosnian Serbs. As a result, thousands of Muslims were massacred when the Serbs overran the Srebrenica safe area in mid-1995. There are a variety of other reports suggesting that the Muslims did all they could to draw the UN and the West into the Bosnian conflict.[29]

The Fall of Srebrenica and the End of UNPROFOR

Nationwide warfare and escalating violence resumed in Bosnia in April 1995 after a tenuous four-month cease-fire broke down. A Croatian attack on the Krajina forced Croatian Serbs to flee to Bosnia. Bosnian Muslims and Croats in turn were evicted from their homes by Bosnian Serbs to accommodate the fleeing Croatian Serbs. The Bosnian Serbs also restricted access to UN safe areas and increased their harassment of UN humanitarian convoys across the country. In May 1995, the Bosnian Serbs stepped up their shelling of Sarajevo and removed heavy weapons from a UN collection area. The UN responded by warning the Serbs that if these weapons were not returned, they would be attacked from the air. The Serbs ignored two deadlines, and NATO bombed a half dozen Serb ammunition bunkers. The Bosnian Serbs responded to the May 1995 NATO airstrikes with a

Photo 8.2: UNPROFOR peacekeeper chained to a pole by Bosnian Serbs as a "human shield" to protect a Serb ammunition depot, 1995. (AP/Wide World Photos)

vengeance. They attacked vulnerable civilians across the country and fired an air burst weapon at a crowded downtown area in the city of Tuzla, killing 71 and injuring almost 200 others. The Serbs also took 370 UN peacekeepers hostage, some of whom were handcuffed as "human shields" to Serb military equipment to deter further NATO airstrikes. The UN negotiated a deal with the Serbs for the release of the hostages that reportedly included a promise that NATO air power would not be used again against the Bosnian Serbs. It is not clear that the UN actually made this promise or, if it was made by a UN negotiator, whether such a promise was approved by UN headquarters. (According to a UN report on the fall of Srebrenica, Russian President Yeltsin and French President Chirac believed that this promise had been made.)[30] Unfortunately, the resolution of the hostage crisis emboldened the Bosnian Serbs and spelled the end of UNPROFOR.

In June 1995, the Bosnian Serbs overran Zepa and Srebrenica, two Muslim enclaves inside Bosnia Serb territory which had been declared "safe areas" by the Security Council and supposedly were under the protection of the UN. The Serbs ignored understrength UNPROFOR garrisons and killed thousands of Muslim inhabitants in the Srebrenica enclave.

The Srebrenica fiasco, coming on the heels of the peacekeeper hostage fiasco, forced world leaders to finally acknowledge that the situation in Bosnia-Herzegovina was beyond the capability of peacekeeping. UNPRO-FOR was withdrawn and NATO conducted a massive six-week air campaign, Operation Deliberate Force. Coupled with gains on the ground by a rebuilt Croatian Army—which routed two Krajina Serb UNPAs in August 1995—the Bosnian Serbs were forced to agree to a stiff peace treaty, the Dayton Accords, on November 21, 1995. This agreement ended the Bosnian Serbs' political independence and their ability to threaten Sarajevo. Dayton created one Bosnian state with two entities—the Muslim-Croat Bosnian Federation and the Bosnian Serb Republic. Both sides agreed to withdraw heavy weapons to cantonment areas and demobilize forces. The Dayton Accords also created a war crimes tribunal to prosecute parties responsible for war atrocities.

The most intrusive aspect of the Dayton Accords was the deployment of the International Force in Bosnia (IFOR), a large (50,000 troops) NATO-led peace enforcement mission. U.S. troops initially made up the majority of IFOR, which was renamed the Stabilization Force (SFOR) in 1996. The IFOR and SFOR missions are officially "NATO-led" rather than "NATO operations" because they included troops from Russia and several other non-NATO European countries. NATO commanded both operations, although Russian troops have a separate command structure answering to a Russian general, who answers to the IFOR/SFOR NATO commander and to Moscow.

The IFOR/SFOR effort was responsible for overseeing the 1995 cease-fire and separating forces of the Croat-Muslim Federation and the Bosnian Serb Republic. As explained earlier, the IFOR/SFOR is a virtual NATO occupation force with wide-ranging powers. Typical for peace enforcement missions, these powers have been used almost exclusively against one party—in this case, the Bosnia Serbs. For example, on several occasions, IFOR/SFOR has barred elected radical Serb leaders from taking office. The Bosnian Serbs have offered little resistance to IFOR and SFOR. The few violent incidents that did occur petered out by 1998.

Macedonia

The UN effort to prevent war from spilling into the Former Yugoslav Republic of Macedonia was one small bright spot to emerge from the UN effort in the Balkans. UNPROFOR was tasked with patrolling Macedonia's border with Serbia in 1993 to prevent Serbian infiltrations of Macedonia that could cause hostilities to break out between the two countries or unrest that could threaten the Macedonian government. This unique mission was called preventive deployment, a peacekeeping operation sent to an area of instability to discourage parties from instigating hostilities. In many ways, this operation resembled the UNFICYP preventive deployment around the

Nicosia airport in Cyprus in 1974 described in Chapter 4. U.S. troops were part of the Macedonia mission, making a Serb action against Macedonia tantamount to a Serb attack on the United States. In 1995, the Macedonia mission was renamed the UN Preventive Deployment Force (UNPREDEP). UNPREDEP was disbanded after China vetoed its renewal on February 25, 1999 to protest Macedonia's decision to exchange ambassadors with Taiwan.[31] It was replaced by a similar operation conducted by NATO.

In February 2001, Macedonia was brought to the brink of civil war after Albanian Kosovars infiltrated the country to promote "minority rights" for ethnic Albanians in Macedonia. Macedonia's Slavic government has resisted negotiating with the ethnic Albanian rebels because it believes the violence is a actually prelude to an effort by Albanian-dominated areas of Macedonia to secede and form an independent state with Kosovo. The violence decreased by mid-2001 after NATO negotiated a cease-fire agreement, which included the deployment of a NATO force of about 3,000 troops. The situation in Macedonia is likely to remain volatile for some time.

Assessment of UNPROFOR and Related Missions

The UN peacekeeping missions in Croatia and Bosnia were abysmal failures and provided expensive lessons of the limits of peacekeeping in areas rent by civil war and ethnic conflict. UNPROFOR and UNCRO were operations equipped to deal only with parties who wanted peace. Unfortunately, the parties in Croatia and Bosnia wanted war. Complicating the UN's effort in these countries was the fact that warring parties not only did not respect the UN but actively plotted to undermine and manipulate UN forces. Simply put, disputants brazenly took advantage of peacekeepers' trust and good will. The *Wall Street Journal* gave a good synopsis of the UNPROFOR fiasco in a May 1995 editorial.

The saga of the United Nations' peacekeeping mission in Bosnia is surely one that will go down in history as an example not to be followed. You do not attempt to appease an aggressor by giving him humanitarian aid, replenishing his fuel supplies and turning a blind eye when he raids weapons depots. Do not attempt to avoid offending the aggressor by letting him attack the people most in need of protection. Do not prevent these people from fighting back. Do not put non-combat-ready peacekeeping forces in places where they cannot defend themselves. Do not be surprised when the troops you have made hostage to your non-policy become real hostages.[32]

Combat forces, of course, cannot be so easily taken advantage of. Expanded peacekeeping operations in Croatia and Bosnia had combat mandates but peacekeeping equipment and mindsets. While the Bosnian Serbs knew that defying UNPROFOR would at most cause the UN Security Council to pass meaningless cease-and-desist resolutions, defying IFOR or

SFOR would have grave consequences, such as the destruction of infrastructure and replacement of Bosnian Serb elected leaders.

UN peacekeeping in Bosnia may have done more damage than other peace enforcement operations to the reputations of the UN and peacekeeping because of the substantial time and money invested as well as the scale of the atrocities committed during UNPROFOR's watch. Like UNOSOM II, UNPROFOR's collapse provided lessons on how to manipulate and exploit UN peacekeeping. Although the UN's failure in Bosnia largely reflected limitations on the UN imposed by weak Western leaders, UN peacekeeping missions in the Balkans provided compelling evidence as to why expanded peacekeeping cannot work in civil war situations and why peacekeepers must have the full consent and cooperation of disputants.

ANGOLA

Angola was a major peacekeeping fiasco and a lost opportunity. Peace and reconciliation might have been possible if a realistic and well-designed force had been deployed and if the UN and the United States had agreed to be honest brokers. Instead, a flawed force was deployed whose mandate was seriously eroded by the United States to pursue a political agenda.

Angola has been torn by civil war since it gained independence from Portugal in 1975. Two parties have dominated the battle for control of the country since independence: the MPLA (Movimento Popular de Libertação de Angola) and UNITA (Unitão Nacional para a Indêpendencia Total de Angola). The MPLA is a Marxist party installed with Soviet bloc support. Its leadership is largely composed of educated Angolans from coastal tribes who worked closely with the Portuguese colonial government. UNITA, which had in the past briefly dallied with Maoism and communist China, is largely composed of less-educated Bantu tribesmen from the Angolan interior.

The UNITA/MPLA conflict became a Cold War battleground for Washington and Moscow as well for American conservatives and liberals. Moscow supported the MPLA and sent it large amounts of weapons and Cuban troops. The United States and South Africa backed UNITA. American liberals, however, fell in love with the MPLA, both because they were more cosmopolitan and well spoken than UNITA and due to liberal disagreement with the campaign by American conservatives against international communism. Black African states and many in the United States and Europe also rejected UNITA because it was allied with South Africa's racist white minority government. American conservatives accused U.S. liberals of ignoring repression and human rights violations by the MPLA. U.S. liberals made the same accusation against UNITA. In truth, there is ample evidence that both parties have atrocious human rights records.

The first Angolan peacekeeping mission, the First UN Angola Verification Mission (UNAVEM I), was a traditional peacekeeping effort deployed from

1989 to 1991 to oversee the withdrawal of Cuban troops from the country. UNAVEM I was successful and achieved its mandate one month ahead of schedule.[33]

UNAVEM II was deployed to Angola from May 1991 until December 1994 to oversee a peace plan agreed to by the MPLA and UNITA that called for a cease-fire, the demobilization of troops, combining MPLA and UNITA forces into a joint army, monitoring of the Angolan police, and national elections.[34]

The mandate of UNAVEM II was similar to UNTAC in Cambodia. Like UNTAC, UNAVEM II was deployed in response to a comprehensive peace agreement, signed by MPLA and UNITA in Estoril, Portugal, on May 1, 1991. Also similar to the UN Cambodia mission, UNAVEM II was charged with monitoring troop assembly areas and oversight of the Angolan government before and during national elections. UNAVEM II differed from UNTAC in that it was considerably smaller (only 655 troops versus 22,000 for UNTAC) and was a lightly armed observer mission.

Like UNTAC, UNAVEM II had a civilian contingent to organize national elections and oversee the national government. However, UNAVEM II did not perform either mission as well as UNTAC. Election monitors were few in number and often incompetent. Moreover, given UN hostility toward UNITA, many UN personnel reportedly were far from objective and refused to investigate UNITA claims of massive electoral abuses by the MPLA.

The MPLA won the legislative elections, 53.74 percent to 34.1 percent for UNITA. In the presidential vote, incumbent MPLA President José Eduardo dos Santos defeated UNITA leader Jonas Savimbi 49.57 percent to 40.07 percent. However, Savimbi and UNITA rejected the election results, claiming massive electoral abuses by the MPLA. Eight smaller Angolan political parties made the same claim and also rejected the election outcome. In an October 17, 1992 statement, the secretary general's special representative to Angola admitted that there had been irregularities in the voting but claimed they had not been of a magnitude to have had a significant effect on the official results and characterized the elections as "free and generally fair."[35] Savimbi and his backers in the United States rejected this statement as a whitewash. The Western media sided against UNITA's claims of MPLA electoral fraud because of its preexisting bias against Savimbi and superior MPLA public relations, according to Margaret Hemenway, an American who observed the Angolan elections in 1993.[36] Perhaps UNITA's strongest argument was their protest of the MPLA's absolute refusal to allow UN oversight of the Angolan government before and during the elections, a major violation of the Angola peace accord.

UNITA's rejection of the election results caused a 16-month cease-fire to break down in late October 1992. The MPLA responded by launching a "seek and destroy" operation in Luanda, the Angolan capital, that killed an estimated 20,000 UNITA supporters and some high-level UNITA officials. In 1994, UNITA and the MPLA signed the Lusaka Protocol ("Acordos de Paz") that led to a shaky peace until 1998. Principal elements of this agreement included:

- UNITA forces would withdraw from territory taken since hostilities broke out.
- UNITA troops would move to quartering areas and demobilize. MPLA troops would move to barracks.
- A cease-fire would be monitored by UN peacekeepers.
- The UN would monitor the state administration throughout the country.
- The UN would lend its good offices to mediate disputes and assist national reconciliation.
- The UN would monitor the neutrality of the Angolan police.

To support the Lusaka Protocol, 7,000 combat troops were added to the UN's Angola operation and it was renamed UNAVEM III.[37]

UNAVEM III and the Lusaka Protocol brought about a decrease in fighting but little stability to Angola. The cease-fire was frequently violated by both sides. UNITA and the MPLA used this time to rearm; UNITA using its diamond revenues, the MPLA using its income from oil. There was some progress in the Angolan peace process in 1997 when Savimbi sent 63 UNITA deputies to take their seats in the National Assembly in Luanda. However, both parties were still far apart in meeting elements of the Lusaka Protocol concerning the demobilization of armed forces and the formation of a joint military. Nevertheless, the West, which was unwilling to support the large UNAVEM III force indefinitely, seized on reports of progress to scale back the UN presence in Angola to a 220-man observer force, renamed the UN Observer Mission in Angola (MONUA).[38]

On June 12, 1998, the UN Security Council passed Resolution 1173 imposing Chapter VII sanctions against UNITA for resisting the full implementation of the Lusaka Protocol. The resolution froze UNITA assets and barred foreign officials from meeting with UNITA representatives in areas of Angola not under the control of the Luanda government. Less than a week later, the MPLA, realizing that UNITA had become diplomatically isolated, broke the cease-fire and launched massive attacks on UNITA strongholds. The government claimed it took this action because UNITA was not honoring the Lusaka Protocol. The resumption of the civil war initially was a disaster for the MPLA, since UNITA was well-prepared for war and seized two-thirds of the country by January 1999. However, government forces gained the initiative later in the year. In 2000, UNITA suffered numerous major defeats and was rumored to be on the brink of defeat. Fueled by growing oil revenues, mercenaries, and political support from the Clinton administration, the MPLA gained a decisive advantage over UNITA by 2001. By 2002, UNITA controlled isolated pockets of Angola and was being aggressively attacked by MPLA forces. On February

23, 2002, MPLA troops killed UNITA Leader Jonas Savimbi during a raid, shooting him 15 times, including twice to the head, according to press accounts.

The Clinton Effect

The outbreak of violence in 1998 reflected new dynamics of the Angolan civil war due to the election of William Clinton as president in November 1992. Mr. Clinton withdrew U.S. support for UNITA in 1993 and backed UN sanctions against it. The Clinton administration also established diplomatic relations with the MPLA and turned a blind eye toward MPLA efforts to exterminate UNITA, including massive arms purchases and the hiring of mercenaries.[39] In 1997, U.S. Secretary of State Madeleine Albright visited Angola but refused to meet with Savimbi unless he met her in Luanda, a trip that would have been suicide for Savimbi, given the political situation at the time. By 1999, because of the policies of the Clinton administration, the MPLA army, which rarely had been able to defeat UNITA in battle, had become a formidable military force. In November 1999, the Angolan government asked the UN to withdraw MONUA, claiming that its presence was "no longer needed."[40] In reality, Luanda almost certainly desired MONUA withdrawn because it was impeding successful operations by the MPLA army and its mercenaries against UNITA. By 2000, the MPLA military was a regional menace and had intervened in conflicts in both Congos and Namibia.

UN peacekeeping in Angola failed because of unworkable mandates and incoherent policies by the West. There may have been a chance for peace if both parties had a true desire to abide by the peace plans and if UNAVEM II had been better designed and capable of sending sufficient numbers of qualified troops and observers and if such a force had remained until the peace plan took hold. Of course, none of these things happened. Like other expanded peacekeeping operations, the UN mistakenly assumed warring parties in a civil war would defer to UN troops and not attack them. UN troops did not have the equipment nor the mandate to compel UNITA or MPLA troops to abide by the peace accord. UNAVEM III, deployed after the Angolan situation had broken down, simply maintained the status quo until one party—the MPLA—was ready to return to war. The UN Security Council facilitated the MPLA's aggression by passing large numbers of resolutions that singled out UNITA for obstructing the peace process but ignored similar actions by the MPLA.

A serious failing of the UN effort in Angola was lack of planning for the possibility that political and ethnic differences would prevent either party from accepting a loss in the national elections. The first Bush administration recognized this problem in late 1992 and discussed a possible dos Santos-Savimbi power sharing arrangement with UN officials. However, the Clinton administration abandoned this idea in 1993, a decision that was in stark contrast with its position in Cambodia where it promoted a power-sharing agreement in similar circumstances for Hun Sen after he was defeated in the 1993 Cambodian elections.

The UN's troubled effort in Angola was undermined further by waste and corruption. Tens of millions of dollars were wasted due to procurement fraud involving corrupt UN officials and suppliers, according to an April 28, 1995 report by the UN under secretary for internal oversight services.[41] The fraud robbed the UN of funds that might have been used for peacekeeping and humanitarian efforts and resulted in purchases of substandard tents and vehicles.

One significant achievement the UN accomplished in Angola was providing humanitarian assistance. In 1993, an estimated 1,000 people a day died from the direct or indirect effects of the war. Malnutrition and starvation were rampant in many areas. The UN began intensive humanitarian efforts across Angola in 1993. By 1995, some 3.5 million Angolans living in accessible areas were receiving humanitarian aid.[42] Unfortunately, the UN had little success in removing Angola's millions of landmines, which still pose a serious threat to Angolan children. The UN Development Program (UNDP) took over humanitarian assistance from UNAVEM III in 1997. The UN's aid program expanded until 1998, when civil war returned to the country. When the MPLA government asked the UN to withdraw MONUA in 1999, it allowed UNDP to remain. UNDP continues its humanitarian effort in Angola today in areas where it can gain access, although it is likely that the MPLA is preventing UNDP from entering UNITA-held areas.

Prospects for Angola as of early 2002 were bleak. Although the MPLA called for a cease-fire and peace negotiations after Savimbi's death, there were no indications that it intended to change its ways and embrace democracy. The Clinton administration's Angola policy and a series of ill-considered peacekeeping efforts made the Angolan situation worse and extended the civil war. The Angolan government installed by UN-monitored elections is a Marxist kleptocracy using oil revenues to purchase weapons and to support a life of privilege for the MPLA elite while ordinary Angolans live in squalor. Angola and southern Africa are significantly more unstable now because of foreign adventurism by the strengthened MPLA army and its mercenaries. Like other failed 1990s expanded peacekeeping operations, it is unfair to call Angola principally a UN failure. It was the West—especially the Clinton administration—that promoted policies that aggravated the Angola morass.

RWANDA

The 1994 Rwanda peacekeeping fiasco was the tragic result of naive attempts to use negotiations and expanded peacekeeping to resolve a civil war and build a democratic nation in a country bitterly divided between two Rwandan ethnic groups. According to two independent investigations, the Rwanda tragedy was exacerbated by feckless policies by the West that prevented the UN from taking steps that might have substantially reduced the number of genocidal killings.[43] Former Secretary General Boutros-Ghali made similar accusations in his memoirs.[44] The repercussions of the Rwanda fiasco are enormous and include large numbers of displaced persons spread across southern Africa and the civil war in Zaire (now known as the Democratic Republic of the Congo).

Rwanda is a small country in south central Africa slightly smaller than the U.S. state of Maryland. With a population of 7.2 million, Rwanda is one of the most densely populated countries on earth. The Rwandan population consists of two groups, the Hutu majority (about 85 percent) and the Tutsi minority (about 15 percent.) Until 1961, the Tutsis dominated the upper classes of Rwandan society and worked closely with the European colonial governments (the Germans until World War I and then the Belgians) that ruled Rwanda since the 1800s. During colonial rule, the Hutus became an oppressed majority in a system that resembled apartheid. Rwandans were issued ethnic identity cards and the best of the country was reserved for the Tutsi minority and European colonialists. When decolonization came to Rwanda in 1961, it was as a Hutu-led revolt for "majority rule." The apartheid-like system remained, except that the Hutus took power and suppressed the Tutsis. Hundreds of thousands of Tutsis fled to neighboring states to escape Hutu violence against them in the 1960s and early 1970s.

Better times came to Rwanda in 1973, when Juvenal Habyarimana, head of the Rwandan army, became president. Tutsis were still discriminated against but violence against them abated. Ethnic peace lasted until the late 1980s, when economic problems coupled with an invasion of Rwanda from Uganda by a Tutsi exile group, the Rwandan Patriotic Front (RPF), rekindled tensions. The Habyarimana government used the RPF invasion to make the Tutsis scapegoats for the country's economic problems. This precipitated at least six mass murders of Tutsis between 1990 and 1993.[45] Violence against Tutsis and fighting between the RPF and Hutu groups continued until a peace agreement was signed in Arusha, Tanzania, in 1993.

The Arusha Peace Agreement

Negotiations to resolve the Rwandan situation began after the RPF invasion in 1990. The final agreement, signed in August 1993, was an extremely ambitious plan that called for Tutsi-Hutu power sharing, an integrated Hutu-Tutsi army, democratic elections, and a transitional government. The agreement also called for the UN to send peacekeepers to help implement the peace plan and monitor a cease-fire.

The Arusha Agreement failed, since its promoters, principally France, the United Kingdom, United States, and the Organization of African Unity (OAU), portrayed the Rwandan conflict as a small-scale civil war rather than a nation with irreconcilable and dangerous ethnic divisions stemming from the desire of powerful Hutu extremist groups to exterminate the Tutsi minority. The peace plan made the same mistakes as previous nation building/expanded peacekeeping efforts, such as trusting non-state parties in ethnic conflicts to abide by a peace agreement and assuming that such parties would respect and defer to UN peacekeepers. As happened in Somalia and Bosnia, no one planned for the contingency that warring parties would try to manipulate or attack UN forces.

The Arusha Agreement was greatly influenced by the Clinton administration, which in mid-1993 was in the midst of preaching its assertive multilateralism gospel. U.S. officials at that time were promoting UN peacekeepers as tools to build nations, establish democracies, and end post–Cold War civil and ethnic conflicts. France jumped on the American assertive multilateralism bandwagon and pushed for a UN force in Rwanda, mostly due to the French parliament's eagerness to end France's military commitment in the country.

The UN Assistance Mission for Rwanda (UNAMIR) was deployed to Rwanda to implement the Arusha Agreement.[46] Although flawed, the Arusha plan recognized that bringing peace to Rwanda would not be easy and anticipated an expanded peacekeeping force with a "Chapter VII" mandate[47] that would guarantee security throughout the country, assist in tracking arms caches, neutralize armed gangs, and provide security for civilians.

UNAMIR had the misfortune of coming before the Security Council for a formal authorizing vote on October 5, 1993, two days after 18 American troops and 500 Somalis were killed in Somalia. After the Somalia fiasco, the United States and other major powers were no longer willing to support the expanded peacekeeping mandate envisioned for UNAMIR in the Arusha Agreement. Instead, a weak observer force mandate was approved and UNAMIR was mostly restricted to operating in Kigali, the Rwandan capital. There also was significant disagreement as to UNAMIR's size. Western leaders favored a force of less than 3,000 troops. The United States proposed 100.[48] UN officials in Rwanda, alarmed at growing violence against Tutsis by Hutus, asked for 4,500 to 8,000 troops.[49] After considerable debate, the Security Council passed Resolution 872 which fixed UNAMIR at 2,548 troops.

The UN had great difficulty finding peacekeepers for UNAMIR, given that three large missions in Somalia, Cambodia, and Yugoslavia were deployed simultaneously and that there was a reluctance by many states to involve themselves in what they believed was a dangerous mission. Moreover, peacekeeping funds were short and UN delays in reimbursing peacekeeping contributors were increasing. UN members also were slow to send promised troop commitments. Most UNAMIR troops arrived several months later; some only a couple of weeks before the genocide began. The UNAMIR budget was not approved until April 4, 1994, two days before genocide broke out. As a result, UNAMIR operated on a shoestring budget and lacked essential supplies, equipment, and vehicles. As a result of these deployment problems, a vastly understrength peacekeeping force lacking both weaponry and a mandate to keep order was deposited inside an ethnic powder keg that was about to explode.

Genocide

On April 4, 1994, a plane carrying Rwandan President Juvenal Habyarimana and Burundi President Cyprien Ntaryamira was shot down over Kigali. Both presidents were killed. This event touched off several months of extreme violence and instability. On April 5, Hutus beat and killed 10 Belgian UNAMIR troops, spurring the Belgian government to withdraw its troops, which comprised one-third of the 1,260 UNAMIR forces deployed at the time. On April 6, Hutus, led by youth militias and the Rwandan presidential guard, began a campaign to exterminate all Tutsis in the country and Hutus sympathetic to Tutsis. This campaign lasted for 100 days and resulted in the murder of an estimated 800,000 people, mostly Tutsis. Also in early April 1994, the Tutsi-dominated RPF launched an offensive and occupied half of the country.

Two independent investigations conducted on behalf of the UN and the OAU concluded that the UN and Western states had clear warning as early as January 1994 that mass murder was being planned by Hutu groups in Rwanda.[50] Moreover, these investigations concluded that Western states including the United States knew by mid-April 1994 that the Hutus had initiated a campaign to wipe out Rwandan Tutsis.[51] Although UNAMIR has been widely blamed for not stopping the bloodshed, most of the blame falls on the United States, France, and the United Kingdom for setting in motion the flawed plan that led to this fiasco and then refusing to step in and stop the violence in Rwanda, which each of these states knew amounted to genocide.

UNAMIR's limited mandate and small size rendered it irrelevant and incapable of stopping Hutu killings of Tutsis. Shortly after the Habyarimana/Ntaryamira plane crash, UNAMIR Commander Romeo Dallaire requested more troops and greater authority to stop what he believed was a dire situation unfolding before his eyes. UN officials in New York rejected Dallaire's request. UNAMIR was instead told that it could not fire on Hutus unless fired upon. Given this mandate, some UNAMIR troops stood by and did nothing as violence broke out around them. On April 7, 1994, Hutu radicals entered the UN compound in Kigali and murdered Rwandan

Prime Minister Agathe Uwilingiyimana who had sought refuge from UN-AMIR. Other former Rwandan officials were murdered in mid-April after UNAMIR troops abandoned them.[52]

The UN received information from an informant in January 1994 that radical Hutus concluded from the October 1993 ambush in Somalia that Western countries had a low tolerance for casualties and were contemplating driving the Belgian UNAMIR contingent out of Rwanda by killing Belgian troops.[53] This is exactly what the Hutus did one day after the Habyarimana/Ntaryamira plane crash. As the Hutus expected, Belgium quickly withdrew its troops. This development draws into question the UN's decision to accept Belgian troops as part of UNAMIR, since Belgium is one of Rwanda's former colonial powers and was hated by the Hutus.[54] As I argued earlier in Chapters 4 and 7, the UN established during the Cold War that peacekeepers must be neutral and acceptable to all parties to a given dispute. Belgian troops clearly did not meet this standard for participation in UNAMIR.

With violence rising and Belgium's decision to withdraw its troops, Secretary General Boutros-Ghali was pressured by all sides to make recommendations to the Security Council on a course of action. He presented the council with three options: (1) sending several thousand troops to Rwanda with a Chapter VII mandate, (2) drawing UNAMIR down to 270 troops and changing its mandate to a force that would try to mediate a peace agreement between Hutus and Tutsis, or (3) completely withdrawing UNAMIR. On April 21, 1994, the Security Council passed Resolution 912, endorsing the second option. However, General Dallaire refused to abide completely by this resolution and only reduced UNAMIR to 540 troops.

The UN was unsuccessful in its attempts to negotiate a cease-fire and an end to the killing. By the end of April, as many as 200,000 had been killed and UNAMIR's new mandate was viewed by UN officials as a colossal mistake. As a result of the failure of the new UNAMIR mandate, Secretary General Boutros-Ghali and African UN members began to push for a beefed up UNAMIR force in late April. The Security Council, for reasons I will explain, was in no hurry to act on this request. The council did not approve it until May 17, 1994, and the new force (a 5,500-man "Chapter VII" effort informally known as UNAMIR II) was not permitted to deploy until July 1994, after the genocide had ended.

UNAMIR and UN officials in New York came under heavy criticism for not stopping the Rwandan genocide. UN officials were condemned for the terms of the Arusha peace plan and for not speaking out against Hutu genocide in mid-to-late April 1994. UNAMIR has been criticized for being badly organized and having a poor chain of command.

These criticisms were misplaced. Western states specified a mandate and size for UNAMIR that made its task impossible. Moreover, even with ethnic harmony, it is hard to see in hindsight how the 2,500 men approved

Photo 8.3: Rwandan government troops killed more than 150 civilians seeking refuge in a school near Kigali, April 1994. (Robert Patrick/Corbis Sygma)

by the Security Council could have implemented as complex a peace agreement as the Arusha Plan. Some UNAMIR troops and their commander, General Dallaire, deserve credit for defying the instructions of UN Headquarters that UNAMIR not take an active role in protecting civilians, actions that saved the lives of 20,000 to 25,000 Rwandans.[55]

The United States and PDD-25

Independent investigations by the OAU and the Carnegie Commission on Preventing Deadly Conflict concluded that the presence of 5,000 well-armed troops in Rwanda in April 1994 would have deterred the Hutus from killing Tutsis and saved hundreds of thousands of lives.[56] Although many players—UN officials, Belgium, the United Kingdom, and France—played a role in delaying the deployment of additional UN troops until it was too late, the main obstacle was the United States.

The Clinton foreign policy team knew it was in trouble in September 1994. Expanded peacekeeping missions deployed in response to President Clinton's assertive multilateralism policy had resulted in violence and high casualties. Peacekeeping casualties in Somalia were a particular problem that was drawing strong criticism from the U.S. Congress.

Another major headache for Clinton officials was its draft policy document on peacekeeping, Presidential Decision Directive 25 (PDD-25). Until late 1993, this policy directive was Wilsonian in outlook and viewed UN peacekeeping as a virtual panacea for all international conflicts. While PDD-25 was officially in draft form until President Clinton signed it in May 1994, numerous aspects of it were implemented before that time. PDD-25 became controversial during the summer of 1993 when members of the U.S. Congress began attacking the document as naive, contrary to U.S. interests, and responsible for ongoing peacekeeping problems.

The October 1993 ambush in Mogadishu that killed 18 U.S. Army Rangers outraged the U.S. Congress and the American press. This situation was exacerbated when a ship carrying U.S. peacekeepers to Haiti was turned back by armed thugs on the docks of Port-au-Prince. Bipartisan opposition arose to PDD-25 and to assertive multilateralism, led by Senator Robert Byrd (D-WV).[57]

The Clinton administration quickly realized the enormity of the Somalia fiasco placed it in grave political danger that threatened the president's entire agenda, his reelection chances, and his party's prospects in the November 1994 congressional elections. It took several steps to mitigate the damage. First, as explained earlier, Clinton officials, especially UN Ambassador Madeleine Albright, tried to pin sole responsibility for the October Mogadishu ambush on Secretary General Boutros-Ghali. Second, it attempted to create the public appearance that PDD-25 had been revised into a new policy calling for peacekeeping reform and limits on the deployment of peacekeepers to areas where they stood a reasonable chance of success.

The Clinton administration announced in late 1993 that it was revising PDD-25 into a new policy to reform UN peacekeeping. A close look at the revised PDD-25 suggested this was mostly a public relations ploy. The administration did not actually abandon assertive multilateralism, but put this policy "on the shelf" until the domestic political situation in the United States was more favorable.[58] (As I will discuss later in this chapter, Clinton officials apparently felt this more favorable time arrived in 1999.) The Clinton administration also did nothing to reform peacekeeping. While Clinton officials did lay down a set of prerequisites for deploying new peacekeeping missions and another set for U.S. participation, they made little use of these prerequisites—except in Rwanda.

In October 1993, because of growing congressional criticism of its troubled peacekeeping policy and the Mogadishu ambush, the Clinton administration tried to severely limit the size of UNAMIR to only 100 troops and abandoned its prior support for giving the mission a "Chapter VII" expanded peacekeeping mandate. After the genocide broke out in Rwanda in April 1994, President Clinton was on the verge of signing the final reworked version of PDD-25. To prove to a skeptical Congress that PDD-25 had in fact been revised, Albright in April and May 1994 claimed to use new PDD-25 language to block expansions of UNAMIR's mandate and size.[59] Eventually, when it was clear that the Rwandan situation was spin-

ning out of control, the United States agreed to vote for a beefed-up UN-
AMIR force (UNAMIR II). However, Washington (with the support of
London) used its influence to delay the deployment of this mission until
mid-July 1994, after the genocide had ceased.[60]

Operation Turquoise

France, frustrated with American tactics to obstruct UNAMIR II, offered
to conduct a French-led "multilateral" mission to protect civilians in
Rwanda. (The mission was actually a French operation with token participation by Senegal, which sent 32 troops.) After the Security Council approved Paris's offer, French troops deployed to Rwanda on June 23,
1994.[61] The mission, known as "Operation Turquoise," consisted of 2,500
troops who established a humanitarian protected zone in southwest
Rwanda. More than 1 million Rwandans sought refuge in the zone.

The legacy of Operation Turquoise is a matter of considerable debate.
There is no doubt that the operation saved lives, perhaps tens of thousands.
But it also provided a refuge for Hutu leaders who organized the killing of
Tutsis. RPF forces were denied access to the humanitarian zones, even after
they seized control of the Rwandan government in July 1994. The French
also refused to turn over Hutus accused of participating in genocide to the
RPF or the UN.[62] When it became clear that France could not stop an RPF
advance on the humanitarian zone, Operation Turquoise arranged the
movement of the Hutus from the humanitarian zone to camps in neighboring Zaire.[63]

Regional Instability and the End of UNAMIR

Approximately 1,200,000 Rwandan Hutus settled in Zaire in July 1994
under French protection. This had profound implications for the security
of the southern half of the African continent that are still being felt today.
France placed the Hutu refugees under the protection of Zairian President
Mobutu, a longtime supporter of Rwandan President Habyarimana. The
Rwandan Hutus used their camps in Zaire to launch raids into Rwanda.
They also, with the support of Mobutu, began ethnic cleansing efforts
against Zairian Tutsis. These actions caused Rwanda and Uganda to back
four anti-Mobutu exile groups, who began a violent campaign in the fall
of 1996 that precipitated a civil war in Zaire, brought down the Mobutu
government, and caused massive humanitarian crises. Civil war in Zaire,
now known as the Democratic Republic of the Congo, continues to this
day. A new UN peacekeeping operation (MONUC) was proposed in 1999
to address the Congo turmoil. MONUC is discussed later in this chapter.

"UNAMIR II" was not fully deployed until October 1994. It remained until late 1995 and worked to prevent ethnic violence, facilitate humanitarian relief, protect internally displaced persons (mostly Hutus in remaining refugee camps), and facilitate the return of refugees. UN forces were unable to address attacks into Rwanda from Zaire by Rwandan Hutu refugees. While there was some internal instability and ethnic violence for several months after the RPF took power in October 1995, the Security Council praised progress made toward national reconciliation. Although the UN wanted to remain in Rwanda through 1996, UNAMIR II was withdrawn in December 1995 at the RPF's request.

It is unfair to call the 1994 events in Rwanda a UN fiasco because the UN played only a supporting role. These events were the results of an ill-conceived peace plan and the mistaken notion that expanded peacekeeping could help bring an end to a civil and ethnic conflict. While UNAMIR could not have solved the Rwandan crisis, it may have averted the genocide and saved a substantial number of lives. Because of lack of Western will, UN forces in Rwanda were so few and weak that they were irrelevant.

Clinton administration officials tried to deflect criticism of their efforts to obstruct and delay the deployment of additional UN troops to Rwanda in 1994 by arguing that Rwanda was an inappropriate location for peacekeepers and that they were only abiding by the wishes of the American people and the U.S. Congress. This was a deliberate effort to confuse the issue.

The author certainly agrees that the Rwandan situation in 1993 and 1994 was an inappropriate place for peacekeepers. However, the Clinton administration promoted a peace plan for Rwanda in 1993 that foreclosed a variety of other possible options and magnified ethnic hatreds. It called for sending UN forces to Rwanda that genocidal parties found they could easily manipulate. Having helped set up and promote a UN scheme to address the Rwandan situation, the United States had a moral responsibility to see through the commitment it made or come up with an alternative plan. Instead, in October 1993, the Clinton administration abdicated its responsibility by backing away from the terms of the Arusha Agreement to score political points at home. Even worse, Clinton officials blocked, also for domestic political reasons, the deployment of additional UN troops from April to July 1994, despite clear evidence that genocide was taking place in Rwanda.[64]

The Rwanda crisis in April 1994 was a time for the United States to make some painful decisions. Living up to the commitments Clinton officials made at the Arusha talks almost certainly would have cost President Clinton politically and spurred sharp criticism from Congress. To avoid this possibility, President Clinton reversed course and abandoned Rwanda. This was a shameless decision that hundreds of thousands of Rwandans paid for with their lives.

LIBERIA

Similar to Rwanda, UN peacekeeping in Liberia contributed to a tragedy of regional instability and widespread human suffering. The civil war in Liberia killed between 100,000 and 150,000 people and forced 700,000 to seek refuge in neighboring countries.[65] Also similar to Rwanda, murderous and criminal elements in Liberia benefited from weak Western leadership and neglect.

Liberia was torn in 1990 by a three-sided civil war between the government and two rebel groups when its president, Samuel Doe, agreed to the deployment of a non-UN expanded peacekeeping force conducted by the Economic Community of West African States (ECOWAS). This force, known as the Economic Community of West African States Monitoring Group (ECOMOG), was comprised initially of about 4,000 troops from Gambia, Ghana, Guinea, Sierra Leone, and Nigeria. Nigeria commanded ECOMOG and provided the bulk of the troops.

In November 1992, after ECOMOG failed to bring stability to Liberia, the Security Council approved an arms embargo against the country.[66] In March 1993, Secretary General Boutros-Ghali proposed in a report to the Security Council a UN role in Liberia, including political reconciliation, election monitoring, and humanitarian assistance.[67] Peacekeeping in Liberia also was a priority of the Clinton administration, which saw a good opportunity to employ its assertive multilateralism policy and send U.S. troops as part of a UN peacekeeping force. The Clinton administration hoped to quietly send American troops as UN peacekeepers to Liberia but was stopped at the last minute due to the intervention of former U.S. Congressman Jim Lightfoot (R-IA).[68]

In July 1993, the Cotonou Peace Agreement was signed in Cotonou, Benin between the Liberian government and the two rebel groups, the National Patriotic Front of Liberia (NPFL) and the United Liberation Movement for Democracy (ULIMO). The Cotonou agreement called for a cease-fire, disarmament, demobilization of all parties, and national elections. Four thousand additional ECOMOG troops were to be sent under the agreement as well as a 400-man UN peacekeeping force known as the UN Observer Mission in Liberia (UNOMIL), which was officially approved by Security Council Resolution 866 on September 22, 1993.

UNOMIL and ECOMOG generally worked closely together. UNOMIL was an observer force charged with verifying the cease-fire and the demobilization and disarmament of combatants. It also had a civilian electoral assistance element. ECOMOG was a more heavily armed force deployed to maintain order and separate combatants. Unfortunately, like Rwanda, the Liberian peacekeeping efforts failed because warring parties did not live up to the terms of the Cotonou agreement and other peace agreements.

Charles Taylor and the NPFL

The leader of the National Patriotic Front of Liberia (and Liberia's current president) is Charles Taylor, an alumnus of the Libyan secret-service camp al-Mathabh al-Thauriya (World Revolutionary Headquarters).[69] In the 1980s, he escaped from a prison in Plymouth, Massachusetts, on charges of embezzlement in Liberia. The United States was about to extradite Taylor to Liberia when he escaped. In 1989, Taylor formed a small rebel group in Liberia and began a civil war in the country.

Taylor was a ruthless rebel leader who used bands of small boys high on crack cocaine as soldiers. His "troops" were vicious and allegedly engaged in cannibalism. While the NPFL was no match for ECOMOG in open warfare, it excelled at guerrilla tactics. From 1991 to 1996 ECOMOG defended a weak Liberian government in Monrovia, the capital, while Taylor's forces controlled 90 percent of the country. From 1989 to 1996, Taylor earned hundreds of millions of dollars by selling off Liberia's natural resources and by drug trafficking. In 1991, to gain control of neighboring Sierra Leone's diamond mines, Taylor sent Foday Sankoh, a former Liberian photographer who attended the al-Mathabh al-Thauriya camp with Taylor,[70] into Sierra Leone with some of the NPLF's fiercest fighters. (Some accounts contend that an additional reason Taylor sent forces into Sierra Leone was to punish it for participating in ECOMOG.) Sankoh took control of the diamond mines and began his own insurgency in Sierra Leone that continues to this day. More on Sierra Leone later in this chapter.

How much the UN and the Clinton administration knew about Taylor when they negotiated with him in 1993 is unclear. Although there were as many as six factions fighting for control of Liberia in the 1990s, the NPFL was the strongest and was primarily responsible for gutting 13 peace agreements from 1993 to 1996. As happened with other failed peacekeeping missions in the 1990s, UN and Western leaders tried to forge a peace agreement with a rebel leader who could not be trusted to keep his word. They then followed up with peacekeeping forces incapable of implementing peace agreements or keeping order. ECOMOG and UNOMIL were attacked and UN aircraft were shot at. ECOMOG and UN troops were kidnapped, beaten, and killed. As a result of the violence, UNOMIL reduced its size to 90 troops in October 1994. It was reduced further in May and July 1995.

The July 1993 Cotonou Peace Agreement was also undermined by the corruption and poor performance of ECOMOG, which earned the nickname, "Every Car Or Moving Object Gone." ECOMOG troops were underpaid and ill-fed, leading them to pillage areas where they were deployed. ECOMOG also suffered from all the problems of UN expanded peacekeeping operations. It was not neutral—ECOMOG deployed at the behest of the Liberian government and was detested by Liberian rebel groups.

ECOMOG used military force to defend Monrovia but had no consistent standards for its use. ECOMOG's bad reputation led the United Kingdom to insist that the UN not use the force to help implement a 1999 peace plan for Sierra Leone. (ECOMOG forces were deployed in Sierra Leone from 1991 to 1999.)

In 1996, with the country in ruins, Charles Taylor decided to run for president of Liberia in "democratic" elections. The NPLF controlled most of the country at that time and had the largest army. Moreover, Liberians knew that if Taylor did not win the election, he would resume the killing. Exhausted by the civil war, Charles Taylor was elected president on May 30, 1997. UNOMIL and ECOMOG withdrew from the country in the fall of 1997.

Charles Taylor today is a regional menace. Liberia continues to be the main supporter of Foday Sankoh's vicious RUF rebel force in Sierra Leone. Since September 2000, Liberia and the RUF have been at war with Guinea and Liberian opposition groups that fled to Guinea. The Liberian economy has collapsed and is dominated by diamond smuggling from Sierra Leone and drug trafficking.

In December 2000, an independent panel commissioned by the Security Council issued a damning report on Taylor's support of the RUF that included this finding:

The Panel found unequivocal and overwhelming evidence that Liberia has been actively supporting the RUF at all levels, in providing training, weapons, and related materiel, logistical support, a staging ground for attacks, and a safe haven for retreat and cooperation.[71]

Reacting to the panel's report, the UN Security Council passed Resolution 1343 on May 7, 2001, that imposed an arms embargo, a travel ban, and a ban on diamond sales if Liberia did not agree to cease its support for the RUF and end its illegal trade in Sierra Leonean diamonds. When Liberia refused to comply with Resolution 1343, the UN implemented the sanctions in July 2001.

Expanded peacekeeping and a peace agreement with all parties obviously was not the answer to the Liberian crisis in 1993. The only solution that would have had any chance of success was a military occupation of the country and the arrest of Charles Taylor. Since the political will did not exist to take such drastic and expensive action, a UN/ECOWAS option was attempted. Scholars will debate for years to come whether this decision made the situation in Liberia worse or made no difference. A strong case could be made that if ECOWAS and the UN had stayed out of Liberia and simply let Charles Taylor take power, thousands of Liberians would not have been killed. Clearly, the UN and ECOWAS did not improve the Liberian situation.

LESSONS NOT LEARNED

After the collapse of UNPROFOR in 1995, the expanded peacekeeping concept was on life support for several years. No significant missions using this operational model were deployed, mostly because of outrage by the U.S. Congress over expanded peacekeeping fiascoes. However, expanded peacekeeping was revived in late 1999 when the Security Council voted to send large new missions to East Timor, Congo, Sierra Leone, and Kosovo. The U.S. General Accounting Office (GAO) reported to Congress that new expanded peacekeeping operations increased the authorized number of UN peacekeepers from 15,000 in June 1999 to 48,000 in October 2000. Annual UN peacekeeping costs increased during that period from $800 million to $2.7 billion, according to GAO.[72]

Peacekeepers Fighting Evil

Expanded peacekeeping missions approved in 1999 marked a quiet return to the doctrine employed in 1993 for UN missions to Somalia, Yugoslavia, and Haiti. As part of this policy reversal, both UN Secretary General Kofi Annan and the Brahimi Report[73] in 2000 called for making peacekeeping forces more "robust" so that they might better address dire humanitarian situations and "evil." Annan and the Brahimi Report contended that peacekeeping is the international community's only response to many serious crises in "failed" states and therefore must be capable of using offensive military force to carry out their mandates. References to "evil" stem from allegations that peacekeepers in Bosnia and Rwanda, due to their light armaments and neutral mandates, stood by and did nothing while innocent civilians were raped and killed. For this reason, Annan and the Brahimi panel contended that peacekeepers should be given the ability to enforce peace agreements and peacekeeping mandates.

For several reasons, robust peacekeepers heavily armed to oppose "evil" is a recipe for disaster. First of all, this concept is no different from the formula that led to ill-fated expanded peacekeeping missions like UNOSOM II and UNPROFOR. While Annan and the Brahimi Report panel claimed to support traditional preconditions for peacekeeping (consent, impartiality, and use of force only in self-defense), at the same they were promoting a dangerous proposal to again draw UN peacekeeping missions into limited warfare that rejected these principles and completely ignored events of the previous eight years.

In addition, the Brahimi panel also took the contradictory position that local consent is a bedrock principle of peacekeeping while also calling for peacekeepers to be prepared to defend UN mandates if local parties manipulate consent or withdraw it.[74] Under this formulation, UN peacekeepers would be like houseguests who, once invited, refuse to leave. Such a doctrine would discourage warring parties from ever permitting the deployment of peacekeepers on their territory.

The Brahimi Report also rejected the long-standing UN conception of impartiality, discussed earlier in Chapter 4, by calling on UN peacekeepers to use force when disputants are not "moral equals."[75] One wonders how an international force could be called peacekeeping and based on consent when it also has a mandate to identify, punish, and possibly attack malefactors. Like its new consent principle, the Brahimi Report's ideas on impartiality would discourage states from turning to peacekeeping to resolve their disputes. For example, just as Egyptian President Nasser insisted in 1956 that UNEF I be strictly neutral, it is hard to imagine how any future leaders will allow UN peacekeepers into their countries if they suspect that peacekeepers could be used against them.

THE 1999 EXPANDED PEACEKEEPING REVIVAL

Beliefs explained above by UN and American officials that expanded peacekeeping still had a future led to the deployment of four new expanded peacekeeping efforts in 1999. Two of these operations—in Kosovo and East Timor—represented unusual improvements on the expanded peacekeeping model and are essentially UN trusteeships. Two other operations, in Sierra Leone and Congo, tried to use the same expanded peacekeeping model that failed so miserably in Rwanda, Haiti, Somalia, and other places. The colossal collapse of expanded peacekeeping in Sierra Leone, the resulting strong opposition from the U.S. Congress, and the election of George W. Bush as president of the United States—who has publicly expressed skepticism of expanded peacekeeping missions—puts the future of these new expanded peacekeeping efforts in doubt. Below is a short description of these missions as of late 2001.

KOSOVO

The UN Mission in Kosovo (UNMIK) was deployed in mid-1999 with a so-called "Chapter VII" mandate to rebuild Kosovo after Operation Allied Force, a 77-day NATO air campaign, ended Serbian persecution of Kosovar Albanians and expelled Serbian military forces from Kosovo. UN Resolution 1244 (June 10, 1999) placed Kosovo under an "interim UN administration" after the NATO air campaign. UNMIK works closely with KFOR, a NATO-led peace enforcement operation, which has primary responsibility for maintaining order in Kosovo, and the OSCE, which is conducting its own humanitarian and nation-building efforts. Like the IFOR/ SFOR missions in Bosnia, KFOR includes troops from Russia and other non-NATO European states.

The UNMIK mission is a new departure for multilateral operations that reflects lessons the West learned from prior expanded peacekeeping missions in Somalia, Cambodia, and other places. UNMIK, KFOR, and OSCE work together as part of what is essentially an occupation force that treats Kosovo as a UN trusteeship. These operations maintain order in Kosovo and perform most governmental functions. They do not rely on the consent of local parties and in theory are deployed indefinitely.

The challenge for the multinational forces in Kosovo today is not protecting Kosovar Albanians from Serbs but preventing Albanian retaliation against the few remaining ethnic Serbs. Driving this problem are Kosovar militia groups who have refused to disarm and hope to use military action to drive remaining Serbs from Kosovo and win Kosovo its independence. The remaining ethnic Serbs in Kosovo want it to remain a southern province of Serbia, and refused to participate in province elections conducted by UNMIK in November 2001 which were intended to prepare Kosovo for "provisional self-government." While the international community has tried to avoid taking a position on whether Kosovo should be independent or remain part of Serbia, it eventually will need to take a stand.

U.S. Troops in the Balkans: Perpetual Deployments?

America's troop commitments in Bosnia and Kosovo—about 11,000 soldiers—were an issue during the 2000 presidential campaign because of statements by the George W. Bush campaign that it favored withdrawing U.S. forces from Bosnia and Kosovo. Critics claimed such action would be shirking U.S. responsibilities and damage its relations with NATO states, who would have to replace U.S. forces. In early 2001, Secretary of State Colin Powell made it known that the United States would not withdraw its troops from Bosnia or Kosovo without consulting with America's NATO allies.

The Clinton administration deployed U.S. troops to the IFOR/SFOR mission in Bosnia by assuring the U.S. Congress that they would be staying for only one year. That was in 1995. Clinton officials also represented the U.S. contribution to the KFOR mission, deployed to Kosovo in 1999, as temporary, although they did not specify the projected length of this deployment.

By 2001, it was becoming clear that supporting U.S. operations in Bosnia and Kosovo will become more and more difficult for the United States. While these operations succeeded in ending open conflict and ethnic cleansing, both have failed to create democratic governments or bring about ethnic reconciliation. Instead, SFOR and KFOR are essentially occupation forces. The "Bosnian state" exists only on paper. In Kosovo, KFOR is mostly concerned with restraining Albanian Kosovars from exacting revenge on the few remaining ethnic Serbs. Violence was increasing in Kosovo and Macedonia as radical ethnic Albanian insurgents—with whom the

United States allied during the war against Serbia—are engaged in a violent campaign in Macedonia that many experts believed was aimed at uniting Albanians in Kosovo and Macedonia in a new ethnic Albanian state. Both SFOR and KFOR are very unpopular with American soldiers and the U.S. Congress and represent a drain on U.S. military resources. Given these factors and a European Union (EU) initiative to start fielding its own peacekeeping operations, it is conceivable that a U.S. president over the next five to 10 years could turn these operations over to an EU peacekeeping mission on the grounds that the Balkans are an area where European security interests are more at stake.[76]

EAST TIMOR

The former Portuguese colony of East Timor was subjected to decades of oppression by Indonesia, which occupied the territory in 1974. In 1999, Indonesia permitted the citizens of East Timor to vote on whether they wished autonomy within Indonesia or independence. After 78 percent of East Timor residents voted for independence, pro-integration militias and Indonesian security personnel conducted a reign of terror that killed thousands and displaced 500,000 from their homes. The violence provoked international condemnation of Indonesia. On September 12, Indonesia accepted an offer by Australia to lead an international peace enforcement operation, International Force East Timor (INTERFET). By late September 1999, INTERFET had replaced Indonesian forces and restored order.

The UN Transitional Administration in East Timor (UNTAET) is a UN expanded peacekeeping mission deployed to East Timor in October 1999 to replace INTERFET. The transition was completed in February 2000. UNTAET is a heavily armed peacekeeping force charged with providing law and order throughout East Timor, administering the territory, helping develop democratic institutions, facilitating the delivery of humanitarian aid, and helping establish a market economy. UNTAET is similar to the multilateral missions in Kosovo except that it conducts civil and governmental functions on its own. The fact that the UN is the government of the East Timor "state" was made clear on June 28, 2001 when Mr. Vieira de Mello, special representative of the secretary general for East Timor, delivered the first East Timor "State of the Nation" address to the East Timor national council.

The UN conducted elections in East Timor in August 2001 for an 88-member constituent assembly and will conduct national elections for a head of state in 2002. However, because of the devastation done to East Timor by the Indonesians and the danger of invasion by Indonesian forces, UNTAET probably will need to remain in place for many years to come.

Photo 8.4: Well-armed UNTAET peacekeeper escorts children in East Timor, 2000. (UN/DPI Photo by Eskinder Debebe)

SIERRA LEONE

UN peacekeeping in Sierra Leone has been a monumental fiasco indicating that the Clinton administration learned nothing from the breakdown of peacekeeping missions in Liberia and Rwanda. Just as UN and American diplomats did in these previous cases, a flawed peace plan was foisted on a broken country divided by civil war between Foday Sankoh's Revolutionary United Front (RUF) and the Sierra Leone government. An expanded peacekeeping force, the UN Assistance Mission in Sierra Leone (UNAMSIL) was to be deployed to implement the peace plan. The absurdity of the U.S.-negotiated peace plan, the ruthlessness of the RUF, and numerous problems with the UN peacekeeping effort proved to be a recipe for a spectacular peacekeeping disaster.

As discussed earlier, the civil war in Sierra Leone began in 1991 when Liberian rebel leader Charles Taylor sent some of his forces led by Foday Sankoh from Liberia to seize control of Sierra Leone's diamond mines. Sankoh organized his own insurgency in Sierra Leone, the RUF, composed largely of young boys fed crack cocaine. The RUF became infamous for its viciousness and a practice of cutting off the limbs of civilians.

In February 1998, the Security Council approved the UN Observer Mission in Sierra Leone (UNOMSIL). UNOMSIL, a small observer mission, was sent to work with ECOMOG, which deployed to the country in 1991.

In December 1998, UNOMSIL was evacuated because of an imminent military coup. Shortly thereafter, a military junta backed by the RUF seized power, and RUF forces advanced on Freetown surrounded by a "shield" of civilians to prevent ECOMOG from attacking them. The RUF committed large numbers of atrocities in the three weeks the junta held the city, including rape, chopping off the limbs of civilians, gouging out eyes, and killing an estimated 6,000 people. ECOMOG and Executive Outcomes, a South African mercenary group, eventually recaptured Freetown, restored the elected government, and drove the junta and the RUF into the jungle. Foday Sankoh was captured and placed under house arrest in Nigeria. UNOMSIL returned to the country but had no effect on improving the security situation.

The United States was working before the fall of Freetown to negotiate a peace settlement with Sankoh. The Clinton administration named Reverend Jesse Jackson its "Special Envoy for the President for the Promotion of Democracy in Africa" in late 1997. Jackson's primary objective was bringing peace to Sierra Leone. The Clinton administration and Jackson undoubtedly knew about Sankoh's record but negotiated with him anyway on at least two occasions in 1998.

The United States became deeply involved in what became one of the most absurd peace accords ever negotiated, the Lome Peace Agreement, in the spring of 1999. Despite the well-publicized barbarity of the RUF campaign to seize Freetown, Jesse Jackson and U.S. Secretary of State Madeleine Albright forced the Sierra Leone government to pardon Sankoh and offer him a post in a new government responsible for Sierra Leone's diamond mines. RUF members also were offered amnesty for all crimes. ECOMOG troops were to leave the country and a large UN peacekeeping force, the UN Assistance Mission for Sierra Leone (UNAMSIL) would be deployed to help monitor the peace agreement.

The Lome Agreement led to a catastrophe. When Sankoh was released from prison, he reorganized his army with help from his patron, Charles Taylor, who had become Liberia's president. (What makes this story even more bizarre is that American and UN officials tried to use Taylor as an interlocutor to assure Sankoh's good behavior.)[77] Sankoh's troops resumed killing and maiming civilians and refused to disarm or allow UN troops into RUF-held areas. Clearly, Sankoh had no interest in peace and was not a party with whom the United States should have been negotiating. Sankoh was captured in June 2000 and likely will be tried as a war criminal. However, the RUF lives on, probably under the command of a Sankoh crony hiding in Liberia.

UNAMSIL was a poorly run and incompetent peacekeeping force that made the Sierra Leone situation worse. Some UNAMSIL troops who entered RUF areas in mid-2000 were stripped of their weapons by the RUF (and often their clothes) and taken hostage because these troops, primarily

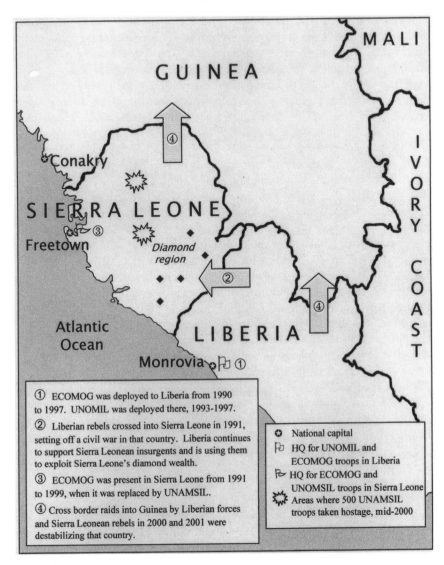

Map 8.2: Peacekeeping in Liberia and Sierra Leone, 1990–2001. (Julie Fleitz)

from Kenya and Zambia, immediately surrendered. (As stated in Chapter 5, some sources claimed that both contingents were, in fact, well-trained elite troops who went to Sierra Leone only to collect UN paychecks and were told they would not have to fight.) Stolen UN weapons and vehicles significantly strengthened the RUF. The RUF took almost 500 UNAMSIL troops hostage in May 2000. In June 2000, UNAMSIL and Freetown would have been overrun if it were not for the deployment of 800 British marines who made a show of force and drove the RUF back. UNAMSIL hostages were released by July 2000; however, more were taken during the fall of 2000. As mentioned in Chapter 5, UNAMSIL also was seriously undermined by fierce bureaucratic infighting by its commanders.

In mid-2001, the Sierra Leone government controlled Freetown and limited areas of the country's interior. Government-controlled areas were protected by UNAMSIL, the Sierra Leone army, former RUF troops, mercenaries, and British troops. Although the government and the RUF signed a cease-fire agreement in November 2000, the RUF did not abide by the pact, especially its disarmament provisions. The RUF still controlled the majority of the country, although it was keeping a low profile, in large part due to the fact that it was fighting alongside Liberian forces in Guinea. As stated earlier, the Security Council imposed sanctions on Liberia in July 2001 for supporting the RUF and trafficking in Sierra Leonean diamonds.

Prospects for UNAMSIL are improving somewhat. The operation had acquired better troops and reached its full strength of 17,500 by July 2001. UNAMSIL had made significant progress increasing its presence into the interior of the country, although it is currently unable to deploy in the diamond-producing regions. The RUF released about 600 of its estimated 1,400 child soldiers. However, there was no indication that the UN had solved the operation's leadership and procurement problems. Moreover, Britain's 600 marines continue to form the backbone of the international effort in Sierra Leone that keeps the RUF at bay.

Prospects for UNAMSIL as of late 2001 were mixed at best. The force appeared capable of maintaining order in the country. UNAMSIL still was unable to gain access to most of the diamond-producing areas, and its "control" of the country did not extend far beyond major roads. Although the UN claimed it had made significant progress disarming the RUF, this was impossible to confirm. It also was an open question as to the RUF's future plans and how Charles Taylor would use it in the future. As of December 2001, the RUF was maintaining a low profile.

UN plans to conduct presidential and parliamentary elections in the spring of 2002 had slipped to May 2002. Although national elections for Sierra Leone appeared to be ill-advised at this time due to ongoing turmoil in the country, not conducting them could lead to violence. President Ahmad Tejan Kabbah's five-year term of office expired in February 2001 and has already been extended twice on security grounds. The RUF and other opposition politicians oppose further extensions of President Kabbah's term and have long called for an interim government.

The outlook for national elections was unclear as of early 2002. UNAMSIL initiated a questionable effort to "mainstream" the RUF and convert it into a political party. However, fearing that RUF leader Foday Sankoh might win the presidential election, in March 2002 the UNAMSIL-controlled electoral commission barred the jailed Sankoh from competing in the election bacause he had never been a registered voter in the country.

Although the RUF planned to run candidates for the Sierra Leone parliament, anger by RUF members at the exclusion of Sankoh from the presidential ballot and allegations by the RUF that UNAMSIL was not providing it with adequate preparations for the election could make it difficult to get the RUF to accept the results of the elections, possibly driving them to resume their war against the government.

The Sierra Leone tragedy is another example of failed leadership. The United States employed policies in 1999 and 2000 not to solve the Sierra Leone problem, but to make it go away. It used a failed multilateral force model in order to be seen as doing something. Clinton officials held their noses and negotiated with a bloodthirsty rebel leader and his bloodthirsty, kleptocratic patron. Like so many other peacekeeping failures in the 1990s, Sierra Leone is not primarily a UN failure—it also is an American failure.

CONGO

Events in Sierra Leone had a profound effect on UN and Clinton administration efforts to send a peacekeeping force resembling UNAMSIL to the Democratic Republic of the Congo (formerly Zaire). As discussed earlier, the Rwandan Hutu cross-border attacks on Rwanda and their ethnic cleansing of Tutsis in Zaire spurred Rwanda and Uganda to back anti-Mobutu rebel groups to invade Zaire in 1999. The Mobutu government was overthrown and Laurent Kabila, leader of one of the rebel groups, took power. (Joseph Kabila took control of the Congo government in January 2001 after his father was assassinated.) In November 1999, after months of intense UN-brokered negotiations, the Security Council authorized the UN Mission in the Democratic Republic of the Congo (MONUC) with a strength of 500 military observers. On February 20, 2000 the Security Council passed Resolution 1291 increasing MONUC to 5,537 troops.

By January 2001, MONUC numbered only 231 troops. That number had increased to 3,225 by October 31, 2001. Difficulty in staffing MONUC stemmed from concerns by the U.S. Congress and many other countries of the UN mission in Congo devolving into another UNAMSIL or UNOSOM II. Noting that the Congo was divided between several warring states and the absence of a cease-fire, Congress blocked the Clinton administration from spending U.S. funds on MONUC[78] and few nations were willing to provide troops. As a result, the deployment of UN troops to Congo was slow. John R. Bolton echoed congressional skepticism of a proposed Congo peacekeeping operation in testimony to a congressional subcommittee in September 2000:

In the proposed Congo operation, while a threat to international peace and security is much stronger, the mission is ill-defined, potentially endless in duration, and with long-term financial costs that defy quantification. The persistent inability of the parties to come to a true meeting of the minds in a sustainable peace agreement brings forebodings of Somalia.[79]

Fighting continued as of late 2001 in the Congo, placing the future of MONUC in doubt. Uganda and Rwanda were fighting on the side of the rebels; Zimbabwe, Angola, and Namibia were on Kabila's side. Burundi had troops in the Congo to protect its border. News that that regional states were preparing to withdraw their troops from Congo was met by a new campaign by rebels based in Rwanda and Burundi to step up attacks on their home countries. (This development led to talk in mid-2001 of a new OAU-Belgian expanded peacekeeping mission in Burundi.) In December 2001, Uganda, which had withdrawn some of its troops, was considering sending them back after anarchy broke out in areas Ugandan troops had been occupying and Rwanda reinforced its military presence in eastern Congo. Lack of support for a large-scale military intervention led by the West has essentially left the peace process in the hands of Joseph Kabila and what is left of his government.

CONCLUSION

Lacking sound theoretical concepts, plagued by incoherent mandates, and ignoring the need for leadership and good management, expanded peacekeeping was doomed to fail. Larger missions like UNPROFOR and UNOSOM II put lightly armed UN troops in the middle of civil and ethnic conflicts. Not surprisingly, both operations were disasters. UNTAC in Cambodia achieved the temporary illusion of success by dropping important parts of its mandate and quickly withdrawing before the mission fell apart. Similarly, missions like UNOMIL, UNAVEM III, and UNAMSIL were politically expedient forces hurled at intractable problems and not serious and sustained responses to conflicts.

Expanded peacekeeping appeared to die in 1995 after the safe areas fiasco in Bosnia. However, it rose from the dead in 1999. Its resilience represents the inability (or refusal) of liberal internationalists to recognize the power realities of the post–Cold War era and the fallacies in their peacekeeping theories. Early reports suggest that expanded peacekeeping efforts deployed in 1999 are likely to suffer the same fate for the same reasons as their predecessors.

Expanded peacekeeping failures damaged UN prestige and the organization's ability to play a useful role in helping resolve international conflicts. But a close look at most expanded peacekeeping fiascoes reveals that these missions did not fail merely because they were based on bad theory. In many cases—especially in Rwanda, Angola, Sierra Leone, and Haiti— they failed because of weak and incoherent leadership by the United States. The effect of this variable is not generally understood and unfairly tarnished UN missions that otherwise might not have been such spectacular failures.

NOTES

1. Abba Eban, "The Slow Death of Collective Security," *Foreign Affairs* 74, no. 5 (September–October 1995), p. 52.

2. *New York Times* editorial, July 10, 1997.

3. John M. Sanderson and Michael Maley, "Elections and Liberal Democracy in Cambodia," *Australian Journal of International Affairs* 52, no. 3 (November 1998), pp. 241–253.

4. Sanderson and Maley source this allegation to Eric Pape, "Will Voters Agree to Bite the Bullet," *Phnom Penh Post* (May 22–June 4, 1998).

5. UN Security Council Resolution 694, December 3, 1992.

6. See the authorizing resolution for UNOSOM II, Resolution 814 (March 26, 1993) and Security Council Resolution 865 (September 22, 1993), which expanded UNOSOM II's nation-building mandate.

7. Sir Brian Urquhart, "Mission Impossible," book review of *Black Hawk Down* by Mark Bowden, *New York Review of Books*, November 18, 1999.

8. Julia Preston, "Waste in Somalia Typifies Failings of UN Management," *Washington Post*, January 3, 1995, p. A11.

9. George Melloan, "New Lessons on the Use and Misuse of Troops," *Wall Street Journal*, October 18, 1993, p. A17.

10. Security Council Resolution 867, September 23, 1993. See also UNMIH Fact Sheet, UN Department of Peacekeeping Operations, Internet website: http://www.un.org/Depts/dpko/dpko/co_mission/unmih.htm.

11. *New York Times* editorial, August 2, 1994, p. 20A.

12. See Lally Weymoth, "Yalta II," *Washington Times*, July 24, 1994, p. C7; "Haiti Isn't UN Business," *Guardian* (London), August 2, 1994.

13. According to Reuters, several United States senators were given a CIA briefing in mid-October 1993 that contended that Aristide was a "psychopath" and had been treated in a psychiatric hospital for mental illness. There also was an allegation that Aristide favored "necklacing" of his opponents, a brutal form of assassination where a tire is filled with gasoline, placed around the neck of a person, and set ablaze. See Reuters story a1350, October 22, 1993.

14. Mary Anastasia O'Grady, "Clinton's Haiti Policy Deserves Prompt Scrutiny," *Wall Street Journal*, January 26, 2001, p. A15.

15. Mary Anastasia O'Grady, "Haiti's Aristide Says 'Show Me the Money,'" *Wall Street Journal*, July 6, 2001, p. A9. O'Grady's reference to Aristide's "telephone company associates" refers to allegations that Aristide had entered into a deal with several Democratic Party officials to loot long distance telephone revenues from Haitian Telco, the Aristide government's monopoly-owned telephone company.

16. "Haitian Connections," *Wall Street Journal*, May 29, 2001.

17. Security Council Resolution 743, February 21, 1992.

18. See Security Council Resolutions 981, 982, and 983, March 31, 1995.

19. Secretary General Report to the Security Council, S/23592, February 15, 1992, paragraph 28.

20. Author correspondence with OSCE Mission in Croatia, March 2001.

21. Safe areas differed significantly from UN Protected Areas. Safe areas were

small enclaves in the middle of Bosnia Serb territory, usually a five- to ten-mile zone drawn around a Muslim town. UN Protected Areas (UNPAs) were up to 75 miles long and 25 miles wide. UNPAs were Croatian territory with Serb majorities or large Serb minorities where most of the fighting between Serbia and Croatia took place.

22. According to former UN Secretary General Boutros-Ghali, the Clinton administration's decision to reject the Vance-Owen Peace Plan and to add offensive missions to UNPROFOR's mandate—such as calling in airstrikes—spurred violence to escalate against UNPROFOR and is the reason it failed. See Boutros Boutros-Ghali, *Unvanquished: A U.S.–U.N. Saga* (New York: Random House, 1999), pp. 68–71. John Bolton, assistant secretary of state for international organizations under President Bush, told the author in June 1999 that he and former Secretary of State James Baker also hold this view and believe that the Bush administration would have signed onto the Vance/Owen Plan if Mr. Bush had been reelected in 1992.

23. Lewis MacKenzie, "What Best Hope for Peace in Bosnia?" *Washington Times*, February 8, 1993, p. E1.

24. Stanley Meisler, "From Great Hope to Scapegoat," *The Washington Monthly*, (July/August 1996), p. 32.

25. Brian Urquhart echoes this view in his review of Boutros-Ghali's memoirs. See Urquhart, "The Making of a Scapegoat," *The New York Review of Books*, August 12, 1999, pp. 32–35.

26. *Report of the Secretary General Pursuant to General Assembly Resolution 53/35: The Fall of Srebrenica*, United Nations document A/54/549, November 15, 1999, p. 20, paragraphs 59–62.

27. Patrick Bishop, "Rose Reveals His Contempt for Bosnian Leaders," *London Telegraph*, November 12, 1998.

28. Secretary General Report to the Security Council, S/1994/300, March 16, 1994.

29. The Secretary General's Report on the *Fall of Srebrenica* gives several examples of this. For example, on February 5, 1994, a mortar round exploded in the Markale marketplace in Sarajevo, killing 68 people and injuring 200. The Bosnian Serbs were blamed and television coverage of this incident provoked worldwide outrage. Initial investigations suggested that the mortar had been fired from Muslim territory or detonated in place. Subsequent investigations disputed this finding, however (paragraph 117). In another incident, UNPROFOR officials claimed Bosnian troops deliberately retreated in the Gorazde area in April 1994, despite having a superior battlefield position, in hopes of embroiling NATO and the United Nations in the war (paragraph 137). Finally, several civilians who survived the Srebrenica massacre charged that Bosnian President Izetbegovic told them before the Serbs overran Srebrenica that a NATO intervention in Bosnia was possible, but only if the Serbs took Srebrenica and killed at least 5,000 of its people. Izetbegovic denied making this statement (paragraph 115).

30. Secretary General's Report on the *Fall of Srebrenica*, paragraphs 194–197.

31. See draft Security Council Resolution S/1999/201.

32. *Wall Street Journal* editorial, "Peacekeeping's End," May 30, 1995, p. A14.

33. UNAVEM I was in part a product of the peace process in neighboring Na-

mibia. It was formally created by the Security Council by Resolution 626, December 20, 1988.

34. See UN Security Council Resolution 696, May 30, 1991.

35. *The Blue Helmets: A Review of United Nations Peacekeeping*, 3rd ed. (New York: UN Department of Public Information, 1996), p. 244.

36. Author interview and communications with Margaret Hemenway, October 2000 and February 2001.

37. See Security Council Resolution 976, February 8, 1995.

38. MONUA was established by UNSC Resolution 1118, June 30, 1997.

39. The MPLA government reportedly has hired Military Personnel Resources Incorporated (MPRI), a U.S.-based mercenary group, and Executive Outcomes, a South African mercenary company composed of veterans who served in the South African Defense Force under South Africa's white minority government. Some reports claim the MPLA began to hire mercenaries in 1993 or earlier. See *Johannesburg Electronic Daily Mail*, October 20, 1999, http://www.mg.co.za/news/99oct2 /20oct-angola; *Johannesburg Electronic Daily Mail*, November 13, 1998, http:// www.mg.co.za/news/98nov1/13nov-angola-html.

40. "Angola Rejects Peacekeeping Role for UN," CNN.com, November 3, 1999, http://www.cnn.com/world/africa/9911/03/angola.un.01/.

41. George Archibald, "UN Officials Wasted Millions on Supplies; Corruption Flourished on Annan's Watch," *Washington Times*, May 29, 1998, p. A1.

42. *The Blue Helmets*, 3rd ed., p. 254.

43. See Organization of African Unity, *Report of the International Panel of Eminent Personalities to Investigate the 1994 Genocide in Rwanda and Surrounding Events* (June 2000), Chapters 9, 10, and 12 (hereafter referred to as the "OAU Rwanda Report"); *Report of the Independent Inquiry into the Actions of the United Nations during the 1994 Genocide in Rwanda*, December 15, 1999 (hereafter referred to as the "UN Rwanda Report"), http://www.un.org/News/ossg/rwanda_ report.htm, pp. 22, 27, 29, and 31.

44. Boutros-Ghali, *Unvanquished*, pp. 134–140.

45. OAU Rwanda Report, paragraph ES.25.

46. Actually, two peacekeeping forces were sent to Rwanda. The first, the UN Observer Mission Uganda-Rwanda (UNOMUR), was deployed along the Uganda-Rwanda border in June 1993 to verify Uganda's claim that it was not supporting RPF forces in Rwanda. UNOMUR probably succeeded in achieving its mandate but had little impact on instability in Rwanda.

47. OAU Rwanda Report, paragraph 13.22.

48. UN Rwanda Report, p. 22.

49. UNAMIR General Romeo Dallaire requested only 4,500 troops because he thought this was the largest number the Security Council would approve. OAU Rwanda Report, paragraph 13.14.

50. OAU Rwanda Report, Chapters 9, 12, 13, and 15; UN Rwanda Report, pp. 6–10.

51. OAU Rwanda Report, Chapter 15; UN Rwanda Report, pp. 25–28.

52. OAU Rwanda Report, paragraph 15.14.

53. UN Rwanda Report, p. 6.

54. Ibid., p. 24.

55. OAU Rwanda Report, paragraph 10.12.

56. See OAU Rwanda Report, Chapter 10; Scott R. Feil, *Preventing Genocide: How the Early Use of Force Might Have Succeeded in Rwanda* (Washington, DC: Carnegie Commission on Preventing Deadly Conflict, 1998).

57. On October 15, 1993, the U.S. Senate adopted an amendment by Senator Robert Byrd cutting off funds for U.S. military operations in Somalia after March 31, 1994 unless the president obtained further spending authority from Congress. See P.L. 103-139, Section 8151.

58. This judgment is based on the author's experience as a member of the PDD-25 drafting committee. Boutros-Ghali made a similar comment in his memoirs when he quoted a Clinton administration official as saying that PDD-25 (known as PRD-13 in the fall of 1993) had been "put on the shelf forever." The author believes the person who made this remark said this instead of saying PDD-25 and assertive multilateralism was dead because the Clinton administration held out the hope that they would one day be able to revive this policy. See Boutros-Ghali, *Unvanquished*, p. 116.

59. Secretary General Boutros-Ghali describes his outrage at Albright's use of the supposedly revised PDD-25 to block sending peacekeepers to stop ongoing genocide in Rwanda in *Unvanquished*, pp. 135–139.

60. The OAU Rwanda Report contends that there is evidence that Clinton administration officials knew that bona fide genocide had broken out at an early stage when it might have been stemmed. However, the report claims Washington dismissed these reports and U.S. officials were told, probably by the White House, to downplay the bloodletting and not use the word "genocide" to describe it. See OAU Rwanda Report, paragraph 15.16. One the most regrettable statements about this episode was made by Albright when she contended in mid-2000 that the Rwanda genocide occurred too rapidly to be addressed. This assertion was clearly false since the 1994 genocide occurred over a 100-day period. See "Albright: U.S. Not to Blame in Rwanda," *Newsday*, July 10, 2000, p. A15.

61. The Security Council accepted France's offer by passing a resolution authorizing members states to take all necessary means to resolve the humanitarian catastrophe in Rwanda. See UNSC Resolution 929, June 22, 1994.

62. The Tutsis and the RPF deeply distrusted the French, whom they believed were pro-Hutu. The RPF condemned Operation Turquoise as a French effort to prop up the tottering Hutu government, which they claimed Paris had done in the early 1990s. The OAU Rwanda Report shared these views and accused the French of providing arms to the Hutus in mid-1994 and mistreating Tutsis. See OAU Rwanda Report, Chapter 15.

63. OAU Rwanda Report, paragraphs 15.67 and 15.58.

64. President George W. Bush was criticized in the U.S. media when he said in response to a question posed to him at an October 2000 presidential debate that he would not have sent peacekeepers to Rwanda. This criticism was unfair because, based on statements made by Bush officials during the 2000 campaign and in early 2001, it is unlikely that the Bush administration would have been a party to an agreement like the Arusha Agreement, nor would it have agreed to send large a peacekeeping effort to an unstable area like Rwanda in the first place.

65. Source: *The Blue Helmets*, 3rd ed., p. 377.

66. UNSC Resolution 788, November 19, 1992.

67. Secretary General Report to the Security Council S/25402, March 12, 1993.

68. The Clinton administration was reluctant to admit publicly that it planned to send U.S. troops to Liberia and hoped to send them quietly without notifying Congress. UN Ambassador Madeleine Albright was forced to confirm this policy in September 1993 when confronted about it by Congressman Jim Lightfoot (R-IA). Albright admitted under questioning by Lightfoot that the United States was planning to send U.S. troops to Liberia—Albright claimed only about a dozen—armed only with sidearms. Because of Lightfoot's dogged pursuit of the truth on this issue and the hard work of his staff, the Clinton administration was forced to agree not to send U.S. troops to Liberia. Given that peacekeeping in Liberia broke down and peacekeepers were taken hostage, Lightfoot's action, in the author's opinion, probably saved the lives of U.S. soldiers, who would have been targeted by Liberian rebel groups. Source: William Deere, professional staff member, Office of Congressman Jim Lightfoot. A confidential source also confirmed this account.

69. This has been widely reported in the media. See Ryan Lizza, "Where Angels Fear to Tread: Sierra Leone, the Last Clinton Betrayal," *The New Republic*, July 24, 2000. p. 22; Douglas Farah, "Sierra Leone's Rebel Without a Home," *Washington Post*, January 22, 2001, p. A13.

70. Lizza, "Where Angels Fear to Tread."

71. *Report of the Panel of Experts on Sierra Leone Diamonds and Arms*, UN document S/2000/1195, December 20, 2000, p. 33.

72. *Preliminary Observations about the U.S. Process for Deciding to Support UN Peace Operations*, briefing handout for GAO Briefing for U.S. House of Representatives International Relations Committee Hearing, GAO-01-100T, October 4, 2000.

73. *Report of the Comprehensive Review of the Whole Question of Peacekeeping Operations in All Their Respects*, UN document A/55/305–S/2000/809, August 21, 2000, paragraph 50. Hereafter referred to as the "Brahimi Report."

74. Brahimi Report, paragraph 48.

75. Brahimi Report, paragraph 50.

76. A prominent advocate of withdrawing U.S. troops is Paula Dobriansky, former vice president and Washington director of the Council on Foreign Relations. Dobriansky argued in a January 2001 article that the withdrawal of U.S. troops from the Balkans was a serious concept and would not destroy NATO, destabilize Europe, or undermine U.S. global leadership. Dobriansky is now U.S. under secretary of state for global affairs. See Paula J. Dobriansky and David B. Rivkin, "Out of the Balkans," *Washington Times*, January 30, 2001, p. A17.

77. See Norimitsu Onishi, "UN's Unlikely Ally for Sierra Leone," *New York Times*. May 16, 2000.

78. U.S. funds for UN peacekeeping in the DROC were withheld in 2000 mostly due to the efforts of Senator Judd Gregg (R-NH).

79. John R. Bolton, Statement to the U.S. House of Representatives Subcommittee on International Organizations and Human Rights Hearing on the Millennium Summit and Current United States Policy on United Nations Peacekeeping, September 20, 2000.

Part III

Assessment and Outlook

The [Clinton] Administration's current deliberations, centering on conditions under which the U.S. might or might not grace international peacekeeping forces with its presence, are sterile. No UN peacekeeping operation anywhere should go forward without our explicit approval and guidance.

—Richard L. Armitage, 1994[1]

Chapter 9

American Foreign Policy and the Future of Peacekeeping

But yet the light that led astray was light from Heaven.
                                    —Robert Burns, "The Vision"

Walk into any college library and one can find dozens of newly issued books explaining how expanded versions of peacekeeping are the wave of the future of "conflict resolution." Clearly, 1990s peacekeeping setbacks failed to discredit expanded peacekeeping in the eyes of many experts. While the Bush administration is justifiably skeptical about using peacekeeping to address civil wars and ethnic conflicts, former Clinton administration officials and UN Secretary General Kofi Annan remain stalwart supporters.

But no matter how elegant their arguments, one thing is clear: expanded peacekeeping simply does not work. It had a chance to prove itself between 1992 and 1995 and failed utterly. Its second chance in Sierra Leone in 2000 rivaled earlier expanded peacekeeping fiascoes. Peacekeeping failures in the 1990s had a profound impact on post–Cold War international relations by causing greater global instability, undermining U.S. influence abroad, damaging peacekeeping as a viable diplomatic tool, and undermining the UN.

INCREASED INSTABILITY

Expanded peacekeeping in the 1990s contributed a significant amount of instability to already unstable political situations. The civil war in Congo is a direct result of an ill-considered expanded peacekeeping peace plan in

Rwanda. Genocide that occurred on the UN's watch in Bosnia and Rwanda created ethnic hatreds that may cause regional instability for generations. Despots and kleptocrats in Angola, Liberia, Haiti, and Cambodia took office by way of corrupt elections monitored by the UN. This undermined respect for democracy in these countries and probably guaranteed that they will not develop democratic institutions for 10 to 20 years or more. Liberia and Angola are regional menaces who have invaded neighboring states. Ill-considered UN peace plans drove large numbers of people from their homes in Congo, Sierra Leone, Rwanda, Angola, and Liberia. Despite the investment of enormous sums and high peacekeeping fatalities, Somalia in 2002 is just as unstable and anarchic as it was when UN troops first deployed there in 1992. The world will be paying for these consequences of 1990s expanded peacekeeping missions for years to come.

DAMAGE TO U.S. INTERESTS

The breakdown of expanded operations resulted in part resulted from faulty theory that did not take account of past peacekeeping experiences and the limitations of the UN. However, an indivisible component of expanded peacekeeping failures from 1993 to 2000 was a lack of Western leadership and resolve.

It was irrational for politicians and diplomats to believe in the 1990s that lightly armed peacekeepers would bring peace to areas engulfed in civil war and anarchy like Bosnia, Croatia, Somalia, Rwanda, Liberia, Angola, Haiti, and Sierra Leone. While peacekeeping brought temporary peace to Cambodia, the country returned to internal conflict and despotism soon after peacekeepers withdrew. All these cases ignored peacekeeping prerequisites established by UNEF I and Dag Hammarskjöld: acceptance by disputants, impartiality, and minimum use of force.

Requiring the consent of warring parties and a cease-fire before deploying peacekeeping was scoffed at by internationalists and American officials in 1993. They considered this requirement as passe for what they believed was a new world order. The Clinton administration's initial approach to international relations—assertive multilateralism—anticipated an active and interventionist UN to resolve post–Cold War ethnic and civil wars. This is not to say that expanded peacekeeping was not also promoted by other countries, including the United Kingdom, Germany, and France. However, these countries generally followed Washington's lead or supported selected operations for their own reasons.

While the Clinton administration had ambitious plans for UN peacekeeping, it was not prepared to expend political capital to achieve them. President Clinton knew in 1993 that finding funding and congressional support for well-armed UN armies to implement his UN-based foreign policy would be difficult. Instead of making a public appeal for funds and troops to implement Mr. Clinton's ambitious international agenda, his administration advocated that the UN pursue it "on the cheap" using modified forms of UN peacekeeping. A side benefit of this scheme was that it proved to be a perfect surrogate for Clinton officials to pursue foreign policy objectives, such as nation building, intervening in Bosnia, and defeating Angola's Jonas Savimbi, that would not have been otherwise possible because of congressional oversight.

Thus a flawed foreign policy backed by weak American leadership was born. Expanded peacekeeping efforts often made little sense militarily and were hamstrung by contradictory political goals. When UN operations begotten of assertive multilateralism failed, the Clinton administration was quick to deny responsibility and blame the UN. This pattern exacerbated several dire situations, especially in Rwanda.

Expanded peacekeeping failures had significant consequences for the United States. The bobbing and weaving by U.S. diplomats proposing poorly thought-through peacekeeping missions and then running away from them when they failed did not go unnoticed by America's allies or at the UN. This behavior harmed America's prestige on the world stage and convinced many UN members that the United States could not be trusted to keep its word. One result was the unanimous opposition to UN Ambassador Albright's 1996 campaign to deny Boutros-Ghali reelection as secretary general.[2] UN members knew very well that the rhetoric by Albright and President Clinton blaming Boutros-Ghali for peacekeeping failures was false. Incredibly, even the British made the unprecedented decision to vote against the United States on Boutros-Ghali's reelection. A similar incident occurred in 1997 when the United States for the first time in the UN's history was voted off the main UN budget-making committee.

Clinton defenders may dispute the above reasons as to why the United States became diplomatically isolated at the UN in the 1990s and attribute this problem to congressional withholding of America's UN payments. I am not convinced that this was the actual reason. America has had UN debts since the 1980s. Most congressional actions from 1993 to 2000 to cut off U.S. payments to the UN were reactions to failures of expanded peacekeeping efforts initiated by the Clinton administration but not vetted with Congress. In several cases, such as Congo in 2000, congressional action put a stop to UN missions that probably would have been fiascoes. Other U.S. withholding was in response to reports of UN corruption and mismanagement. The Clinton administration, by initiating dubious expanded peacekeeping efforts over strong congressional objections, invited intervention by the U.S. Congress. As a congressional aide working UN issues explained to me, "adult supervision was needed."

FORGING A NEW AMERICAN POLICY ON UN PEACEKEEPING

The aftermath of expanded peacekeeping, assertive multilateralism, PDD-25, and a foreign policy littered with expanded peacekeeping fiascoes left a policy vacuum for the George W. Bush administration. The challenge for Bush policymakers in this new decade will be to forge a more responsible policy toward UN peacekeeping that reflects U.S. national interests and maintains peacekeeping as a foreign policy tool the United States can use when appropriate. Below are some elements Bush policymakers might consider in forging this policy.

- American national interests must be at the center of any U.S. foreign policy. While the majority of the American people are not isolationists, they believe that the United States has finite resources and cannot afford to be engaged in every conflict around the world.

- U.S. troops participating in peacekeeping missions frequently are at great—and often unjustifiable risk—since they are rarely seen as neutral and non-threatening arbiters. American military support to peacekeeping should be limited to support roles, such as providing air transport and logistics support. U.S. military doctrine must be changed to reflect this reality. This means U.S. military training programs teaching U.S. troops how to be peacekeepers must be radically changed to stress support roles and not serving as peacekeepers on the ground.

- If for some extraordinary reason the United States must send ground troops as peacekeepers—such as in Western Sahara in 1991—those troops must be given specialized training by a nation with significant peacekeeping experience to learn the intricacies of peacekeeping doctrine and practice. If deployed, American peacekeepers also must receive special training in maintaining a low visibility and avoiding terrorist threats. The Weinberger and Powell doctrines are time tested guides that provide good justification for keeping American ground troops out of peacekeeping missions.[3]

- U.S. logistic and transport support to UN peacekeeping must be factored into America's official financial contribution to UN peacekeeping and not be "off the books" as it often has been in the past.

- The United States will share sensitive American intelligence with the UN only on a case-by-case basis and only with trusted foreign nationals.

- Consent of warring parties is an absolute prerequisite for the United States to support a peacekeeping mission. This consent must be linked to a peace plan and a stable cease-fire.

- U.S. leaders must be wary of the "spoilers" theory, which tries to pin the blame for failed expanded peacekeeping missions deployed in civil war situations on terrorist groups, militias, and other non-state actors not under the control of disputant leaders who sign or agree to UN peace plans. Advocates of this theory claim that by making UN peacekeepers more "robust" they would be able to deal with "spoilers" who might attack peacekeepers or take other steps to undermine peacekeeping missions. The real answer to this problem is not to arm peacekeepers to do battle with hoodlums and thugs, but to keep peacekeeping missions out of situations where they should not have been deployed in the first place.

• The United States must cease using confusing and intellectually dishonest peacekeeping terminology. The United States will use foreign relations terms with precision and mean what it says. The United States will no longer refer to SFOR and KFOR as peacekeeping missions. America will call these operations what they are: peace enforcement missions. The United States will stop lumping peacekeeping and peace enforcement together under the vague title "peace operations."

• Sometimes the United States may charge peacekeeping missions with ancillary duties such as facilitating the delivery of aid or conducting elections. However, such tasks will not be a peacekeeping mission's primary purpose, and America will not deploy peacekeepers to conduct such missions in lieu of or in hopes of obtaining the consent of warring parties and/or a cease-fire.

• American policy on peacekeeping must be modest, fair, and humble. U.S. leaders will not use peacekeeping as a proxy to send foreign troops to perform dangerous military missions the U.S. Congress will not support. The United States most certainly will not use peacekeeping to impose its values on the world by using the troops of other states. America will not use peacekeeping to promote one-sided policies weighted against one disputant in a given conflict. Finally, while there may be a time and place for the United States to force a rogue state to adopt Western concepts of democracy and human rights, the United States will not use peacekeeping for such a purpose.

• The United States must attempt to obtain "sunset provisions" with end dates when voting for peacekeeping missions. However, if the United States has given its word that it will support a given peacekeeping operation indefinitely, America will support that mission except under the most dire of circumstances.

• The United States will support new peacekeeping operations only if they are on a small scale until the UN reforms itself and demonstrates the capability and competence to operate large-scale peacekeeping missions. At present, that day appears to be a long way off.

• The United States must never support charging the UN with commanding or conducting offensive military operations. When such operations are necessary, they must be conducted and commanded by competent national authorities.

• The United States recognizes that bringing democracy to "failed" states, ending civil wars, and creating market economies are generally outside the capabilities of UN peacekeeping missions and are more appropriate for peace enforcement operations. When such missions are attempted, the United States will make it clear that it considers them to be long-term commitments.

DAMAGE TO THE UN

Expanded peacekeeping did significant damage to the UN by harming the integrity of the institution. Thanks to expanded peacekeeping missions,

UN corruption and bureaucracy have grown as has international cynicism toward the organization.

While the UN has long been a poorly run organization, the flood of funds thrown at it during the 1990s caused corruption and mismanagement to increase exponentially. As earlier explained in Chapter 5, the UN peacekeeping department refuses to submit to an independent audit of its finances. Accounts abound of kickbacks and corrupt procurement contracts concerning peacekeeping. Moreover, Secretary General Annan has made the peacekeeping corruption problem worse by using peacekeeping staff slots as a shell game to evade real reforms in the rest of the UN. Given the lack of interest by Kofi Annan and senior UN leaders, significant administrative and budgetary reform across the UN system—especially in the peacekeeping department—are not likely in the foreseeable future.

The reputation of the UN has also been severely tarnished by expanded peacekeeping fiascoes. True or not, efforts by the Clinton administration to pin the blame for the failures of its peacekeeping policies on Boutros-Ghali and the UN were very successful, especially in the United States. Admittedly, former Secretary General Boutros-Ghali assisted this campaign through his imperious style and poor public relations.

America has strong isolationist tendencies that date back to President George Washington, who urged his fellow citizens in his farewell address to avoid foreign entanglements. Although most Americans realize that isolationism is not a viable policy for the United States today, peacekeeping failures were enthusiastically seized upon by Americans who have long been leery of the UN and U.S. commitments abroad. An increase in the number of tales of UN corruption and fraud that accompanied the explosion of UN peacekeeping in the 1990s made this problem worse and generated strong bipartisan opposition to UN peacekeeping.

Countering new American opposition to the UN generated by 1990s expanded peacekeeping fiascoes should be an important goal for the second Bush administration. Although the UN has its limitations and frequently will not do what the United States wants it to do, occasionally, the United States will need it. For example, the UN played a useful role in 1991 in providing a multilateral cover for the American-led campaign to expel Iraq from Kuwait. As explained earlier, at least a dozen traditional peacekeeping missions have been deployed over the last 50 years that have promoted U.S. interests and the security of U.S. allies, often Israel. Finally, since the UN is not going to go away, the United States must engage the organization and not retreat from it to assure that the UN promotes its agenda and not the agendas of America's adversaries.

DAMAGE TO PEACEKEEPING

Expanded peacekeeping failures did significant harm to the peacekeeping concept. Disputants to future international crises likely will be hesitant to enlist the help of UN peacekeepers to monitor truces and cease-fires because peacekeeping during the 1990s became synonymous with international interventions. Where this proves to be the case, crises could spin out of control and require larger scale and more expensive multilateral interventions with the United States bearing much of the costs.

The collapse of expanded peacekeeping missions appeared to validate the traditional peacekeeping model. UN officials and most member states distanced themselves from expanded peacekeeping–like missions by the end of 1993. By late 1995, traditional peacekeeping prerequisites were again the official guidelines for UN peacekeepers.

Unfortunately, there are still plenty of liberal internationalists who have not given up on expanded peacekeeping. UN Secretary General Kofi Annan and the Brahimi Commission panel are among these, advocating in 1999 and 2000 "robust peacekeeping" to fight "evil." Despite the failure of similar operations in Somalia and Bosnia, the "robust peacekeeping" concept was well received by the American press. The rise of this idea and new expanded peacekeeping missions in 1999 indicate that peacekeeping has still not found its moorings. Unless sensible leaders rein in peacekeeping, it will again be used to rationalize UN projects that make regional crises worse and incur high and unnecessary casualties.

CAN TRADITIONAL PEACEKEEPING BE SAVED?

Traditional peacekeeping need not suffer the fate of expanded peacekeeping. While post–Cold War expanded peacekeeping failures illustrate the limits of multilateral interventionism in a world where nationalism and the nation-state system remain strong, it also suggests several lessons to maintain traditional peacekeeping as a useful tool in the quiver of post–Cold War foreign policymakers.

First, peacekeeping works best when it sticks to the traditional model using mission prerequisites developed by Dag Hammarskjöld. Such missions will be rare and should be reserved for international conflicts and deployed only when full consent can be obtained from parties to a dispute. The success of the UNMEE operation sent in 2000 to the Ethiopia-Eritrea border proves that traditional peacekeeping missions still have a place in the post–Cold War world. Traditional peacekeepers can perform ancillary duties such as election monitoring and rebuilding infrastructures so long as the consent of warring parties is obtained and these duties do not compromise the neutrality of the peacekeeping mission.

Second, it must be recognized that peacekeeping in most cases will only help manage international conflicts, not solve them.

Third, the UN's refusal to reform and clean up waste and corruption will erode political and financial support for the deployment of all future UN operations. Pronouncements on this subject by UN Secretary General Kofi Annan have not been encouraging.

Fourth, the events of the 1990s indicate that there is no such thing as Chapter VII peacekeeping and that peacekeeping and peace enforcement are mutually exclusive. It usually will not be feasible or advisable to convert a peacekeeping operation—which is by definition consensual and non-threatening—into an offensive war-fighting force. Peacekeeping missions that try to do so will be unable to achieve the successes scored by most traditional peacekeeping efforts that were born of trust, neutrality, and consent of parties to a dispute. Such efforts also sacrifice the UN's reputation as a neutral arbiter, thus putting all existing and future UN peacekeeping missions at risk.

"BUT HOW CAN WE DO NOTHING WHEN PEOPLE ARE SUFFERING?"

"We must do something!" is the oft-repeated refrain that liberal internationalists like to use to justify sending military force to areas where their nation has no national interests at risk. Those who have advocated expanding peacekeeping mandates to deal with anarchy in Somalia, Sierra Leone, and the Congo and hopeless ethnic divisions in Kosovo and Bosnia did so claiming that there was no other way to address these crises. They insisted that *something* be done and peacekeeping was the only solution.

Of course, peacekeeping is not the only solution to failed states, humanitarian crises, and anarchy. Large-scale invasion under the rubric of peace enforcement would do the trick nicely. But operations of this kind are essentially war and extremely expensive. Since it is rarely politically possible to garner support for these types of missions, peacekeeping has been substituted.

Sometimes, the United States may deem it necessary and appropriate to conduct peace enforcement missions in a failed state or regional humanitarian crisis to end human suffering. If Washington should decide to support such operations, they should be done right and not with half-measures or public relations gestures. They should be multilateral "coalitions of the willing" composed of competently commanded, equipped, and trained soldiers. These operations must take into account the following lessons of 1990s peace enforcement and expanded peacekeeping missions:

- Peace enforcement missions to "failed" states may involve combat and in many cases will require a substantial commitment of troops for many years.
- The best course for humanitarian disasters is for nongovernmental humanitarian aid agencies to deliver emergency assistance. If multinational military operations are needed to set up such efforts, they should be of short duration and withdraw in favor of nongovernmental humanitarian aid agencies as soon as possible.
- Building democratic societies cannot be done quickly or cheaply. National elections in nations divided by civil and ethnic conflicts often should be delayed until

passions have cooled, possibly for several years after a peace treaty is signed. Such delays will require interim international forces. When elections are held they should stress power sharing and not Western-style "winner take all" outcomes, since most Third World societies do not have a tradition of peaceful transfer of power. The United States should not support coalitions or power-sharing arrangements that include extremists or mass murderers.

- If the United States again elects to have the UN conduct a national election in a society torn by civil and/or ethnic conflict, it must not make the mistake made by Clinton and UN officials of making the election the final stage of a multilateral operation after which the society is abandoned to fend for itself. If the United States backs such a mission, it must be prepared to support a respectable post-election international presence to assure democratic government has taken root.

- Establishing market economies in Third World states is a major undertaking that will usually take many years to accomplish. This task will be painful and may cause turmoil in Third World states, since it involves internal competition and social upheavals.

It is unlikely that Washington will lead or set up many "coalitions of the willing" as described above. Given their expense and the likelihood of endless deployments, the American people would be loathe to support such operations. But using this approach would be an honest strategy to address international strife. It is far and away a better plan than intervening in civil wars with combat troops and dishonestly calling such efforts "peacekeeping." If such operations are justifiable, American elected officials should readily and openly make their case to the American people and explain why U.S. troops should be sent and why the U.S. taxpayers should pay the costs. Since such missions are tantamount to war, the U.S. Constitution appears to require that the president obtain the concurrence of the Senate before deploying U.S. troops to peace enforcement operations.

The alternative is to recognize that not all world crises can be addressed by the international community and to do nothing. UN operations deployed between 1993 and 2000 in Haiti and Sierra Leone certainly accomplished nothing. NATO and UN operations in Kosovo made the humanitarian situation in that region worse. Growing violence by ethnic Albanians in Kosovo and Macedonia was threatening the lives of U.S. soldiers in Kosovo in 2001 and causing a policy quandary for the George W. Bush administration. Ironically, "do nothing" could become the standard international response, since the U.S. Congress has grown weary of the plethora of peacekeeping fiascoes in "failed" states. Lewis MacKenzie summed up why the United States should often "do nothing" in a January 2001 article:

[P]ersuasive and emotional cries for U.S. intervention will reverberate around the world. It will be difficult in many cases to decline. But that's what the Bush Administration should do. The United States should not risk further erosion of its war-fighting capabilities; it should not allow its military forces to be drawn into small wars and peacekeeping missions that, history has shown, can last years or even decades.[4]

In mid-2001, the author attended a seminar where a former senior Clinton administration official argued for maximum deployment of peacekeeping operations worldwide, called for peacekeepers to enforce order while "nation-building efforts" rebuild societies, and lamented that peacekeeping was not used more often during the Cold War. Another attendee at this seminar, a prominent liberal internationalist expert on UN peacekeeping, called for making UN peacekeepers more "robust" so they could enforce UN peace agreements and fight evil. Given the experience of the past eight years, following such advice would lead to more expanded peacekeeping fiascoes that would destroy the remaining prestige of the UN and traditional peacekeeping. That would be a pity. The traditional peacekeeping model has proven itself to be a useful foreign policy tool when used in the right circumstances. It is certain to be needed again.

NOTES

1. Richard L. Armitage, "Bend the UN to Our Will," *New York Times*, February 24, 1994, p. A23.

2. Boutros-Ghali decided to drop his reelection bid in December 1996 after President Clinton named Albright secretary of state.

3. Casper Weinberger, President Reagan's secretary of defense, summarized this axiom in 1984 with the following six points on the use of U.S. combat troops that became known as the Weinberger Doctrine: Either the United States' or its close allies' vital interest had to be at risk; the war had to be fought "wholeheartedly, with the clear intention of winning"; we should employ decisive force in the pursuit of clearly defined political and military objectives; we must constantly reassess whether the use of force in necessary and appropriate; there must be a "reasonable assurance" of congressional and public support; force should be used only as a last resort. In 1991, General Colin Powell, then President Bush's chairman of the Joint Chiefs of Staff, slightly amended the Weinberger Doctrine when he argued that American military forces should not be committed to battle without overwhelming force, overwhelming public support, and only when the objectives were clearly defined and the results reasonable achievable. This became known as the Powell Doctrine.

4. Lewis MacKenzie, "A Crucial Job, but Not One for a Superpower," *Washington Post*, January 14, 2001, p. B3.

Appendix

UN Peacekeeping Mission
Data, 1947–2000

AFRICA

UN Operation in the Congo (ONUC)
Dates: 1960–1964
Established: June 14, 1960 by UNSC Resolution 143
Maximum Strength: 19,828 (July 1961)
Participation by U.S. Personnel: No
Cost: $400 million
Mandate: Originally deployed to restore order and facilitate the withdrawal of Belgian troops. UN forces remained and tried to keep order when a four-sided civil war broke out. Final tasks were apprehending, detaining, and deporting foreign mercenaries and preventing the secession of Congo's Katanga province. Authorized by UN Security Council to use force to perform these latter tasks.

UN Transition Assistance Group (UNTAG)
Dates: 1989–1990
Established: February 16, 1989 by UNSC Resolution 632
Maximum Strength: About 8,000
Participation by U.S. Personnel: Yes
Cost: $400 million
Mandate: Observer force deployed to help ensure cessation of hostilities, oversee confinement of combatant troops to bases, and supervise free and fair elections in Namibia.

UN Mission for the Referendum in Western Sahara: (MINURSO)
Dates: 1991–
Established: April 28, 1991 by UNSC Resolution 690
Authorized Strength: 3,000
Maximum Strength: About 700

Strength as of November 2001: 263
Participation by U.S. Personnel: Yes
Gross cost since inception: $430 million
2001 cost: $50 million
Mandate: Buffer force to separate POLISARIO and Moroccan forces and organize and conduct a national election on the future status of Western Sahara.

UN Operation in Mozambique (ONUMOZ)
Dates: 1992–1995
Established: December 16, 1992 by UNSC Resolution 797
Authorized Strength: 7,100
Participation by U.S. Personnel: Yes
Cost: $520 million
Mandate: Buffer, humanitarian, election monitoring, and civil administration operation charged with monitoring the General Peace Agreement for Mozambique. Provided security during national elections. One of the most successful peacekeeping missions deployed within a state.

First UN Operation in Somalia (UNOSOM I)
Dates: 1992–1993
Established: April 24, 1992 by UNSC Resolution 751
Authorized Strength: 4,270
Maximum Size: 500
Participation by U.S. Personnel: No
Cost: $43 million
Mandate: Observer mission deployed to assist the delivery of humanitarian aid in Somalia.

Second UN Operation in Somalia (UNOSOM II)
Dates: 1993–1995
Established: March 26, 1993 by UNSC Resolution 814
Authorized Strength: 28,000
Participation by U.S. Personnel: Yes
Cost: $1.6 billion
Mandate: Expanded peacekeeping mission with "Chapter VII" mandate. UNOSOM II tried to restore order to Somalia, disarm Somalis, and rebuild the country's economy and political institutions.

UN Observer Mission Uganda-Rwanda (UNAMUR)
Dates: 1993–1994
Established: June 22, 1993 by UNSC Resolution 846
Authorized Strength: 81
Participation by U.S. Personnel: No
Cost: $15 million
Mandate: Observer force sent to monitor the Uganda-Rwanda border and ensure that no military assistance was moving into Rwanda from Uganda.

UN Assistance Mission for Rwanda (UNAMIR)
Dates: 1993–1996
Established: October 5, 1993 by UNSC Resolution 872
Authorized Strength: 5,500

Participation by U.S. Personnel: No
Cost: $437 million
Mandate: Observer force charged with providing security for humanitarian areas, protecting relief distribution, and assisting in the training of a new national police force. Also charged with establishing humanitarian safe areas.

UN Observer Mission in Liberia (UNOMIL)
Dates: 1993–1997
Established: September 22, 1993 by UNSC Resolution 866
Authorized Strength: 400
Participation by U.S. Personnel: No
Cost: $85 million
Mandate: Observer force sent to help implement a peace accord and work with ECOMOG, a non-UN regional peacekeeping force.

UN Aouzou Strip Observer Group (UNASOG)
Dates: 1994
Established: May 4, 1994 by UNSC Resolution 915
Authorized Strength: 9
Participation by U.S. Personnel: No
Cost: <$1 million
Mandate: Buffer force to oversee return of Aouzou Strip from Libya to Chad.

UN Mission in the Central African Republic (MINURCA)
Dates: 1998–2000
Established: March 27, 1998 by UNSC Resolution 1159
Authorized Strength: 1,360
Participation by U.S. Personnel: No
Cost: $73 million
Mandate: Observer force sent to assist in maintaining security in capital.

UN Observer Mission in Sierra Leone (UNOMSIL)
Dates: 1998–1999
Established: July 13, 1998 by UNSC Resolution 1181
Maximum Strength: 250
Participation by U.S. Personnel: No
Cost: $40 million
Mandate: Monitor security and humanitarian situation.

UN Assistance Mission in Sierra Leone (UNAMSIL)
Dates: 1999–
Established: September 20, 1999 by UNSC Resolution 1321
Authorized Strength: 17,500
Strength as of November 2001: 17,500
Participation by U.S. Personnel: No
Gross cost since inception: $1.3 billion
2001 cost: $600 million
Mandate: Originally deployed as a buffer and observer force to help warring parties implement the Lome Peace Accords, disarm combatants, facilitate the delivery of humanitarian aid, and assist with national elections. After mission almost collapsed

in May 2000, mandate was changed to maintaining order in the capital and monitoring situation in countryside.

UN Mission in the Democratic Republic of the Congo (MONUC)
Dates: 1999–
Established: November 30, 1999 by UNSC Resolution 1279
Authorized Strength: 5,537
Strength as of November 2001: 2,398
Participation by U.S. Personnel: No
Gross cost since inception: about $450 million
2001 cost: $400 million
Mandate: Buffer, observer, and humanitarian to restore order to the Congo, which is divided by a war between Congolese factions and troops from Rwanda, Burundi, Uganda, and Angola. Given "Chapter VII mandate" to defend civilians, UN personnel, and UN facilities.

UN Mission in Ethiopia and Eritrea (UNMEE)
Dates: 2000–
Established: July 31, 2000 by UNSC Resolution 1312
Authorized Strength: 4,200
Strength as of November 2001: 3,870
Participation by U.S. Personnel: No
2001 Cost: $180 million
Mandate: Monitor buffer zone and cease-fire between Ethiopia and Eritrea.

Angola Missions

First UN Angola Verification Mission (UNAVEM I)
Dates: 1989–1991
Established: December 20, 1988 by UNSC Resolution 626
Authorized Strength: 70
Participation by U.S. Personnel: No
Cost: $16 million
Mandate: Observer force that successfully monitored the withdrawal of Cuban troops from Angola.

Second UN Angola Verification Mission (UNAVEM II)
Dates: 1991–1995
Established: May 30, 1991 by UNSC Resolution 696
Authorized Strength: 655
Participation by U.S. Personnel: No
Cost: $175 million
Mandate: Observer force tasked with monitoring transition to democracy, incorporation of UNITA into Luanda government, verifying Angolan peace plan, monitoring Angolan police, and verifying September 1992 national elections.

Third UN Angola Verification Mission (UNAVEM III)
Dates: 1995–1997
Established: February 8, 1995 by UNSC Resolution 976

Authorized Strength: 4,220
Participation by U.S. Personnel: No
Cost: $890 million
Mandate: Buffer force charged with facilitating the restoration of the 1991 peace plan.

UN Observer Mission in Angola (MONUA)
Dates: 1997–1999
Established: July 1, 1997 by UNSC Resolution 1118
Authorized Strength: 3,575
Participation by U.S. Personnel: No
Cost: $293 million
Mandate: Observer force to assist parties find a peaceful solution to the Angolan conflict. Essentially a token force left by the UN after it gave up on UNAVEM III.

ASIA

UN Military Observer Group in India and Pakistan (UNMOGIP)
Dates: 1948–
Established: April 21, 1948 by UNSC Resolution 47
Authorized Strength: 102
Strength as of November 2001: 45
Participation by U.S. Personnel: Yes, although forced to withdraw by India in the 1970s when Pakistan "allied" with the United States.
Gross cost since inception: $163 million
2001 cost: $3.1 million
Mandate: Observer force charged with overseeing cease-fire between Indian and Pakistani forces in the disputed historical state of Jammu and Kashmir. In 1972, after India and Pakistan had agreed on a "line of control" in the region, New Delhi said that UNMOGIP's mandate had lapsed and asked it to withdraw. Pakistan disagreed and the secretary general ruled that only the UN Security Council could authorize the withdrawal of UNMOGIP.

UN Security Force in West New Guinea (UNSF)
Dates: 1962–1963
Established: September 21, 1962 by UNGA Resolution 1752 (XVII)
Authorized Strength: 1,576
Participation by U.S. Personnel: No
Cost: $26 million
Mandate: Observe peace agreement and keep order during UN-supervised transfer of national administration from Netherlands to Indonesia.

UN India-Pakistan Observer Mission (UNIPOM)
Dates: 1965–1966
Established: September 20, 1965 by UNSC Resolution 211
Authorized Strength: 96
Participation by U.S. Personnel: No
Cost: $2 million

Mandate: Observer force to monitor India/Pakistan border. Terminated after India and Pakistan withdrew their forces from the border.

UN Good Offices Mission in Afghanistan and Pakistan (UNGOMAP)
Dates: 1988–1990
Established: April 25, 1988 by UNSC Resolution 622
Authorized Strength: 50
Participation by U.S. Personnel: No
Cost: $14 million
Mandate: Assist the representative of the secretary general to implement peace accords stemming from the Soviet withdrawal from Afghanistan.

UN Iran-Iraq Military Observer Group (UNIIMOG) (See Middle East Missions)

UN Advance Mission in Cambodia (UNAMIC)
Dates: 1991–1992
Established: October 16, 1991 by UNSC Resolution 717
Authorized Strength: 1,504
Participation by U.S. Personnel: Yes
Cost: (included in UNTAC—see below)
Mandate: Observer force to help Cambodian parties maintain a cease-fire prior to the deployment of UNTAC.

UN Transitional Authority in Cambodia (UNTAC)
Dates: 1992–1993
Established: February 28, 1992 by UNSC Resolution 745
Authorized Strength: 22,000
Maximum Strength: about 20,000 (June 1993)
Participation by U.S. Personnel: Yes
Cost: $1.6 billion
Mandate: Buffer and observer force to oversee implementation of peace agreement, organize free and fair elections, oversee disarmament, repatriate and resettle displaced persons, monitor government administration, and assist rebuilding infrastructure, especially roads.

UN Military Liaison Team (UNMLT)
Dates: 1993–1994
Established: November 1993 by UNSC Resolution 880
Authorized Strength: 20
Participation by U.S. Personnel: Yes
Cost: $5 million
Mandate: Observer force deployed to monitor Cambodian situation after withdrawal of UNTAC at the request of the Cambodian government.

UN Transitional Administration in East Timor (UNTAET)
Dates: 1999–
Established: October 25, 1999 by UNSC Resolution 1272
Authorized Strength: 10,790
Strength as of November 2001: 9,614
Participation by U.S. Personnel: Yes

Gross cost since inception: $1.3 billion
2001 cost: $560 million
Mandate: Buffer and administration force. Keeps order and exercises all legislative and executive authority in East Timor until local control is possible.

CENTRAL AMERICA AND THE CARIBBEAN

UN Observer Group in Central America (ONUCA)
Dates: 1989–1991
Established: November 7, 1989 by UNSC Resolution 644
Authorized Strength: 1,098
Participation of U.S. Personnel: No
Cost: $89 million
Mandate: Verify efforts by Costa Rica, El Salvador, Guatemala, Honduras, and Nicaragua to cease aid to irregular forces and insurrectionist movements in the region and to not use their territory for attacks on other states. Also facilitated the voluntary demobilization of the Nicaraguan Contras.

UN Observer Mission in El Salvador (ONUSAL)
Dates: 1991–1995
Established: May 1991 by UNSC Resolution 693
Authorized Strength: 1,108
Maximum Strength: 685 (February 1992)
Participation of U.S. Personnel: No
Cost: $107 million
Mandate: Buffer, police, and humanitarian observer force sent to facilitate and monitor peace accord. Monitored cease-fire and national elections. Also maintained order during deployment of new national police force.

UN Verification Mission in Guatemala (MINUGUA)
Dates: 1997
Established: 1997 by UNSC Resolution 1094
Authorized Strength: 155
Participation of U.S. Personnel: No
Cost: $5 million
Mandate: Observer force to verify cease-fire between government and rebel group. Also observed cessation of hostilities, separated forces, and demobilized rebel group.

Haiti Missions

UN Mission in Haiti (UNMIH)
Dates: 1993–1996
Approved on September 23, 1993 by UNSC Resolution 867. Not deployed until 1994.
Maximum Strength: 6,800 (June 30, 1995)
Participation by U.S. Personnel: Yes
Cost: $316 million
Mandate: Observer force intended to be deployed in 1993 to monitor human rights,

promote democracy, and provide non-lethal military and police training. Finally deployed in late 1994 with added task of helping organize national elections.

International Civilian Mission in Haiti (MICIVIH) (UN/OAS Mission)
Dates: 1993–2000
Authorized Strength: 100
Participation by U.S. Personnel: No
Cost: Unknown
Mandate: Observe humanitarian situation and run programs to promote democracy.

UN Support Mission in Haiti (UNSMIH)
Dates: 1996–1997
Established: June 28, 1996 by UNSC Resolution 1063
Authorized Strength: 1,500
Participation by U.S. Personnel: Yes
Cost: $56 million
Mandate: Observer force successor to UNMIH. Charged with monitoring conduct of Haitian national police and maintaining a secure and stable environment. Also tasked with promoting institution building, national reconciliation, and economic rehabilitation.

UN Transitional Mission in Haiti (UNTMIH)
Dates: 1997
Established: July 30, 1997 by UNSC Resolution 1123
Authorized Strength: 250
Participation by U.S. Personnel: Yes
Cost: $20 million
Mandate: Observer force tasked with monitoring Haitian national police.

UN Civilian Police Mission in Haiti (MIPONUH)
Dates: 1997–2000
Established: November 28, 1997 by UNSC Resolution 1141
Authorized Strength: 300
Participation by U.S. Personnel: Yes
Cost: $40 million
Mandate: Observer force to assist with professionalization of Haitian national police.

International Civilian Support Mission in Haiti (MICAH)
Dates: 2000–2001
Established: December 17, 1999 by UNGA Resolution A/54/193
Authorized Strength: 100
Participation by U.S. Personnel: No
Cost: $10 million
Mandate: Token observer mission left in Haiti after previous peacekeeping efforts failed. MICAH's mission was to file reports on the situation in Haiti and serve as an advance team for a future UN mission to rebuild the country if and when conditions permit. Withdrawn on February 6, 2001 due to increased violence and instability.

EUROPE

UN Peacekeeping Force in Cyprus (UNFICYP)
Dates: 1964–
Established: March 4, 1964 by UN Security Council (UNSC) Resolution 186
Maximum Strength: 6,411 (June 1964)
Size as of November 2001: 1,246
Gross cost since inception: $980 million
2001 cost: $65 million. (Greece and Government of Cyprus pay almost one-half.)
Participation of U.S. Personnel: No
Mandate: Originally deployed in 1964 as an observer force to monitor relations between the Turkish and Greek communities on the island. After the 1973 Turkish invasion, UNFICYP was converted into a buffer force charged with supervising a cease-fire and demilitarized zone between Turkish Cypriot forces and the Cyprus National Guard.

Balkan Missions

UN Protection Force (Yugoslavia) (UNPROFOR)
Dates: 1992–1995
Established: February 21, 1992 by UNSC Resolution 743
Authorized Strength: 45,000
Maximum Strength: 39,922 (September 30, 1994)
Cost: $4.6 billion
Participation of U.S. Personnel: Yes
Mandate:
  1992–1995: *Croatia*: Buffer force to separate Croatian and Krajina Serbs, monitor cease-fires, monitor demilitarization of UN protected areas, and facilitate return of refugees.
  Bosnia: "Chapter VII" buffer force that escorted humanitarian convoys and monitored exclusion zones. Also tasked with deterring attacks against "safe areas."
  Macedonia: Buffer force performing "preventive deployment" mission along the Serbia/Macedonia border.
  1995: UNPROFOR buffer and humanitarian mandate limited to Bosnia; Croatia and Macedonia operations were made to separate missions.

UN Confidence Restoration Operation in Croatia (UNCRO)
Dates: 1995–1996
Established: March 31, 1995 by UNSC Resolution 981
Maximum Strength: 7,000 (November 1995)
Participation of U.S. Personnel: Yes
Cost: $300 million
Mandate: Buffer force deployed to assist the implementation of a cease-fire between Croatia and Serbia and to control movement across Croatia's international borders.

UN Mission in Bosnia and Herzegovina (UNMIBH)
Dates: 1995–
Established: December 21, 1995 by UNSC Resolution 1035

Authorized Strength: 2,900
Strength as of November 2001: 1,684
Participation of U.S. Personnel: Yes
Gross cost since inception: $810 million
2001 cost: $144 million
Mandate: Composed of UN civilian administration and UN International Police Force (IPTF). Charged with monitoring fair administration of justice within Bosnia-Herzegovina and training law enforcement personnel. Also aids and observes elections.

UN Preventive Deployment Force (UNPREDEP)
Dates: 1995–1999
Established: March 31, 1995 by UNSC Resolution 983
Authorized Strength: 1,106
Participation of U.S. Personnel: Yes
Cost: $570 million
Mandate: Buffer force between Macedonia and Serbia. UNPREDEP was unique in that it was a "preventive deployment"—that is, it was sent prior to conflict breaking out between two states. The presence of U.S. troops made this operation a "tripwire" force that would trigger a vigorous U.S. military response if it was attacked by Serbia. UNPREDEP was disbanded after China vetoed its renewal on February 25, 1999 to protest Macedonia's decision to exchange ambassadors with Taiwan. It was replaced by a NATO operation.

UN Mission of Military Observers in Prevlaka (UNMOP)
Dates: 1996–
Established: January 15, 1996 by UNSC Resolution 1038
Authorized Strength: 28
Strength as of November 2001: 26
Participation of U.S. Personnel: No
Gross cost since inception: about $26 million (UNMOP costs are included in UN-MIBH)
2001 cost: less than $1 million
Mandate: Observer force deployed on the Prevlaka Peninsula, a narrow strip of land between Serbia and Croatia.

UN Transitional Administration for Eastern Slavonia, Baranja, and Western Sirium (UNTAES)
Dates: 1996–1998
Established: January 15, 1996 by UNSC Resolution 1037
Authorized Strength: 5,177
Participation of U.S. Personnel: Yes
Cost: $350 million
Mandate: "Chapter VII" buffer and observer force deployed to oversee integration of former Serb Krajina into Croatia, demilitarize region, and organize elections.

UN Civilian Police Support Group (Croatia) (UNPSG)
Dates: 1998
Established: December 19, 1997 by UNSC Resolution 1145
Authorized Strength: 233
Participation of U.S. Personnel: No

Cost: $70 million
Mandate: Observer force that succeeded UNTAES, charged with monitoring Croatian police in Danube region. The UN turned this responsibility over to the Organization for Security and Cooperation in Europe (OSCE) in October 1998.

UN Interim Administration in Kosovo (UNMIK)
Dates: 1999–
Established: June 10, 1999 by UNSC Resolution 1244
Authorized Strength: 6,000
Strength as of November 2001: 4,489
Participation of U.S. Personnel: Yes
Gross cost since inception: $1.2 billion
2001 cost: $400 million
Mandate: Police monitoring and civil administration mission with "Chapter VII" mandate. Tasked with performing governmental functions, building a legal system, restoring public services, monitoring human rights, facilitating humanitarian assistance, "institution building" (establish television and radio stations and political parties), and reconstruction.

FORMER SOVIET UNION

UN Observer Mission in Georgia (UNOMIG)
Dates: 1993–
Established: August 1993 by UNSC Resolution 858
Authorized Strength: 136
Strength as of November 2001: 106
Participation of U.S. Personnel: Yes
Gross cost since inception: $250 million
2001 cost: $28 million
Mandate: Originally charged with facilitating a negotiated settlement of Georgian civil war. Since a cease-fire and separation of forces agreement was signed in 1994, UNOMIG has monitored a weapons exclusion zone and cease-fire. Also acts as a liaison with other Commonwealth of Independent States (CIS) "peacekeeping" missions.

UN Mission of Observers in Tajikistan (UNMOT)
Dates: 1994–2000
Established: December 1994 by UNSC Resolution 968
Maximum Strength: 120 (September 1997)
Participation of U.S. Personnel: No
Cost: $70 million
Mandate: Deployed to observe a September 1994 cease-fire agreement.

MIDDLE EAST

UN Truce Supervision Organization (UNTSO)
Dates: 1948–
Established: May 29, 1948 by UNSC Resolution 50
Authorized Strength: 572

Strength as of November 2001: 152
Participation by U.S. Personnel: Yes
Gross cost since inception: $592 million
2001 cost: $23 million
Mandate: Observer mission deployed after Arab/Israeli War of 1948. Now assigned to provide ad hoc support to UNDOF and UNIFIL. Often used as advance force for newly-approved peacekeeping missions.

First UN Emergency Force (UNEF I)
Dates: 1956–1967
Established: November 4, 1956 by UNGA Resolution 998
Authorized Strength: 6,073
Participation by U.S. Personnel: No
Cost: $214 million
Mandate: Buffer force separating Israeli and Egyptian forces in the Sinai Peninsula and the Gaza Strip after the Suez Crisis.

Second UN Emergency Force (UNEF II)
Dates: 1973–1979
Established: October 25, 1973 by UNSC Resolution 340
Authorized Strength: 6,973
Participation by U.S. Personnel: No
Cost: $446 million
Mandate: Buffer force separating Israeli and Egyptian forces after the 1967 Six Day War. UNEF II was a successful operation that was replaced by MFO, a non-UN peacekeeping mission, as part of the Camp David Accords in 1979.

UN Observation Group in Lebanon (UNOGIL)
Dates: 1958
Established: June 11, 1958 by UNSC Resolution 128
Authorized Strength: 591
Participation by U.S. Personnel: No
Cost: $4 million
Mandate: Observer force deployed along Lebanon-Syria border to monitor for illegal infiltration of arms or insurgents into Lebanon from Syria.

UN Yemen Observation Mission (UNYOM)
Dates: 1963–1964
Established: June 11, 1963 by UNSC Resolution 179
Authorized Strength: 189
Participation by U.S. Personnel: No
Cost: $2 million. (Costs were borne by disputants.)
Mandate: Observer force to monitor disengagement agreement between Saudi Arabia and Egypt.

UN Disengagement Observer Force (UNDOF)
Dates: 1974–
Established: May 31, 1974 by UNSC Resolution 350
Authorized Strength: 1,454
Strength as of November 2001: 1,032
Participation by U.S. Personnel: No
Gross cost since inception: $732 million

2001 cost: $36 million
Mandate: Buffer force to oversee cease-fire between Israel and Syria in the Golan Heights. Progress has been made since 1999 toward withdrawing UNDOF and replacing it with a non-UN peacekeeping force.

UN Interim Force in Lebanon (UNIFIL)
Dates: 1978–
Established: March 19, 1978 by UNSC Resolution 425
Authorized Strength: 7,000
Strength as of November 2001: 5,851
Participation by U.S. Personnel: No
Gross cost since inception: $3.2 billion
2001 cost: $212 million
Mandate: Buffer force sent to confirm withdrawal of Israeli troops from southern Lebanon and to assist government of Lebanon in regaining control of this area. Israel refused to completely withdraw from southern Lebanon or to disband the Army of Southern Lebanon, a pro-Israel militia, until May 2000. UNIFIL was expanded at that time to better patrol areas formally occupied by Israel and the Army of Southern Lebanon.

UN Iran-Iraq Military Observer Group (UNIIMOG)
Dates: 1988–1991
Established: July 20, 1987 by UNSC Resolution 598
Authorized Strength: 399
Participation by U.S. Personnel: No
Cost: $190 million
Mandate: Observer force to monitor cease-fire ending Iran-Iraq War.

UN Iraq-Kuwait Observer Mission (UNIKOM)
Dates: 1991–
Established: April 3, 1991 by UNSC Resolution 687
Authorized Strength: 1,100
Strength as of November 2001: 1,099
Participation by U.S. Personnel: Yes
Gross cost since inception: $496 million
2001 cost: $53 million. (Kuwait pays two-thirds.)
Mandate: "Chapter VII" observer force charged with monitoring a demilitarized zone between Iraq and Kuwait.

Sources: United Nations, *The Blue Helmets: A Review of United Nations Peacekeeping*, 3rd ed. (New York: UN Department of Public Information, 1996); UN Department of Peacekeeping Operations Internet homepage, http://www.un.org/Depts/dpko/; UN Department of Public Information Fact Sheet, DPI/1634/Rev.19, March 1, 2001; Central Intelligence Agency, Worldwide Peacekeeping Charts 1992–1995; General Accounting Office, *United Nations: Limitations in Leading Missions Requiring Force to Restore Peace* (Washington, DC: Government Printing Office, 1997); General Accounting Office, *UN Peacekeeping: Status of Longstanding Operations and U.S. Interests in Supporting Them* (Washington, DC: Government Printing Office, 1997); Organization of American States Internet homepage, http//:www.oas.org/.

Selected Bibliography

BOOKS AND MONOGRAPHS

Acheson, Dean. *Present at the Creation: My Years in the State Department*. New York: Norton, 1969.

Akehurst, Michael. *A Modern Introduction to International Law*. London: George Allen and Unwin, 1984.

Allen, James H. *Peacekeeping: Outspoken Observations by a Field Officer*. Westport, CT: Praeger, 1996.

Bailey, Sydney D. *The United Nations: A Short Political Guide*. New York: Praeger, 1964.

Bennis, Phyllis. *Calling the Shots: How Washington Dominates Today's United Nations*. New York: Olive Branch, 1996.

Benton, Barbara (ed.). *Soldiers for Peace*. New York: Facts on File, 1996.

Blechman, Barry M. and J. Matthew Vaccaro. *Training for Peacekeeping: The United Nations Role*. Washington, DC: Henry L. Stimson Center, July 1994.

Boutros-Ghali, Boutros. *Unvanquished: A U.S.–U.N. Saga*. New York: Random House, 1999.

Bowden, Mark. *Black Hawk Down: A Story of Modern War*. New York: Atlantic Monthly, 1999.

Buckley, William F., Jr. *United Nations Journal: A Delegate's Odyssey*. New York: Anchor Books, 1977.

Buckley, William Joseph. *Kosovo: Contending Voices on Balkan Interventions*. Grand Rapids, MI: William B. Erdmans, 2000.

Burns, James MacGregor. *Roosevelt: The Soldier of Freedom, 1940–1945*. New York: Harcourt Brace Jovanovich, 1970.

Campbell, Thomas. *Masquerade Peace*. Tallahassee: Florida State University Press, 1973.

Carpenter, Ted Galen (ed.). *Delusions of Grandeur: The United Nations and Global Intervention*. Washington, DC: Cato Institute, 1997.

Carter, Barry E. and Phillip R. Trimble. *International Law*. Boston: Little, Brown, 1995.

Charters, David A. (ed.). *Peacekeeping and the Challenge of Conflict Resolution*. New Brunswick: University of New Brunswick, 1994.

Claude, Inis L., Jr. *Swords Into Plowshares*, 4th ed. New York: Random House, 1971.

Connally, Thomas. *My Name Is Tom Connally*. New York: Crowell, 1954.

Crocker, Chester A. *High Noon in Southern Africa: Making Peace in a Rough Neighborhood*. New York: Norton, 1992.

Dallek, Robert. *Franklin D. Roosevelt and American Foreign Policy, 1932–1945*. New York: Oxford University Press, 1979.

Damrosch, Lori Fisler and David J. Scheffer (eds.). *Law and Force in the New International Order*. Boulder, CO: Westview Press, 1991.

Daniel, Donald C. F. *U.S. Perspectives on Peacekeeping: Putting PDD-25 in Context*. Strategic Research Department, Research Memorandum 3-94. Newport, RI: U.S. Naval War College, 1994.

Diehl, Paul F. *International Peacekeeping*. Baltimore: Johns Hopkins University Press, 1993.

Doughterty, James E. *Security through World Law and World Government: Myth or Reality*. Philadelphia: Foreign Policy Research Institute, 1974.

Durch, William J. (ed.). *The Evolution of UN Peacekeeping*. New York: St. Martin's Press, 1993.

———. *UN Peacekeeping, American Policy, and the Uncivil Wars of the 1990s*. New York: St. Martin's Press, 1996.

Erskine, Emmanuel A. *Mission with UNIFIL: An African Soldier's Reflections*. London: Hurst, 1989.

Evans, Gareth. *Cooperating for Peace: the Global Agenda for the 1990s and Beyond*. St. Leonards, Australia: Allen and Unwin, 1993.

Feil, Scott R. *Preventing Genocide: How the Early Use of Force Might Have Succeeded in Rwanda*. Washington, DC: Carnegie Commission on Preventing Deadly Conflict, 1998.

Fetherston, A. B. *Towards a Theory of United Nations Peacekeeping*. New York: St. Martin's Press, 1994.

Findlay, Trevor. *Challenges for the New Peacekeepers*. Oxford: Oxford University Press, 1996.

Gilbert, Martin. *Winston S. Churchill*. Boston: Houghton Mifflin, 1986.

Goodrich, Leland M. and Edvard Hambro. *Charter of the United Nations: Commentary and Documents*. Boston: World Peace Foundation, 1949.

Halperin, Morton H. and David J. Scheffer. *Self-Determination in the New World Order*. Washington, DC: Carnegie Endowment for International Peace, 1992.

Hederstedt, Johan et al. *Nordic UN Tactical Manual*, Vols. I and II, Joint Nordic Committee for Military UN Matters. Jyvaskyla: Gummerus Kirjapaimo Oy, 1992.

Heininger, Janet E. *Peacekeeping in Transition: The United Nations in Cambodia*. New York: Twentieth Century Fund, 1994.

Higgins, Rosalyn. *UN Peacekeeping: Documents and Commentary*, vol. 4. Oxford: Oxford University Press, 1981.

Hilderbrand, Robert C. *Dumbarton Oaks: The Origins of the United Nations Search for Postwar Security*. Chapel Hill: University of North Carolina Press, 1990.

Hillen, John. *Blue Helmets: The Strategy of UN Military Operations*. Washington, DC: Brassey's, 1998.

Hirsch, John L. and Robert B. Oakley. *Somalia and Operation Restore Hope: Reflections on Peacemaking and Peacekeeping*. Washington, DC: U.S. Institute of Peace Press, 1995.

Hoopes, Townsend and Douglas Brinkley. *FDR and the Creation of the UN*. New Haven, CT: Yale University Press, 1997.

Hull, Cordell. *The Memoirs of Cordell Hull*. New York: Macmillan, 1948.

Hume, Cameron. *The United Nations, Iran, and Iraq: How Peacemaking Changed*. Bloomington: Indiana University Press, 1994.

The International Institute for Strategic Studies. *The Military Balance 1999–2000*. Oxford: Oxford University Press, 1999.

The International Institute for Strategic Studies. *The Military Balance 2000–2001*. Oxford: Oxford University Press, 2000.

Jacobson, Harold K. *Networks of Interdependence: International Organizations and the Global Political System*. New York: Knopf, 1984.

James, Alan. *Peacekeeping in International Politics*. New York: St. Martin's Press, 1990.

Jett, Dennis C. *Why Peacekeeping Fails*. New York: St. Martin's Press, 1999.

Joint Military Doctrine–Peace Support Operations. Swedish Armed Forces. Internet website http://www.mil.se.FM.doctrines/chapter1.htm.

Joint Warfare Publication 3.50: Peace Support Operations. Northwood: UK Ministry of Defence, 1998.

Kalb, Madeleine. *The Congo Cables: The Cold War in Africa from Eisenhower to Kennedy*. New York: Macmillan, 1982.

Kelen, Emery. *Hammarskjold*. New York: Putnam, 1966.

Lee, John M., Robert Von Pagenhardt, and Timothy W. Stanley. *Strengthening United Nations Peacekeeping and Peacemaking: A Summary*. Washington, DC: International Economic Studies Institute, 1992.

Lowerheim, Francis L., Harold D. Langley, and Manfred Jones (eds.). *Roosevelt and Churchill: Their Secret Wartime Correspondence*. New York: Saturday Review Press, 1975.

Luard, Evan. *The United Nations: How It Works and What It Does*. New York: St. Martin's Press, 1979.

Luck, Edward C. *Mixed Messages: American Policy and International Organization*. Washington: Brookings Institution Press, 1999.

Mackinlay, John. *A Guide to Peace Support Operations*. Providence, RI: Thomas J. Watson Institute for International Studies, 1996.

Mackinlay, John, and Jarat Chopra. *A Draft Concept of Second Generation Multilateral Operations, 1993*. Providence, RI: Thomas J. Watson Institute for International Studies, 1993.

MacKinnon, Michael G. *The Evolution of US Peacekeeping Policy Under Clinton: A Fairweather Friend?* London: Frank Cass, 2000.

Marks, Edward. *Complex Emergencies: Bureaucratic Arrangements in the UN Secretariat.* Washington, DC: National Defense University Press, 1996.

Maynes, Charles William and Richard S. Williamson (eds.). *U.S. Foreign Policy and the United Nations System.* New York: Norton, 1996.

Meisler, Stanley. *The United Nations: The First Fifty Years.* New York: Atlantic Monthly Press, 1995.

NATO, Peacekeeping, and the United Nations. London: British-American Security Information Council, 1994.

Nicholas, H. G. *The United Nations as Political Institution,* 4th ed. London: Oxford University Press, 1971.

Nordquist, Myron H. *What Color Helmets: Reforming Security Council Peacekeeping Mandates.* Newport Paper Number 12. Newport, RI: U.S. Naval War College, 1997.

Oakley, Robert B., Michael J. Dziedzic, and Eliot M. Goldberg (eds.). *Policing the New World Disorder: Peace Operations and Public Security.* Washington, DC: National Defense University Press, 1998.

O'Brien, Conor Cruise. *The Siege: The Saga of Israel and Zionism.* New York: Simon and Schuster, 1986.

———. *To Katanga and Back: A UN Case History.* New York: Simon and Schuster, 1962.

Pickert, Perry L. (ed.). *Intelligence for Multilateral Decision and Action.* Washington, DC: Joint Military Intelligence College, 1997.

Pirnie, Bruce R. and William E. Simons. *Soldiers for Peace: An Operational Typology.* Santa Monica, CA: Rand Corporation, 1996.

———. *Soldiers for Peace: Critical Operational Issues.* Santa Monica, CA: Rand Corporation, 1996.

Pugh, Michael Pugh (ed.). *The UN, Peace, and Force.* London: Frank Cass, 1997.

Quinn, Dennis (ed.). *Peace Support Operations and the U.S. Military.* Washington, DC: National Defense University Press, 1994.

Reston, James. *Deadline: A Memoir.* New York: Random House, 1991.

Ritke, Indar Jit, Michael Harbottle, and Bjorn Egge. *The Thin Blue Line: International Peacekeeping and Its Future.* New Haven, CT: Yale University Press, 1974.

Roberts, Adam and Benedict Kingsbury (eds.). *United Nations, Divided World: The UN's Roles in International Relations.* Clarendon: Oxford University Press, 1994.

Rosner, Gabriella. *The United Nations Emergency Force.* New York: Columbia University Press, 1963.

Shevchenko, Arkady. *Breaking with Moscow.* New York: Knopf, 1985.

Sköld, Nils. *United Nations Peacekeeping after the Suez War: UNEF: The Swedish Involvement.* New York: St. Martin's Press, 1996.

Snow, Donald M. *Peacekeeping, Peacemaking, and Peace Enforcement: The U.S. Role in the New International Order.* Carlisle Barracks, PA: U.S. Army War College, 1993.

Stern, Brigitte (ed.). *United Nations Peace-keeping Operations: A Guide to French Policies.* Tokyo: United Nations University, 1998.

Summers, Harry G. *On Strategy: A Critical Examination of the Viet Nam War.* New York: Dell, 1984.

Thakur, Ramesh Thakur. *International Peacekeeping in Lebanon.* Boulder, CO: Westview Press, 1987.

Thant, U. *View from the UN.* New York: Doubleday, 1978.

The United Nations Association. *Partners for Peace: Strengthening Collective Security for the 21st Century.* New York: UNA-USA, 1992.

Urquhart, Brian. *A Life in Peace and War.* New York: Norton, 1987.

———. *Ralph Bunche: An American Life.* New York: Norton, 1993.

Vandenberg, Arthur, Jr. and Joe Alex Morris (eds.). *The Private Papers of Senator Vandenberg.* Boston: Houghton Mifflin, 1952.

Weinstein, Allan. *Perjury: The Hiss-Chambers Case.* New York: Knopf, 1978.

Weiss, Thomas G., David P. Forsythe, and Roger A. Coate. *The United Nations and Changing World Politics.* Boulder, CO: Westview Press, 1996.

Woodhouse, Tom and Oliver Ramsbotham (eds.). *Peacekeeping and Conflict Resolution.* London: Frank Cass, 2000.

Zacker, Mark W. *Dag Hammarskjöld's United Nations.* New York: Columbia University Press, 1970.

U.S. GOVERNMENT DOCUMENTS

Central Intelligence Agency

"Worldwide Peacekeeping, 1992." Document EUR 92-10007. Washington, DC: Central Intelligence Agency, May 1992.

"Worldwide Peacekeeping, 1993." Document EUR 93-10008. Washington, DC: Central Intelligence Agency, May 1993.

"Worldwide Peacekeeping, 1994." Document EUR 94-10001. Washington, DC: Central Intelligence Agency, February 1994.

"Worldwide Peacekeeping, 1995." Washington, DC: Central Intelligence Agency, 1995.

Congressional Research Service

Bite, Vita. *UN and International Organization Arrears: Paying U.S. Outstanding Dues.* Congressional Research Service, Report 97-347 F. Washington, DC: Library of Congress, 1997.

———. *UN Funding, Payment of Arrears and Linkage to Reform: Legislation in the 105th Congress.* Congressional Research Service, Report 97-711 F. Washington, DC: Library of Congress, 1997.

Browne, Marjorie Ann. *United Nations Peacekeeping: Issues for Congress.* Congressional Research Service, Report IB90103. Washington, DC: Library of Congress, 1998.

Browne, Marjorie Ann and Ellen Collier. *Peacekeeping Options: Considerations for U.S. Policymakers and the Congress.* Congressional Research Service, Report 97-454 F. Washington, DC: Library of Congress, 1997.

Katsouris, Andreas and Nina M. Serafino. *Peacekeeping Training in the U.S. Army.* Congressional Research Service, Report 98-477. Washington, DC: Library of Congress, 1998.

Selected Bibliography

Serafino, Nina M. *Peacekeeping: Issues of U.S. Military Involvement.* Congressional Research Service, Report IB94040. Washington, DC: Library of Congress, 1997.

Department of State

U.S. Department of State, Office of Inspector General. *Report of Audit: Peace Operations Reform: Implementation of PDD-25 and Related Issues.* Report 7-CI-003. Washington, DC: U.S. Department of State, March 1997.

———. *PDD-25 U.S. Policy Considerations and PDD-56 Interagency Management of Complex Contingency Operations.* Briefing handout. International Organizations Bureau. July 13, 2000.

———. *Presidential Decision Directive 25. U.S. Policy on Reforming Multilateral Peace Operations.* May 6, 1994, http://www.fas.org/irp/offdocs/pdd25.htm.

———. *Presidential Decision Directive 56. Managing Complex Contingency Operations.* May 1997. http://www.fas.org/irp/offdocs/pdd56.htm.

———. *Presidential Decision Directive 71. Strengthening Criminal Justice Systems in Support of Peace Operations.* February 24, 2000. http://www.fas.org/irp/offdocs/pdd/pdd-71.htm.

GENERAL ACCOUNTING OFFICE

U.S. General Accounting Office. *Peace Operations: Estimated Fiscal Year 1995 Costs to the United States.* GAO/NSIAD-95-138BR. Washington, DC: Government Printing Office, May 1995.

———. *Peace Operations: U.S. Costs in Support of Haiti, Former Yugoslavia, Somalia, and Rwanda.* GAO/NSIAD-96-38. Washington, DC: Government Printing Office, March 1996.

———. *Peace Operations: Withdrawal of U.S. Troops from Somalia.* GAO/NSIAD-94-175. Washington, DC: Government Printing Office, June 1994.

———. *Preliminary Observations about the U.S. Process for Deciding to Support UN Peace Operations.* Briefing handout for U.S. House of Representatives International Relations Committee Hearing. GAO-01-100T. October 4, 2000.

———. *UN Peacekeeping.* Handout for U.S. Senate Committee on Foreign Relations Staff Briefing, March 15, 2000.

———. *UN Peacekeeping: Efforts to Improve Management.* Briefing handout, December 1998.

———. *UN Peacekeeping: Issues Related to Effectiveness, Cost, and Reform.* GAO/NSIAD-97-139. Washington, DC: Government Printing Office, April 9, 1997.

———. *UN Peacekeeping: Lessons Learned in Managing Recent Missions.* GAO/NSIAD-94-9. Washington, DC: Government Printing Office, December 1993.

———. *UN Peacekeeping: Status of Long-standing Operations and U.S. Interests in Supporting Them.* GAO/NSIAD-97-59. Washington, DC: Government Printing Office, April 1997.

———. *United Nations: Reform Initiatives Have Strengthened Operations, but Overall Objectives Have Not Yet Been Achieved.* GAO/NSIAD-00-150. Washington, DC: Government Printing Office, May 2000.

———. *United Nations Limitations in Leading Missions Requiring Force to Restore Peace.* GAO/NSIAD-97-34. Washington, DC: Government Printing Office, March 1997.

U.S. CONGRESS

Defining Purpose: The UN and the Health of Nations: Final Report of the United States Commission on Improving the United Nations. September 1993.

United States Senate Committee on Foreign Relations Subcommittee on International Operations. *United Nations Peacekeeping Missions and Their Proliferation.* Record of hearing held April 5, 2000. S. Hrg 106-573.

SELECTED UN DOCUMENTS

An Agenda for Peace: Preventive Diplomacy, Peacemaking, and Peacekeeping. June 17, 1992.

The Blue Helmets: A Review of United Nations Peacekeeping. 2nd ed. New York: UN Department of Public Information, 1991.

The Blue Helmets: A Review of United Nations Peacekeeping. 3rd ed. New York: UN Department of Public Information, 1996.

Certain Expenses of the United Nations. ICJ Reports, 1962. http://www.icj-cij.org.

Comprehensive Report on Lessons Learned from United Nations Mission for Rwanda (UNAMIR), October 1993–April 1996. December 15, 1999.

The Geneva Accords: Agreements on the Settlement of the Situation Relating to Afghanistan. 1988.

Report of the Comprehensive Review of the Whole Question of Peacekeeping Operations in All Their Respects. A/55/305–S/2000/809. August 21, 2000.

Report of the Panel of Experts on Sierra Leone Diamonds and Arms. S/2000/1195. December 20, 2000.

Report of the Secretary General: [Final] Report on MONUA. S/1999/49. January 17, 1999.

Report of the Secretary General: Final Report on the UN Observer Mission in Liberia. S/1997/712. September 12, 1997.

Report of the Secretary General: [Final] Report on UNAVEM II. S/1995/97. February 1, 1995.

Report of the Secretary General: [First] Report on MONUC. S/2000/30. January 17, 2000.

Report of the Secretary General: Progress Report on UNAVEM III. S/1997/304. April 4, 1997.

Report of the Secretary General: Second Report on the UN Preliminary Deployment in the Democratic Republic of the Congo. S/1999/1116. November 1, 1999.

Report of the Secretary General on the MONUC. S/2000/1138. December 1, 2000.

Report of the Secretary General Pursuant to General Assembly Resolution 53/35: The Fall of Srebrenica. A/54/549. November 15, 1999.

Report of the Secretary General Pursuant to Security Council Resolutions 982 and 987. S/1995/444. May 30, 1995.

UNOMIG Background Paper. UN Department of Peacekeeping Operations website http://www.un.org/Depts/DPKO/Missions/unomig/unomigB.htm. Accessed March 15, 2001.

ARTICLES

Bandow, David. "Avoiding War." *Foreign Policy* no. 89 (Winter 1992–1993), pp. 156–174.

Bishop, Patrick. "Rose Reveals His Contempt for Bosnian Leaders." *London Telegraph*, November 12, 1998, http://www.portal.telegraph.co.uk.

Boutros-Ghali, Boutros. "An Agenda for Peace: One Year Later." *Orbis* 37, no. 3 (Summer 1993), pp. 323–332.

———. "Towards a New Generation of Peacekeeping Operations." *Bulletin of Arms Control* (May 1993), p. 7.

Center for Security Policy. "Clinton Legacy Watch #1: Acquiescence to Hun Sen's 1993 Power-Play Ensured Present Meltdown in Cambodia." Number 97-D 95. July 10, 1997.

———. "Clinton Legacy Watch #15: Invitation to Genocide in Angola." Number 97-D. December 10, 1997.

———. "Clinton Legacy Watch #52: The Perils of "Nation Building." Number 00-F 57. December 1, 2000.

———. "Unlucky Number: Con Job on PDD-13 Can't Conceal Unacceptability of Clinton Peacekeeping Doctrine." Number 94-D. April 28, 1994.

———. "Voodoo Foreign Policy: How Not to Invade Haiti." Number 94-D 51. May 17, 1994.

Chayes, Abram. "Perspective on the Gulf: Gulf War Isn't Possible Without the UN." *Los Angeles Times*, November 9, 1990, p. 7.

Clark, Mark T. "The Trouble with Collective Security." *Orbis* (Spring 1995), pp. 237–258.

Claude, Inis L., Jr. "The Management of Power in the Changing United Nations." *International Organization* 15 (Spring 1961), pp. 219–235.

———. "The New International Security Order: Changing Concepts." *Naval War College Review* 47, no. 2 (Winter 1994), p. 14.

Durch, William J. "Building on Sand: UN Peacekeeping in the Western Sahara." *International Security* 17, no. 4 (Spring 1993), pp. 151–171.

———. *Discussion of the Brahimi Report of the Panel on UN Peace Operations*. Briefing handout. Washington, DC: The Stimson Center, November 10, 2000.

Eban, Abba. "Interest and Conscience in Diplomacy," *Society* 15, no. 3 (April 1986), p. 19.

———. "The Slow Death of Collective Security." *Foreign Affairs* 74, no. 5 (September–October 1995), p. 52.

Fauriol, Georges. "A Look at the Record of Clinton's Protégé in Haiti." *Wall Street Journal*, November 3, 2000, p. A21.

Flynn, Gregory and David J. Scheffer. "Limited Collective Security." *Foreign Policy* no. 80 (Fall 1990), pp. 77–101.

Foss, John et al. "U.S. Forces on the Golan Heights." *Commentary* 98, no. 6 (December 1994), pp. 73–89.

Heilbrunn, Jacob. "Albright's Mission." *The New Republic*, August 22 and 29, 1994, pp. 19–27.

Hendrickson, David, C. "The Recovery of Internationalism." *Foreign Affairs* 73, no. 5 (September/October 1994), pp. 26–43.

Hillen, John. "Peace(keeping) in Our Time: The UN as a Professional Military Manager." *Parameters* (Autumn 1996), pp. 17–34.

James, Alan. "The Congo Controversies." *International Peacekeeping* (London) 1, no. 1 (Spring 1994), pp. 44–58.

———. "Is There a Second Generation of Peacekeeping?" *International Peacekeeping* (University of Frankfurt) 1, no. 4 (September–November 1994), pp. 110–113.

Kirkpatrick, Jeane J. "Boutros-Ghali, Gunslinger of the World." *Los Angeles Times*, March 11, 1993, p. B7.

———. "Review Essay: The Use of Force in the Law of Nations." *Yale Journal of International Law* 16, no. 2 (Summer 1991), p. 594.

Kristol, Irving. "A Post-Wilsonian Foreign Policy." *Wall Street Journal*, August 2, 1996, p. A14.

Lind, Michael. "Twilight of the UN." *The New Republic*, October 30, 1995, pp. 25–33.

Lizza, Ryan. "Where Angels Fear to Tread: Sierra Leone, the Last Clinton Betrayal." *The New Republic*, July 24, 2000, p. 22.

LoBaido, Anthony. "Cold War Alive, Battles in Africa." WorldNetDaily.com, May 15, 2000.

Luck, Edward. "Making Peace." *Foreign Policy* no. 89 (Winter 1992–1993), pp. 137–155.

MacKenzie, Lewis. "A Crucial Job, but Not One for a Superpower." *Washington Post*, January 14, 2001, p. B3.

Mandelbaum, Michael. "Foreign Policy as Social Work." *Foreign Affairs* (January/February 1996), pp. 16–32.

Maynes, Charles William. "America Without the Cold War." *Foreign Policy* no. 78 (Spring 1990), pp. 3–25.

McCain, John. "In Bosnia, Another Mistake." *Wall Street Journal*, April 15, 1994, p. A8.

McNeill, Terry. "Humanitarian Intervention and Peacekeeping in the Former Soviet Union and Eastern Europe." *International Political Science Review* 18, no. 1 (1997), pp. 95–113.

Meisler, Stanley. "From Hope to Scapegoat." *The Washington Monthly* (July–August 1996), pp. 30–34.

———. "Is It Mission Impossible for the UN?" *Los Angeles Times*, November 15, 1992, p. 1.

Melloan, George. "Bosnia Strips Bare the 'Peacekeeping' Illusion." *Wall Street Journal*, August 10, 1993, p. A11.

———. "Gorazde's Lessons About Foreign Policy Drift." *Wall Street Journal*, April 25, 1994, p. 9.

———. "New Lessons on the Use and Misuse of Troops." *Wall Street Journal*, October 18, 1993, p. A17.

Meron, Theodor. "Exclusive Preserves and the New Soviet Policy Toward the Secretariat." *American Journal of International Law* (April 1991), pp. 322–329.

Murphy, Sean D. "The Security Council, Legitimacy, and the Concept of Collective Security after the Cold War." *Columbia Journal of Transnational Law* 32, no. 2 (1994), pp. 201–288.

Nachmias, Nitza. "UNIFIL: When Peace Is Non-Existent, Peacekeeping Is Impossible." *International Peacekeeping* 6, no. 3 (Autumn 1999), pp. 95–112.

Odom, William E. "How to Create a True World Order." *Orbis* (Spring 1995), pp. 155–172.

O'Grady, Mary Anastasia. "Clinton's Haiti Policy Deserves Prompt Scrutiny." *Wall Street Journal*, January 26, 2001, p. A15.

———. "Haiti's Aristide Says 'Show Me the Money.' " *Wall Street Journal*, July 6, 2001, p. A9.

Paris, Roland. "Peacebuilding and the Limits of Liberal Internationalism." *International Security* 22, no. 2 (Fall 1997), pp. 54–89.

The Perils of Peacekeeping. Transcript of NewsHour with Jim Lehrer Program. http:www.pbs.org. Broadcast date: May 9, 2000.

Perlmutter, Amos. "Chaos, Kleptocracy, and Gems." *Washington Times*, May 16, 2000, p. A16.

Peters, Ralph. "Sierra Leone Is Blood on America's Hands." *Wall Street Journal*, May 11, 2000, p. A26.

Preston, Julia. "Waste in Somalia Typifies Failings of UN Management." *Washington Post*, January 3, 1995, p. A11.

Rieff, David. "The Bill Clinton of the UN." *The New Republic*, August 5, 1996, pp. 16–20.

Roberts, Adam. "The Road to Hell . . . A Critique of Humanitarian Intervention." *Harvard International Review* 16, no. 1 (Fall 1993), pp. 10–13.

Rostow, Eugene V. "Is UN Peacekeeping a Growth Industry?" *Joint Forces Quarterly* (Spring 1994), pp. 100–105.

Ruggie, John Gerard. "Multilateralism: The Anatomy of an Institution." *International Organization* 46, no. 3 (Summer 1992), pp. 561–598.

———. "Wandering in the Void: Charting the UN's New Strategic Role." *Foreign Affairs* (November–December 1993), pp. 26–31.

Sanderson, John M. and Michael Maley. "Elections and Liberal Democracy in Cambodia." *Australian Journal of International Affairs* 52, no. 3 (November 1998), pp. 241–253.

Scheffer, David J. "United States: Administration Policy on Reforming Multilateral Peace Operations." *International Legal Materials* 33 I.L.M. 705, 1994.

Szamuely, George. "Clinton's Clumsy Encounter with the World." *Orbis* (Summer 1994), pp. 373–394.

Tardy, Thierry. "French Policy Towards Peace Support Operations." *International Peacekeeping* (London) 6, no. 1 (Spring 1999), pp. 55–78.

Touval, Saadia. "Why the UN Fails." *Foreign Affairs* 73, no. 5 (September/October 1994), pp. 44–57.

INTERVIEWS

Colonel Kenneth Allard, U.S. Army (retired), former peacekeeper and MSNBC military commentator.

Mr. Roscoe Bartlett, U.S. Congressman (R-MD).

Mr. Brian Boquist, President, International Charter, Inc.

Staff Sergeant John Burns, U.S. Army Ranger.

Dr. Donald C. F. Daniel, U.S. Naval War College professor and author.

Mr. William Deere, Professional Staff Member, Office of U.S. Congressman James Lightfoot (R-IA).

Mr. Gareth Evans, Former Australian Prime Minister, architect of the 1991 Cambodian peace accord, and author.

Mr. Leonard R. Hawley, Deputy Assistant Secretary of State for International Organization Affairs.

Mrs. Margaret Hemenway, Professional Staff Member, Office of Senator Bob Smith (R-NH) and observer to 1993 Angolan elections.

Mr. John Herzberg, Senior Professional Staff Member, U.S. House of Representatives, International Relations Committee.

Dr. Alan James, author and Professor Emeritus, Keele University.

Ambassador Jeane Kirkpatrick, Senior Fellow, American Enterprise Institute and former U.S. Permanent Representative to the United Nations.

Dr. Mark Lagon, Professional Staff Member, U.S. Senate Foreign Relations Committee.

Ambassador Charles Lichenstein, Senior Fellow, The Heritage Foundation and former Deputy U.S. Ambassador to the United Nations.

Mr. Francesco Manca, Acting Director, UN Peacekeeping Situation Center.

Mr. Stanley Meisler, former *Los Angeles Times* UN correspondent and author.

Mr. Tetsu Miyabara, Senior Analyst, U.S. General Accounting Office.

Mr. Alex Morrison, President, Pearson Peacekeeping Center.

Mr. Daniel New, Project Manager, Michael New Fund.

Colonel George Oliver, Director, U.S. Army War College Peacekeeping Institute.

Mr. Frank Record, Senior Professional Staff Member, U.S. House of Representatives, International Relations Committee.

Dr. Adam Roberts, Oxford University professor and author.

Mr. Michael Rorhback, Senior Analyst, U.S. General Accounting Office.

Mr. Pedro San Juan, former American UN Secretariat Official.

Dr. James Schear, Deputy Assistant Secretary of Defense for Peacekeeping and Humanitarian Assistance.

Ms. Linda Shenwick, U.S. Delegate to the UN Fifth (Budgetary) Committee.

Ms. Pamela Thiessen, Legislative Assistant to U.S. Senator Rod Grams (R-MN).

Sir Brian Urquhart, former UN Under Secretary General for Political Affairs.

Mr. Michael Westphaul, Professional Staff Member, U.S. Senate Foreign Relations Committee.

Index

Note: Page numbers in **bold** indicate detailed information on a topic.

About the Author

FREDERICK H. FLEITZ, JR. is Special Assistant to the Under Secretary of State for Arms Control and International Security. He has studied and worked with the United Nations for many years. From 1981 to 1986 he held several positions, including President of the Board of Directors, with the National Collegiate Conference Association, a nonprofit corporation that sponsors a college-level educational program on the UN. He also has been a UN nongovernmental organization representative. He analyzed the UN and UN peacekeeping issues for the Central Intelligence Agency (CIA) from 1986 to 1994. From 1995 to 1998 he worked on the CIA Balkan Task Force, analyzing the SFOR (Stabilization Force in Bosnia) peace enforcement operation, and later as a Kosovo military analyst. The views expressed in this book are his alone and do not necessarily represent the views of the Department of State, the CIA, or the U.S. government.